R&D Management Practices a
Innovation: A Macroeconom
Perspective

R&D Management Practices and Innovation: A Macroeconomic Perspective

Ellis Gray

NY Research Press
New York

Published by NY Research Press
118-35 Queens Blvd., Suite 400,
Forest Hills, NY 11375, USA
www.nyresearchpress.com

R&D Management Practices and Innovation: A Macroeconomic Perspective
Ellis Gray

International Standard Book Number: 978-1-64725-450-6 (Hardback)

Cataloging-in-Publication Data

R&D management practices and innovation : a macroeconomic perspective / Ellis Gray.
p. cm.
Includes bibliographical references and index.
ISBN 978-1-64725-450-6
1. Research, Industrial--Management. 2. Technological innovations--Management. 3. Macroeconomics. I. Gray, Ellis.
T175.5 .R33 2023
658.57--dc23

Contents

Preface

Research and development (R&D) refers to the process undertaken by businesses in order to learn more about their industry. The new technological or scientific knowledge gained through R&D is then applied to produce new or improved products and services that can be used or sold by the business. It is often classified into three categories, including development research, basic research and applied research. It encompasses tasks such as advanced development, process development, technological development, prototyping, technology transfer, fundamental research, concept development and new product development. R&D and innovation is the act of creating and commercializing novel concepts, introducing novel procedures, or altering the way a business generates revenue. It can also be seen as the necessary activity to keep a company viable and competitive in the long run. This book contains a detailed explanation of the management practices and innovation associated with R&D. It is appropriate for students seeking detailed information in this area as well as for experts.

The information shared in this book is based on empirical researches made by veterans in this field of study. The elaborative information provided in this book will help the readers further their scope of knowledge leading to advancements in this field.

Finally, I would like to thank my fellow researchers who gave constructive feedback and my family members who supported me at every step of my research.

Ellis Gray

1

An Overview of Policy and Innovation

Cristiana Benedetti Fasil and Miguel Sanchez-Martinez

The key role of innovation as a driver of economic development was first described by Schumpeter (1934). In current times, there is widespread consensus among academic economists and policymakers, that research and development (R&D) activities play a decisive role in fostering growth in productivity and, hence, in the standards of living, as innovation intensive industries create highly skilled jobs, exhibit higher wages, are more productive, are often export-led and enhance competitiveness during the thick and thin of business cycles.[1]

The productivity growth slowdown in Europe and other advanced economic blocs experienced since the 2008–2009 economic and financial crisis has further reinforced the interest of policymakers in promoting innovation. Improving innovation performance is complex, not least because of the numerous actors and pieces of the innovation system

[1] See, among others, Kumar and Sundarraj (2018).

C. Benedetti Fasil (Deceased) · M. Sanchez-Martinez (✉)
European Commission, DG JRC, Brussels, Belgium
e-mail: miguel.sanchez-martinez@ec.europa.eu

C. Benedetti Fasil (Deceased)
e-mail: cristiana.benedetti-fasil@ec.europa.eu

involved. Thus, the intricacies surrounding the promotion of innovation, and especially the best approaches to fostering it, play a central role in the European Union's policy landscape. Testament to this are profound debates such as the ones reflected in the European Union's Europe 2020 strategy, which emphasise R&D and innovation as essential means to achieving the overarching goals of jobs, growth and sustainable development. The emphasis of the Europe 2020 strategy is notably on 'improving the conditions for innovation, research and development' (European Council, 2010), with the specific objective of 'increasing combined public and private investment in R&D to 3% of GDP by 2020' (European Commission, 2014).

In the innovation policy debate, the following topics usually take centre stage: (i) best policy practices to spur innovation by the private sector with as large society-wide impacts as possible, (ii) technology diffusion (both across countries and firms), (iii) the apprehension of disruptive innovations, and ways to promote them, iv) the role of non-R&D innovation, v) the role of public versus private R&D.[2] For the specific case of the EU, the most pressing innovation challenges identified include: increasing knowledge-intensive industrial activities, improving access to finance in high growth, highly innovative activities, strengthening the role of higher education institutions in local innovation ecosystems and improving the governance of research and innovation systems.[3]

The increased interest of policymakers in innovation has naturally been accompanied by an increasing need to evaluate the impact of policy measures. EU funding instruments such as the Framework Programme (FP) for research and the regional Europe Structural Investment Funds (ESIF) include legal requirements to collect data on implementation and to undertake evaluations at certain stages of the implementation (mid-term/ex-post, for example). Measuring the impact of innovation is an intricate question compounded by the often relatively long lag between policy initiatives and observed actual impacts. In addition to indicator-based approaches, such as the European Innovation Scoreboard, there has also been mounting interest in undertaking macroeconomic assessments of the impacts on GDP, imports, exports, employment at the EU,

[2] On this last point, see, among others, Mazzucato (2018).

[3] For the most salient documentation on these issues, see European Commission (2015), European Commission (2016), European Commission (2017) and European Commission (2018).

national and regional levels (European Council, 2010). This has provided further momentum to conducting research on the modelling of R&D and innovation policies as an additional way to quantifying the economic impact of innovation policies.

This reader is aimed at bringing to the forefront the latest empirical and theoretical insights stemming from the most recent literature related to the modelling of the macroeconomic impact of R&D policies. The content of this book is thus relevant both to academic and policy-related audiences working in the fields of R&D and innovation. As such, it is a wide-encompassing manuscript containing clear messages and results in the area of R&D and innovation policy and their macroeconomic impact and modelling.

Specifically, the purpose of this volume is threefold. First, to dissect the most relevant empirical facts to date on innovation and growth, and their consequences for policy. Second, to provide an overview of the state-of-the-art of macroeconomic models featuring innovation channels, the new elements of this narrative and their drawbacks. Third, to briefly discuss the models that have been implemented to analyse some of the most relevant innovation policies managed by the European Commission, including succinct examples. Fourth, to bridge the technical discussions offered with precise suggestions on fruitful ways forward, with a view to tackling the most pressing policy demands.

These and other similar questions were the subject of a workshop jointly organised by the International Economic Association and the European Commission's Joint Research Centre in March 2017. Distinguished academics and Commission officials participated and discussed different modelling approaches and issues for modelling R&D and innovation. This book is an off-spring of the discussions in this workshop, and it includes its proceedings.

The book is divided into three parts. In line with the aforementioned objectives, the first part is devoted to overviewing the latest theoretical and empirical contributions in the field of the macroeconomic modelling of R&D and innovation policies.[4] In particular, Chapter 2 overviews the most recent empirical literature and its implications for innovation policy.

[4] Please note that since January 2020, the UK is no longer a member of the EU. However, the contents of this book were written at a time when this status was still not officially recognized. The authors and editors have thus decided to include the UK as part of the EU in all the discussions contained in this reader

Chapter 3 delineates where the literature on DSGE models with innovation dynamics currently stands, the main ingredients of these models, and the paths that the academic literature in this area is set to follow. Chapter 4 presents a succinct summary of the Proceedings of the joint IEA-JRC workshop on 'Macroeconomic Modelling for R&D and Innovation', held in Brussels in March 2017. Part II of the book presents concise overviews of the different macroeconomic models that have been used for innovation policy evaluations by the European Commission in the past. Some examples of such evaluations are also provided, together with brief discussions on them. Finally, Part III presents the main conclusions on the macroeconomic modelling of R&D and innovation policies, and the potential ways forward.

References

European Commission. (2014). *Taking stock of the Europe 2020 strategy for smart, sustainable and inclusive growth*. COM/2014/0130.

European Commission. (2015). *State of the innovation union*. ISBN 978-92-79-52969-6, https://doi.org/10.2777/805999KI-01-15-871-EN-N.

European Commission. (2016). *Better regulations for innovation-driven investment at EU level*. Commission Staff Working Document. ISBN 978-92-79-51529-3, https://doi.org/10.2777/987880KI-04-16-030-EN-N.

European Commission. (2017). *Current challenges in fostering the European innovation ecosystem*. EUR 28796 EN, Publications Office of the European Union, Luxembourg, 2017, ISBN 978-92-79-73862-3, https://doi.org/10.2760/768124, JRC108368.

European Commission. (2018). *A renewed agenda for research and innovation—Europe's change to shape its future*. The European Commission's contribution to the informal EU leaders meeting on innovation. Sofia, 16th of May 2018.

European Council. (2010). *European council conclusions*. 17 June. EUCO 13/10, Brussels, 2010.

Kumar, V., & Sundarraj, R. P. (2018). The Economic Impact of Innovation. In S. Nature (Ed.), *Global innovation and economic value*, Vol. 2, pp. 49–93.

Mazzucato, M. (2018). *The entrepreneurial state*. Penguin Books ISBN 9780141986104.

Schumpeter, J. A. (1934). *The theory of economic development: An inquiry into profits, capital, credit, interest, and the business cycle*. New Brunswick, New Jersey: Transaction Books. ISBN 9780878556984. Translated from the 1911 German original *Theorie der wirtschaftlichen Entwicklung*.

PART I

Macroeconomic Modeling of R&D and Innovation Policies

2

Empirical Literature: Implications for Innovation Policy

Ufuk Akcigit

2.1 Introduction

Innovation and technological progress are the key determinants of long-run economic growth and welfare. For instance, in recent work, Akcigit et al. (2017) (henceforth AGN) show that those states in the US that have innovated more over the twentieth century grew much more rapidly than those that innovated less (see Fig. 2.1). Relatedly, more research effort has been devoted to understanding the social implications of innovation. Does higher GDP per capita or GDP growth increase happiness? The existing empirical literature on happiness and income looks at how various measures of subjective well-being relate to income or income growth. For instance, Aghion et al. (2016) analyze the relationship between creative destruction and subjective well-being. They show that: (i) the effect of creative destruction on expected individual welfare is unambiguously positive if the unemployment rate is controlled for, less so if it is not; (ii) job

U. Akcigit (✉)
University of Chicago, CEPR, and NBER, Chicago, Illinois, USA
e-mail: uakcigit@uchicago.edu

creation has a positive and job destruction a negative impact on well-being; (iii) job destruction has a less negative impact in US Metropolitan Statistical Areas (MSA) within states with more generous unemployment insurance policies; (iv) job creation has a more positive effect on individuals that are more forward-looking.

Given the tight link between innovation, economic growth, and well-being, designing the right public policies to achieve inclusive and sustainable growth requires a good understanding of what lies behind the innovation process. The mapping between innovation and economic growth can be described broadly as

$$\text{Firms} \rightarrow \text{Inventors} \rightarrow \text{Ideas} \rightarrow \text{Aggregate Growth}$$

where firms hire inventors to produce new ideas/technologies which lead to economic growth. In line with this mapping, I will center my discussion in this chapter around three categories: (*i*) firm studies, (*ii*) inventor studies, and (*iii*) idea (patent) studies.

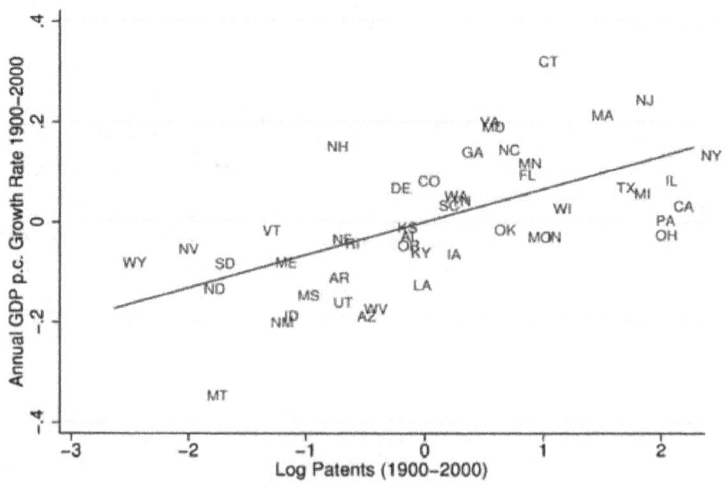

Fig. 2.1 100 Years of Innovation and Economic Growth (US States, 1900–2000) (*Source* Akcigit, Grigsby, and Nicholas [2017])

2.2 Firm Studies

Tax Credit and R&D Incentives of Firms Debates on public policy and economic growth cannot ignore the fact that innovations do not fall from the sky. They are created by firms and inventors who respond to economic incentives and, importantly, incentives are shaped by public policy. A large literature documents the important effects of tax incentives for R&D, thus justifying the detailed study of their optimal design.[1] A recent paper by Akcigit et al. (2017) (henceforth AAI) studies the role of R&D Tax Credit for innovation. In the US, the 1970s was a period of productivity slowdown that raised concerns about the declining international competitiveness of the US. At the time, John McTague of the Reagan White House said, "Foreign competition in the technology intensive industries poses a serious threat to our country's position in the international marketplace than ever before in our history." There are possible policies to deal with this "problem," the most discussed being import tariffs. The result of these debates was the introduction of the Federal R&D Tax Credit for the first time in 1981 (which has been in effect ever since).

Figure 2.2 shows the evolution of average firm-level R&D spending (normalized by firm sales) and the total share of patents at the US Patent Office filed by US firms. There are two facts worth mentioning. First, there had been a massive loss of technology leadership as documented by the rapid decline in the US patent share from 1975 to 1985. Second, US firms showed a large response to policy change. Starting from 1981, firms in the US increased their R&D spending which then translated into more patented innovations and brought international technology catch-up to a halt. How effective were these policies of the 1980s and how do tariffs affect innovation incentives?

Akcigit et al. (2017) assess the effects of import tariffs and R&D subsidies as possible policy responses to foreign technological competition in a dynamic general equilibrium growth model. Their quantitative investigation illustrates that, statically, globalization (defined as reduced trade barriers) has an ambiguous effect on welfare, while, dynamically, intensified globalization boosts domestic innovation through induced international competition. Accounting for transitional dynamics, they compute

[1] Among many others, see Goolsbee (1998), Bloom et al. (2002), Bloom and Griffith (2001), Bloom et al. (2002), and Serrano-Velarde (2009).

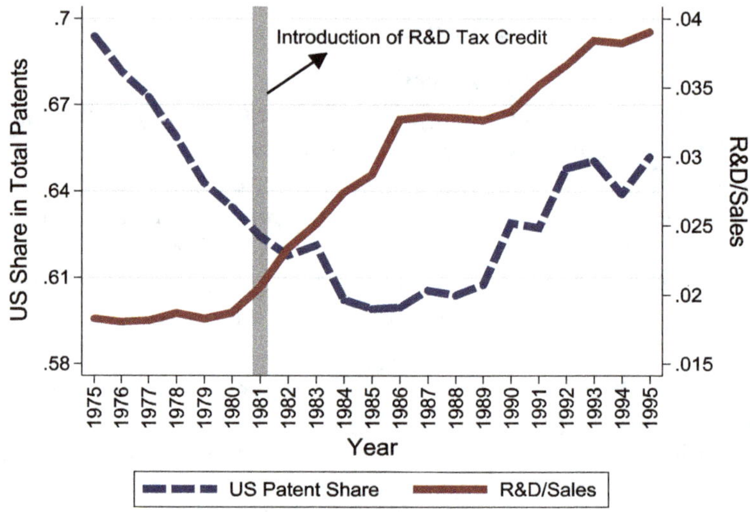

Fig. 2.2 Introduction of R&D Tax Credit, Firm R&D Spending and Innovation in the US (*Source* Akcigit, Ates, and Impullitti [2017])

optimal policies over different time horizons. Their model suggests that the introduction of the Research and Experimentation Tax Credit in 1981 was an effective policy response to foreign competition, generating substantial welfare gains in the long run. A counterfactual exercise shows that increasing trade barriers as an alternative policy response produces gains only in the very short run, and only when introduced unilaterally, while leading to large losses in the medium and long run. Protectionist measures generate large dynamic losses from trade, distorting the impact of openness on innovation incentives and productivity growth. Finally, they show that less government intervention is needed in a globalized world, thanks to intensified international competition as a result of lower trade barriers.

Key takeaway: An important policy message from this example is that tax policy, or specifically the R&D Tax Credit, could contribute to the attractiveness of a country for R&D and be a powerful tool for making firms more innovative and competitive.

Firm Selection and Public Policy The goal of R&D policies is to incentivize firms to undertake greater R&D investment, produce more innovations, increase productivity, and create more jobs. However, these policies do not affect every firm in the economy in the same way. For instance, Criscuolo et al. (2012) have shown that large incumbents are better at obtaining government subsidies. One can argue that R&D subsidies to incumbents might be inefficiently preventing the entry of new firms and therefore slowing down the replacement of inefficient incumbents by more productive new entrants. The turnover and factor reallocation between incumbents and entrants is an important source of productivity growth. Foster et al. (2001, 2006) have shown empirically that the reallocation of factors across firms accounts for more than 50% of productivity growth in the US. Given the empirical importance of this reallocation margin, it is necessary that R&D policy takes into account the interaction between innovation and factor reallocation. This is the focus in Acemoglu et al. (2018) (henceforth AAABK).

AAABK build a model with heterogeneous firm types where type is determined by innovative productivity. For instance, high-type firms produce more innovation for any given level of R&D input than low-type firms. The authors estimate the model by matching various empirical moments capturing key features of firm-level R&D behavior, shipment growth, employment growth, and exit, and the variation of these moments with size and age. They then use the estimated model as a lab to run counterfactual experiments and test the impacts of various observed R&D policies on economic growth and welfare. The policies that the authors consider include a subsidy to new entrants, a subsidy to R&D by incumbents, and a subsidy for the continued operation of incumbents.

The main findings are summarized as follows. Using 1% of the GDP to subsidize new entrants, R&D or continued operations of incumbents have small effects, and some of them even reduce welfare in the economy. This result might suggest that the decentralized equilibrium is already efficient and any subsidy in this environment is making the economy move away from its efficient level. To the contrary, the decentralized equilibrium may be highly inefficient due to the usual intertemporal R&D spillovers and competition (Schumpeterian) effects. However, in this model there is another important margin: *firm selection*.

In order to understand the role of selection, AAABK first solve for the economy's allocation from the viewpoint of a social planner who internalizes all the externalities of R&D spending. What they find is that the social planner forces low-type firms to exit the economy much more frequently, so that all their production resources are reallocated to the high-type firms. Then they turn to the *optimal* public policy experiments in which they assume that the policymaker cannot observe firm types but has access to the usual policy tools such as an R&D subsidy, an entry subsidy, and a subsidy/tax to firm operations. What they find is that the optimal policy requires a substantial tax on the operation of incumbents combined with an R&D subsidy to incumbents. The reason for this result is that taxing operations makes it harder for low-type firms to survive and forces them to exit. The freed-up factors of production are then reallocated to high-type firms, which make use of them much more effectively.

Their general equilibrium analysis, which incorporates both reallocation and selection effects, highlights the fact that the economy in equilibrium might contain too many low-type firms and policies that ignore the selection effect might help low-type firms survive. Another point that is highlighted is the fact that intertemporal spillovers are sizable and overall R&D investment is below the efficient level. Therefore a combination of R&D subsidies and taxes on firm operations could be an effective way of providing innovation incentives to firms, while also leveraging the selection margin in the economy.

Key takeaway: The authors conclude that (i) governments often subsidize industries, (ii) these subsidies typically go to all firms, regardless of performance, (iii) focused subsidies could be more effective since they could redistribute key resources by letting low-type firms exit, and hence exploit the selection of firms in the economy.

2.3 Inventor Studies

Who Becomes an Inventor? Inequality of opportunities to get proper education could prevent the citizens as well as society from realizing their full innovative potential. The strong complementarity between innovation and education is documented by AGN for the US and by Aghion et al. (2017) for Finland.

In Figure 2.3, AGN show that increased education makes it more likely for someone to become an inventor. Figure 2.4, on the other hand, shows that kids with rich parents are also more likely to become inventors. If parental income is the only resource to accessing education, Figures 2.3 and 2.4 suggest that financial constraints could be important impediments to inclusive growth whereby a broader fraction of the society participates in the innovation and growth process.

Key takeaway: An important takeaway from these findings is that public policy needs to ensure access to education for potential future inventors who could generate economic growth through their creative ideas.

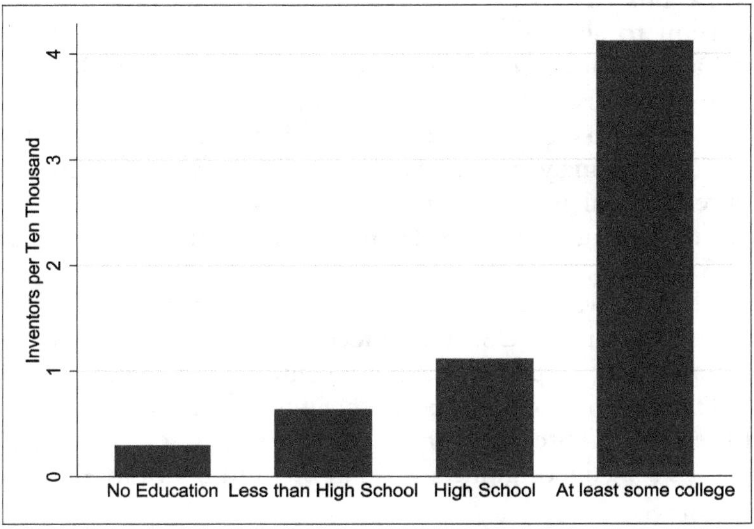

Fig. 2.3 Becoming Inventor and Education (*Source* Akcigit, Grigsby, and Nicholas [2017])

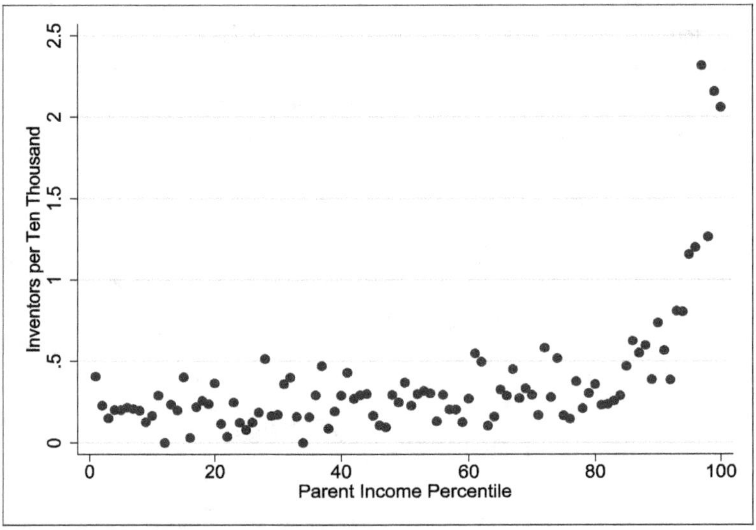

Fig. 2.4 Becoming Inventor and Parental Income (*Source* Akcigit, Grigsby, and Nicholas [2017])

Taxation and Inventor Mobility When it comes to policy debates, it is important to also take into account the disincentive effect of taxes on individuals and inventors in particular. Many of the prolific inventors around the world are international migrants and their location choice is affected by country-specific policies. In their work, Akcigit et al. (2016) (henceforth ABS) analyze the impact of top marginal income tax rates on the international mobility of inventors. Among many other things, they study the changes in tax codes in various countries, as illustrated in Figures 2.5 and 2.6.

Figure 2.5 shows the 1986 Policy Reform that reduced the top marginal tax rate in the US. The effect has been a rise in the number of foreign superstar (highest-quality) inventors who migrate to the US. Similarly, Figure 2.6 shows the policy change in Denmark in 1992 which lowered the top tax rate for high-income foreign researchers. The result of this change is again a significant rise in the number of foreign inventors in the country.

Key takeaway: The analysis by ABS shows the (dis)incentive effects of tax policies. Their findings suggest that some policies (top marginal tax rates, in this case) could impose significant costs on the society through their adverse effects on innovation incentives and economic growth.

Innovation, Inequality and Social Mobility Rising top-income share has been at the center stage of the current policy debates and many of the proposals to combat this trend focus on imposing heavy taxes on top-income groups. These discussions should also take into account

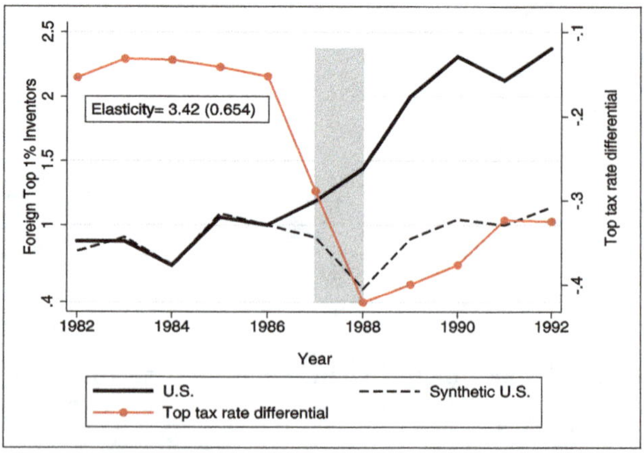

Fig. 2.5 Becoming Inventor and Education (*Source* Akcigit, Baslandze, and Stantcheva [2016])

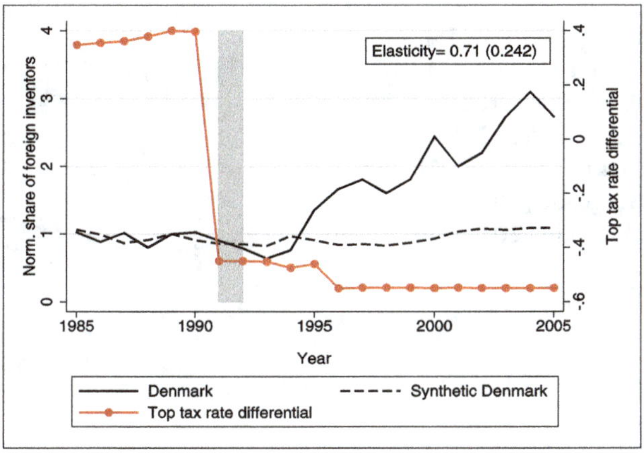

Fig. 2.6 Becoming Inventor and Parental Income (*Source* Akcigit, Baslandze, and Stantcheva [2016])

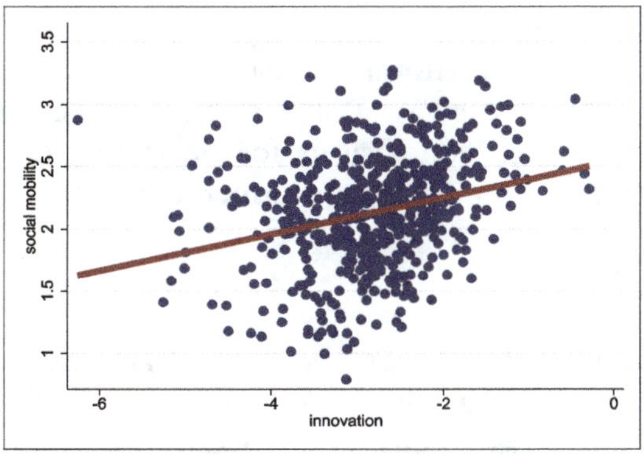

Fig. 2.7 Social Mobility and Patenting across the US Commuting Zones (*Source* Aghion, Akcigit, Bergeaud, Blundell, and Hémous [2018])

the link between top-income inequality and innovation, which has been studied by Aghion et al. (2018) (henceforth AABBH).

Innovation has important and nuanced implications for inequality and social mobility. On the positive side, AABBH show that those US regions (commuting zones) that produced more innovations have also experienced greater social mobility (see Figure 2.7).[2]

Innovation, however, comes with an important trade-off. In Figure 2.8, AABBH also show that the states which had an increase in

[2] Social mobility here is the expected percentile or "rank" (from 0 to 100) for someone aged 30 in 2011–2012 whose parents belonged to some percentile of the income in 1996 when the person was aged 16.

Fig. 2.8 Top-1% Income Share and Patenting across the US States 1980–2005 (*Source* Aghion, Akcigit, Bergeaud, Blundell, and Hémous [2018])

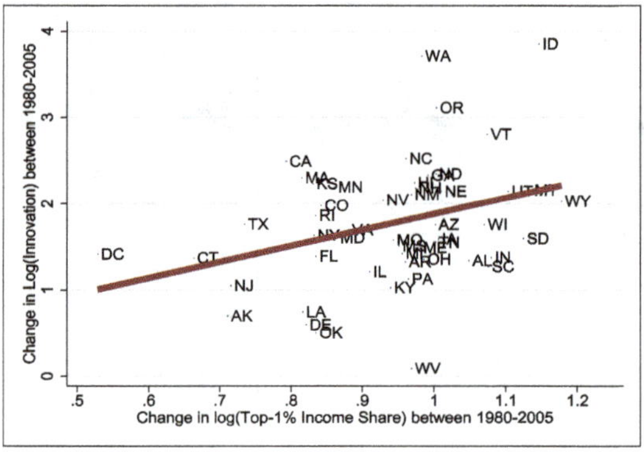

patented innovations also experienced, on average, a rise in top-income share between 1980 and 2005. These findings highlight the fact that while innovation is associated with faster growth and social mobility, it also comes with an increase in top-income inequality.

Key takeaway: Policies should take into account this tradeoff before leaping to conclusions for or against heavy taxation. In particular, high taxation may induce more equality but less social mobility.

2.4 Ideas

Market for Ideas New ideas are the seeds for economic growth. The rise in living standards depends not only on the production of new ideas (as it was discussed in Section 2.2), but also on the effectiveness of transforming new ideas into consumer products or production processes. Incarnating an idea into a product or a production process is by no means immediate. What happens to ideas and patents once they are produced? While a lot of the policy discussions center around increasing the number of ideas/patents/technologies produced, very little attempt is made at understanding how these new ideas are utilized after their invention. Akcigit et al. (2016) fill this gap by studying the secondary market for patents.

Ideas are not necessarily born to their best users and firms often develop patents that are not close to their primary business activity. This initial "mismatch" could potentially be mitigated in a secondary market where firms can buy and sell patents through patent agents (intermediaries). In Akcigit et al. (2016), the authors study the secondary market for ideas (patents) in the US. They build an endogenous growth model where firms invest in R&D to produce new ideas. An idea increases a firm's productivity. By how much depends on the technological distance between an idea and the firm's line of business. Ideas can be bought and sold on a market for patents. A firm can sell an idea that is not relevant to its business or buy one if it fails to innovate. The model is matched to stylized facts from the market for patents in the US. The analysis gauges how efficiency in the patent market affects growth. They find that the contribution of the secondary market for patents to the overall productivity is quantitatively significant.

Key takeaway: The immediate policy implication of this study is that strengthening the market for technologies could make economies use their scarce innovations and ideas better by allocating them to better users.

Patent Trolls The secondary market for patents suffers from various frictions and so-called "patent trolls" or non-practicing entities (NPEs) have emerged due to these frictions. Despite the attention on NPEs in the media and in policy circles, there is almost no systematic evidence on their business activities. How do NPEs impact innovation and technological progress? The question has enormous importance for industrial policy, with virtually no direct empirical evidence to start answering it.

A recent paper (Abrams et al., 2017) takes a major step in this direction by making use of some NPE-derived patent and financial data to answer this question. In doing so the authors inform the debate that has portrayed NPEs alternatively as benign middlemen that help to reallocate IP to where it is most productive or stick-up artists that exploit the patent system to extract rents, thereby hurting innovation. They find that NPEs target patents coming from small firms that are more litigation-prone, and patents from large firms that are not core to a company's business. When NPEs license patents, those that generate higher fees are closer to the licensee's business and more likely to be litigated. These findings suggest that NPEs could serve as middlemen in the market for technologies when frictions like high search costs or informational asymmetry between potential licensors and licensees are present.

Key takeaway: Taken together, the evidence in this paper is mixed and does not solely support the benign middleman or the stick-up artist theory. Rather it suggests that there are some aspects of NPEs that may increase innovation and some that may not. Therefore a more nuanced perspective on NPEs as well as additional empirical work is necessary before informed policy decisions can be made.

2.5 Conclusion

To sum up, innovation is good for society for at least three reasons: it leads to economic growth, social mobility, and happiness.

On the firm side, industrial policies could encourage more innovation, if we guide our innovation policy in an informed way, especially thinking about how the competition will have differential effects in different industries. The analysis on trade and innovation also shows that protectionist policies are detrimental for competition and growth, suggesting that the single-market policies of EU that remove trade barriers would stimulate more innovation and productivity growth. When it comes to individuals, a strong education policy could be a very influential innovation policy. High taxation could have significant disincentive effects for innovators, which could also harm social mobility in the society. Finally, having a well-functioning market for technologies could make economies utilize their scarce innovative ideas much more effectively.

Even though some of these studies use data from the US, their findings are much more general and relevant for all frontier countries that aim to grow through innovations. These findings show that public policy, innovation, market for ideas, and economic growth are tightly interlinked. Therefore any discussion on public policy and growth cannot be pursued in isolation from innovations and their effective use in practice, which are the main sources of long-run economic growth and prosperity.

The main lessons from these studies for Europe can be summarized as follows: First, international competition is healthy for innovation incentives. Second, innovation policies, such as R&D subsidies, require patience on the policymaker side, as these subsidies impact the economy in the medium-to-long run. Third, industrial policy needs to take into account the firm composition and factor reallocation in the economy. Bailing-out unproductive firms could slowdown factor reallocation from unproductive incumbents to more productive entrants. Fourth, education policy could be a very effective innovation policy in Europe. Providing as much equal opportunity for education as possible could improve the quality of the inventor pool and the overall innovation capacity. Fifth, the design of income tax policy has to take into account the fact that inventors do respond to incentives. Therefore one policy direction could be to couple income tax with tax breaks or research grants to inventors in order to undo the potential disincentive effects of taxes. Finally, the use of new technologies is at least as important as their inventions. Hence, Europe might also have to focus on its secondary market for technologies, in particular on technology sale and licensing, in order to improve its overall productivity.

References

Abrams, D. S., Akcigit, U., & Oz, G. (2017). Patent trolls: Benign Middleman or Stick-up artist? University of Chicago, Working Paper.

Acemoglu, D., Akcigit, U., Alp, H., Bloom, N., & Kerr, W. R. (2018). Innovation, reallocation, and growth. *American Economic Review,* 108(11), 3450–91. https://doi.org/10.1257/aer.20130470.

Aghion, P., Akcigit, U., Bergeaud, A., Blundell, R., & Hémous, D. (2018). Innovation and top income inequality. *Review of Economic Studies,* 86(1), 1–45.

Aghion, P., Akcigit, U., Deaton, A., & Roulet, A. (2016). Creative destruction and subjective wellbeing. *American Economic Review, 106*(12), 3869–3897.

Aghion, P., Akcigit, U., Hyytinen, A., & Toivanen, O. (2017). Social origins and IQ of inventors. NBER Working Paper #24110.

Akcigit, U., Ates, S., & Impullitti, G. (2017). Innovation and trade policy in a globalized world. National Bureau of Economic Research Working Paper #24543.

Akcigit, U., Baslandze, S., & Stantcheva, S. (2016). Taxation and the international migration of inventors. *American Economic Review, 106*(10), 2930–2981.

Akcigit, U., Celik, M. A., & Greenwood, J. (2016). Buy, keep or sell: Economic growth and the market for ideas. *Econometrica, 84*(3), 943–984.

Akcigit, U., Grigsby, J., & Nicholas, T. (2017). The rise of American ingenuity: Innovation and inventors of the Golden Age. National Bureau of Economic Research Working Paper #23047.

Bloom, N., Chennells, L., Griffith, R., & Van Reenen, J. (2002). How has tax affected the changing cost of R&D? Evidence from eight countries. In *The Regulation of Science and Technology*, pp. 136–160. Springer.

Bloom, N., & Griffith, R. (2001). The Internationalisation of UK R&D. *Fiscal Studies, 22*(3), 337–355.

Bloom, N., Griffith, R., & Van Reenen, J. (2002). Do R&D tax credits work? Evidence from a panel of countries 1979–1997. *Journal of Public Economics, 85*(1), 1–31.

Criscuolo, C., Martin, R., Overman, H., & Van Reenen, J. (2012). The causal effects of an industrial policy. National Bureau of Economic Research Working Paper #17842.

Foster, L., Haltiwanger, J., & Krizan, C. J. (2006). Market selection, reallocation, and restructuring in the US retail trade sector in the 1990s. *Review of Economics and Statistics, 88*(4), 748–758.

Foster, L., Haltiwanger, J. C., & Krizan, C. J. (2001). Aggregate productivity growth: Lessons from microeconomic evidence. In *New Developments in Productivity Analysis*, pp. 303–372. University of Chicago Press.

Goolsbee, A. (1998). Does R&D policy primarily benefit scientists and engineers? *American Economic Review (Papers and Proceedings), 88*(2), 298–302.

Serrano-Velarde, N. (2009). Crowding-out at the top: The heterogeneous impact of R&D subsidies on firm investment. Bocconi Working Paper.

3

Analyzing Innovation, Endogenous Growth and Firm Dynamics

Omar Licandro

3.1 Introduction

This chapter surveys the literature on innovation, endogenous growth and firm dynamics, aiming to better understand the mechanisms through which innovation policies affect the progress of technology, productivity growth, output growth and welfare. When modeling the macroeconomy with the objective of evaluating the effect of innovation policies, the modeler has to fundamentally understand the different mechanisms through which a policy is expected to affect the dynamics of the economy through innovation. Since innovations fundamentally diffuse through a complex process of firm, plant and product creation and destruction, it is critical to understand the relation between innovation and the dynamics of market selection.

In writing this survey, an effort has been made to keep notation consistent across different models, imposing assumptions and interpreting results under a common framework, making models as comparable as possible. Section 3.2 gives a preliminary picture of these similarities by

O. Licandro (✉)
University of Nottingham, Nottingham, UK
e-mail: Omar.Licandro@nottingham.ac.uk

pointing out some fundamental issues that arise when modeling innovation in a context of heterogeneous firms. It stresses the dynamic nature of the innovation process, describes the usual assumptions about firm heterogeneity in the context of innovation models of perfect, monopolistic and oligopolistic competition, uses aggregation theory to relate models of heterogeneous firms with the one-final-good Neoclassical and endogenous growth models, draws attention to the equivalence between (sunk) entry costs and R&D irreversible investments, as well as the embodied nature of technical progress.

Section 3.3 describes and analyzes firm heterogeneity in models of exogenous growth, starting with the perfectly competitive model of heterogeneous firms first developed by Hopenhayn, to then study a close economy version of the monopolistic competitive model first suggested by Melitz (2003) to finally refer to the close economy version of the oligopolistic model developed by Impullitti and Licandro (2018).

Finally, Sect. 3.4 studies firm heterogeneity in models of endogenous growth in order to understand the role of selection in shaping innovation and productivity growth. This section relates the traditional Romer (1990) and Schumpeterian (Aghion & Howitt, 1992) models to the recent literature on endogenous growth with firm heterogeneity, discussing the selection and imitation mechanism suggested by Luttmer (2007) and Klette and Kortum (2004).

3.2 Preliminaries

Before surveying the literature on firm dynamics and innovation, this section revises some critical concepts.

Time. Since the Industrial Revolution, modern economies live in a permanent state of innovation and progress. In this sense, innovation has to be understood as a dynamic process fueling technological developments. For this reason, the literature on economic growth belongs to the family of dynamic stochastic general equilibrium (DSGE) models where time is a fundamental dimension of the economic system. Static models are some times used as a shortcut, however, by construction they miss a fundamental dimension of the innovation process: It takes a long time to implement, adopt and diffuse new technologies.[1]

[1] Different authors have measured the time it takes for innovation to diffuse. Comin and Hobijn (2010) estimate that new technologies take around fifty years to be adopted

Aggregate macroeconomic and microeconomic data are generally collected monthly, quarterly or annually. As a consequence, models designed to simulate and evaluate innovation policies often assume that time is discrete. In this chapter instead, we choose to follow the main tradition of economic growth theory and assume that time is continuous. Moreover, we abstract from aggregate shocks, even when some of the models reviewed originally embody aggregate stochastic processes.

Firm Heterogeneity. New technologies are fundamentally developed and implemented by the private sector. In a decentralized world, technical progress operates through the creation and destruction of products, plants and firms. In this sense, understanding the innovation process requires a minimum degree of firm heterogeneity and a good understanding of the dynamics of firms and markets.

The recent literature on firm dynamics usually models firm heterogeneity by assuming that the productivity of a firm can be characterized by some variable z. A firm entering the economy at time t draws its initial z, let us denote it by z_t, from some known entry (density) distribution $\psi_t(z)$. The entry distribution may be evolving over time. The support of the entry distribution is usually assumed to be in the real line, with some lower bound $\zeta_t \geq 0$.[2] As time passes, the productivities of these firms evolve following independent Markov processes. Equilibrium at time t will be then characterized as an equilibrium productivity (density) distribution that we denote by $\phi_t(z)$, for $z \geq z_t^*$, where z_t^* is the productivity of the least productive firm still surviving on the market. This is commonly called the cut-off productivity level.

In this review, we mainly concentrate on the study of economies where the productivity of a firm is time invariant, meaning that at entry firms draw a productivity z from $\psi_t(z)$, for $z \geq \zeta_t$, $\zeta_t \geq 0$, and keep this productivity constant all along their active life. In stationary economies, the entry distribution $\psi(z)$ and the lower bound of its support ζ are assumed to be time invariant. Instead, in growing economies the entry distribution $\psi_t(z)$

worldwide after their invention. When compared to the US, Comin et al. (2008) estimate that the lag in the use of new technologies by most countries is measured in decades. Adams (1990) measures in roughly 20 years the time it takes academic knowledge to contribute to productivity growth. Mansfield (1989) quantifies in 8 years the mean adoption delay of twelve mayor 20th-century innovations. Jovanovic and Lach (1997) estimate at 8.1% the annual diffusion rate of new products.

[2] Some papers, like Melitz and Redding (2015), assume also that the support of entry distribution has a finite upper bound.

will move overtime guided by some form of spillover, as well as the lower bound of its support ζ_t. Hence, a stationary entry distribution will not result in growing average productivity.

A standard assumption in this literature is that a firm with productivity z employs some flexible production factor x to produce output y. In the following, inputs and output of a firm with productivity z will be denoted $x(z)$ and $y(z)$, respectively. In perfectly competitive economies, this technology is assumed to have decreasing returns on x. However, under monopolistic competition, including also other forms of imperfect competition, technology is frequently assumed to be linear on x. Hopenhayn and Melitz, respectively assume $y(z) = z\,x(z)^{\alpha}$, $\alpha \in (0, 1)$ and $y(z) = z\,x(z)$. Following Collard and Licandro (2018), we will in some sections assume that $y(z) = F\big(z, x(z)\big)$, with $F(.)$ being a Neoclassical technology.

This literature often abstracts from capital accumulation by assuming that labor ℓ is the sole production factor, i.e. $x = \ell$. Hopenhayn (2014) generalizes it to a two production factor economy, with $x = F(k, \ell)$; k represents capital and $F(k, \ell)$ is assumed to be a Neoclassical technology.

In line with the Neoclassical growth framework, we survey first models where the productivity of firms is stationary or evolves exogenously, to then study models where firm heterogeneity is guided by innovation and technological developments.

Entry Cost, Innovation and Capital Reversibility. It is generally assumed that firms have to pay some entry cost before they draw productivity z from $\psi_t(z)$. On top of that, the entry cost is frequently assumed to be sunk, i.e. the investment realized to create the firm is irreversible: When a firm closes down, nothing is recovered from this investment. Moreover, it is usual that net revenues of operative firms are strictly positive, implying that fixed production costs need to be assumed for the least productive firms to exit.[3]

Interestingly, the sunk entry cost, even when fully irreversible, can be interpreted as a form of intangible investment. Since operative firms make positive profits at equilibrium, the value of the firm, namely the expected

[3] In Hopenhayn (1992), net revenues are strictly concave due to decreasing returns to labor; at equilibrium, low productivity firms optimally hire few workers making net revenues strictly positive. In Melitz (2003), monopoly profits are strictly concave implying that low productive firms also optimally hire few workers making net revenues strictly positive.

discounted flow of profits, is the value of the associated intangible investment. Firms close down and exit when the value of their intangible capital is zero.

As an alternative and consistent with national accounts, Collard and Licandro (2018) assume that the entry cost is a form of capital investment (tangible and intangible), with capital being partially reversible, i.e. it has a market value smaller than the replacement cost. Under very general assumptions about firms'technology, they show that aggregate technology is Neoclassical on aggregate capital and labor. Moreover, since capital is partially reversible, no fixed production cost is needed for the least productive firms to exit: Firms exit when the value of being operative is smaller than the market value of capital.

In the endogenous growth literature, when innovation is assumed to be undertaken by new entrant firms, R&D investment is a form of entry cost.[4] Firms have to invest in R&D in order to innovate and then enter the economy. In Romer (1990), new firms innovate by creating a new variety. Since firms are never displaced in the Romer's model, the R&D investment can be seen as fully reversible. Patents can be transferred at no cost. In the Schumpeterian model of Aghion and Howitt (1992) or in the Grossman and Helpman (1991)'s quality-ladder model the entering firm displaces an incumbent firm, which is known as business-stealing effect. R&D investments are then fully irreversible in these two models.

One-Final-Good Economy. Macroeconomic models are designed to understand the behavior of GDP as measured by national accounts. Consistently, in the tradition of the Neoclassical growth theory, an economy is modeled as producing a sole final good, directly associated to GDP in the data. The final good is then allocated to different uses, such as consumption or investment. Macroeconomic models of heterogeneous firms belong to this tradition.

For example, in Hopenahyn (1992) the production side of an economy is modeled as a mass of heterogeneous firms that produce the sole final good under perfect competition. Hence, in these economies, firm's technology has decreasing returns on labor, in line with the Lucas (1978)'s span of control model.

[4] In Sect. 4.4, some models of innovation by incumbents, where R&D does not play the role of an entry cost, are also surveyed. Another example of such models can be found in Akcigit and Kerr (2017).

Alternatively, in the monopolistic competitive approach inspired in Dixit and Stiglitz (1977), a perfectly competitive, representative firm produces the sole final good by the mean of a constant elasticity of substitution technology defined on a continuum of heterogeneous intermediary inputs, which are assumed to be gross substitutes. The market for intermediary inputs is assumed to be monopolistically competitive. Each heterogeneous intermediary firm has monopoly power on the production of a particular intermediary input and owns a constant return to scale technology defined on a vector of production factors (usually labor only).[5] An alternative and isomorphic way of representing the same economy is to assume that the monopolistically competitive firms produce a continuum of final consumption goods that households order by the mean of a constant elasticity of substitution utility function. Consumption in national accounts is then interpreted as the aggregate of all the different consumption goods, aggregated by the mean of household preferences.

Aggregation. As shown by Hopenhayn and Collard and Licandro (2018), most of these economies share some simple aggregation properties that cause aggregate technology to be Neoclassical in exogenously driven growth models. These aggregation properties are shared with most endogenous growth models, where aggregate technology indeed belongs to the family of AK production functions. The main implication is that aggregate conditions are quite standard despite the complexity added by firm heterogeneity.

Spillovers. In the Neoclassical growth model, technical progress is a gift offered by Nature that instantaneously diffuses over the whole economy without limit: All firms and countries may access the frontier technology. In particular, the representative firm benefits from it without paying any cost. In this sense, technical progress in the Neoclassical growth model is nothing else than spillovers! Of course, since technical progress is part of the environment, and Nature gives rise to it without facing any trade-off, a perfectly competitive economy reacts to it optimally. Hence, in the Neoclassical growth mode technical progress diffuses through inconsequential spillovers.

However, when innovations are added to the picture endogenizing the rate of technical progress, spillovers become consequential. For example,

[5] This framework has been extended to alternative forms of imperfect competition, see Atkeson and Burstein (2008) and Impullitti and Licandro (2018).

endogenous growth in the learning-by-doing model is based on a particular form of spillover: the state of technology depends on past capital production. Consequently, investors (i) do not internalize the effect of their actions on technical progress, (ii) invest less than optimal and (iii) the economy grows at a rate smaller than the optimal growth rate. Similarly, in Romer (1990) expanding-product-variety model, innovators increase the mass of intermediary inputs, which affect the productivity of final producers through another form of spillover externality.

In the Schumpeterian and quality-ladder models, the technology of innovators builds upon the pre-existing state of knowledge. This operates as a form of spillover, since the knowledge that innovators create, indeed, flows back to the economy improving the innovation technology of the following innovators. Hence, when innovators substitute Nature, investing resources to make the technology progress, since they do not internalize knowledge spillovers, spillovers become consequential.

Technological spillovers result from a fundamental property of knowledge, the so-called *non-rivalry*: The use of some knowledge by an individual or firm does not prevent another by using it simultaneously. The fact that an engineer is using the Pythagoras theorem to calculate some structures does not impede others from using it too. For this fundamental reason, a model designed to evaluate innovation policies has to include knowledge spillovers, as well as the potential distortions generated by the policies, in particular those addressed to protect intellectual property rights. In this sense, it is important to understand that innovation policies have to be analyzed in a second-best framework.

Embodied Technical Change. The evidence of a permanent decline in the price of durable goods (including equipment investment, structures, durable consumption and some forms of intangible capital), relative to the price of non-durable consumption and services, gave raise to a large literature stressing the importance of modeling the economy as a two-sector model with durable and non-durable goods. The standard way of modeling is in line with Greenwood et al. (1997).[6]

As aforementioned, in the Neoclassical growth model technical progress is disembodied: new technologies diffuse all over the economy at no cost. Instead, when technical progress is embodied in capital, it requires investments to diffuse. The frontier of technology moves in

[6] See also Felbermayr and Licandro (2005).

the investment sector, but investments are needed to allow for technical progress to diffuse to the consumption sector.

Finally, in the vintage capital literature the gift of Nature is only addressed to new capital units.[7] Investment is key for an economy that wants to benefit from the progress of technology, since technical progress does not spillover previously produced capital. For this reason, technical progress in the vintage capital model, is said to be embodied in new capital. Moreover, a perfectly competitive vintage capital economy optimally reacts to technical change. The fact that the gift of Nature only flows over the capital producing industry is also inconsequential (Solow, 1962).

3.3 Firm Dynamics and the Neoclassical Model

The seminal work of Jovanovic (1982) and Hopenhayn (1992), and the subsequent application to international trade by Melitz (2003), gave raise to an extensive literature on the macroeconomic implications of firm dynamics pointing to the fundamental role of market selection on economic performance and welfare. Even if Jovanovic (1982) stresses the role of incomplete information and learning, in the Hopenhayn (1992) framework heterogeneous firms operate in perfectly competitive markets, making selection to be optimal by construction. In the Melitz (2003) model of monopolistic competition, instead, selection interacts with different types of market frictions, making welfare gains from selection less obvious.

As mentioned, time is assumed to be continuous and denoted by t, with $t = 0$ being the initial time. Population is assumed to be constant and normalized to one, implying that aggregate variables are measured in per capita terms. There is a sole final good which is adopted as numeraire, even if in some sections of the chapter the implications of multiple final goods (consumption and investment, for example) are discussed.

A representative household, with additively separable constant intertemporal elasticity of substitution (CIES) preferences, inelastically offers one unit flow of labor. Households face perfect financial markets with riskless interest rate r_t. The saving behavior of the representative

[7] See Solow (1962) and Solow et al. (1966), and more recently, Boucekkine et al. (1997, 2005) and Gilchrist and Williams (2000). Bambi et al. (2014) develop an endogenous growth model of vintage technologies.

household then reduces to the well-known Euler equation

$$\frac{\dot{c}_t}{c_t} = \sigma(r_t - \rho), \tag{EE}$$

where c_t is per capita consumption, $\sigma > 0$ is the intertemporal elasticity of substitution and $\rho > 0$ is the subjective discount rate. When financial markets value time more than individuals subjectively do, i.e. when $r_t > \rho$, individuals optimally save and postpone consumption, making $\frac{\dot{c}_t}{c_t} > 0$. The intensity of consumption postponement depends on the intertemporal elasticity of substitution. In the extreme case of intertemporal perfect substitutability, when σ goes to ∞, for a given difference $r_t - \rho > 0$, individuals postpone any consumption, making $\frac{\dot{c}_t}{c_t} = \infty$. In the other extreme of perfect complementarity, when σ goes to 0, any given difference $r_t - \rho > 0$ has no effect on the consumption path that will be in any case constant.

3.3.1 Ramsey-Hopenhayn Model

The Economy. A continuum of perfectly competitive heterogeneous firms produces at time t a sole final good using capital as a fixed production factor and labor as a flexible factor.[8]

A firm, when associated to a particular unit of capital, has a time invariant productivity z, with $\phi_t(z)$ representing the equilibrium (density) productivity distribution, for z in the support (z_t^*, ∞); the so-called cut-off productivity z_t^* is endogenous. To fix ideas, let us see each unit of capital as a plant. Firms may own different plants with different productivity. $\phi_t(z)$ is the distribution of productivity across plants. Buying one unit of capital costs η units of the final good, $\eta > 1$. However, when transformed back into the final good, the capital unit is worth just one unit. In line with the misallocation literature, investment distortions are measured by $\eta - 1 > 0$.[9] In this sense, investment is partially sunk, since firms cannot recover their investment fully when a plant closes down.

[8] This section is inspired in Collard and Licandro (2018).

[9] See Hsieh and Klenow (2009). For a survey on this literature, see Restuccia and Rogerson (2017). Hopenhayn (2014) shows the intrinsic relation between the literature on firm dynamics and the literature on misallocation.

A plant with productivity z has access to technology[10]

$$y_t(z) = A_t\, z^{\alpha} \ell_t(z)^{1-\alpha}, \tag{3.1}$$

with $\alpha \in (0, 1)$.[11] The state of technology A_t exogenously grows at the rate $(1-\alpha)\gamma$, $\gamma > 0$. Variables $y_t(z)$ and $\ell_t(z)$ denote output and employment, respectively. It is easy to see that, for a given wage rate w_t, the optimal labor demand is

$$\ell_t(z) = \left(\frac{(1-\alpha)A_t}{w_t}\right)^{\frac{1}{\alpha}} z.$$

Since operative plants produce all the same final good, per capita production (remind that population has been normalized to one) is

$$y_t = k_t \int_{z_t^*}^{\infty} y_t(z)\phi_t(z)\mathrm{d}z,$$

where k_t represents the mass of operative plants, which by assumption is equal to the stock of capital per capita.

Labor market clearing implies that the equilibrium wage rate, plant profits and per capita output are, respectively,

$$w_t = (1-\alpha)A_t\left(\bar{z}_t k_t\right)^{\alpha}, \quad \pi_t(z) = \alpha A_t\left(\bar{z}_t k_t\right)^{\alpha-1} z \ \text{ and } \ y_t = A_t\left(\bar{z}_t k_t\right)^{\alpha}, \tag{3.2}$$

where the average productivity of firms is

$$\bar{z}_t = \int_{z_t^*}^{\infty} z\phi_t(z)\mathrm{d}z.$$

At equilibrium aggregate technology is Cobb-Douglas with total factor productivity given by $A_t\, \bar{z}_t^{\alpha}$.[12] Wages and profits are equal to the marginal product of labor and capital, respectively. Selection raises the average

[10] The argument below applies to any Neoclassical technology $F(z, \ell)$.

[11] This technology is in line with the span of control assumption in Lucas (1978).

[12] Alternatively, Collard and Licandro (2018) interpret productivity z as being embodied in capital, meaning that $\bar{z}$ represents the average quality of the physical capital k and $\bar{z}k$ measures capital in quality adjusted units.

productivity of firms, increasing output y_t, wages w_t, and average profits $\pi_t(\bar{z}_t)$.

Selection. New plants buy one unit of capital and then draw productivity z from the entry distribution $\psi(z)$, for z in the positive real line. Let us assume $\psi(z)$ is Pareto, with tail parameter $\kappa > 1$ and expected productivity at entry equal to one (which implies that the lower bound of the support of z is $\frac{\kappa-1}{\kappa}$). As shown in Collard and Licandro (2018) under some general conditions, for all time $t \geq 0$, the equilibrium cut-off productivity is $z_t^* = z^*$ (time invariant) and the equilibrium productivity distribution is the entry distribution truncated at z^*; i.e.,

$$\phi_t(z) = \frac{\psi(z)}{1 - \Psi(z^*)},$$

for all $t \geq 0$ and for $z \in (z^*, \infty)$, where $\Psi(z)$ is the cumulative of $\psi(z)$.[13]

Since profits are linear on z and the equilibrium z^* is time invariant, the value of any operative plant $v_t(z)$ is linear on z too. Notice that operative plants at $t = 0$ will optimally like to be operative forever. At equilibrium, then

$$v_t(z) = v_t z, \qquad \text{and} \qquad v_t = \int_t^{\infty} \pi_s(1)\, \mathrm{e}^{\int_s^{\infty}(r_h+\delta)\mathrm{d}h} \mathrm{d}s$$

where v_t is the expected discounted flow of profits of a firm with productivity $z = 1$ and $\delta > 0$ is an exogenous exit rate, equivalent to the physical depreciation rate in the Neoclassical model. The path of v_t depends on the path of the aggregates.

The equilibrium cut-off productivity z^* results then from combining the exit and free entry conditions

$$v_t z^* = 1 \qquad (\mathrm{EC_{RH}})$$

$$\Psi(z^*) + \left(1 - \Psi(z^*)\right) v_t \bar{z} = \eta \qquad (\mathrm{FE_{RH}})$$

[13] There are two critical assumptions behind this result. Firstly, the economy is assumed to be at steady state at the initial time $t = 0$. Secondly, a permanent and unanticipated shock makes the economy become more selective. The first is a very usual assumption in macro dynamics. The second restrict the analysis to policies that promote selection, which in this framework, are welfare improving.

From the exit condition (EC_{RH}), the value of the marginal plant, $v_t z^*$, is equal to the value of capital (which is equal to one, since capital can be transformed back into one unit of the final good). From the free entry condition (FE_{RH}), the investment cost η has to be equal to the expected value of entry. Notice that a new plant expects to get a productivity smaller than z^* with probability $\Psi(z^*)$, in which case immediately exits and recovers one. Otherwise, with probability $1 - \Psi(z^*)$, the plant will produce and get an expected value $v_t \bar{z}$.

The equilibrium cut-off productivity results from combining (EC_{RH}) and (FE_{RH}) to get rid of v_t. Collard and Licandro (2018) show that under very general conditions the solution exists and is unique, with $z^* > 1/\eta$ depending only on the entry distribution $\psi(z)$ and the investment distortion $\eta - 1$.[14] Both, a reduction in investment distortions and an increase in the variance of the entry distribution raise z^* by reducing the cost of entry and increasing the likelihood of reaping the benefits of a high productivity draw, respectively.

Aggregate Economy. Since the capital of exiting plants (those with productivity smaller than z^*) is fully recycled, the efficiency condition reads

$$y_t + \Psi(z^*)e_t = c_t + \eta e_t,$$

where e_t represents entry, i.e., the mass of new plants created at time t. Each new plant needs a unit of capital, which costs η. Moreover, a fraction $\Psi(z^*)$ of them close down and their capital reverts to the economy, being consumed or invested.[15]

Capital per capita evolves following

$$\dot{k}_t = \big(1 - \Psi(z^*)\big)e_t - \delta k_t,$$

[14] This result generalizes the separation result in Melitz (2003), making selection to be independent of the path of the aggregates.

[15] It is implicitly assumed that the selection process at any time t repeats infinitely until all firms get a productivity larger than z^*. Collard and Licandro (2018) use the alternative assumption that the capital of plants closing down at t cannot be recycled until $t + dt$, in which case the dynamics of Ramsey-Hopenhayn economy is slightly different even if it still shows standard (saddle-path) monotonic convergence properties.

where $\delta > 0$ is the physical rate of capital depreciation. The feasibility condition results from combining the previous two equations

$$\dot{k}_t = \frac{1 - \Psi(z^*)}{\eta - \Psi(z^*)}\left(A_t\left(\bar{z}k_t\right)^{\alpha} - c_t\right) - \delta k_t. \tag{FC}$$

Notice that the rate at which the final good transforms into physical capital is smaller than one, since investment distortions make the selection process costly.

Combining the exit condition (EC_RH) and the Euler equation (EE), the last one reads

$$\frac{\dot{c}_t}{c_t} = \sigma\left(z^*\alpha A_t\left(\bar{z}k_t\right)^{\alpha-1} - \rho - \delta\right), \tag{EE$'$}$$

where the marginal product of capital corresponds to the profits of the marginal plant z^*.

Given an initial $k_0 > 0$, the equilibrium cut-off z^* and the associated average productivity $\bar{z}$, an aggregate equilibrium of the Ramsey-Hopenhyan model is a path $\{c_t, k_t\}$, for $t \geq 0$, such that both (EE') and (FC) conditions hold (together with a transversality condition) It is important to notice that (FC) and (EE') are the same as in the Neoclassical growth model, with a few constant terms depending on the equilibrium value of z^*. At the balanced growth path the economy then grows at the constant rate γ.

Collard and Licandro (2018) show that a policy that decreases investment distortions, by making the economy more efficient, increases capital, output and consumption (measured in efficiency units) at the balanced growth path, generating steady state welfare gains. Moreover, the dynamic system has standard stability properties, meaning that the economy monotonically converges to a unique balanced growth path.

Transitional Dynamics. Let us assume the economy was initially at steady state with past investment distortions given by $\eta_p > 1$.[16] For simplicity, the rate of technical progress is $\gamma = 0$. Consistently, the economy at the initial time $t = 0$ has a distribution of firms $\phi_p(z) = \psi(z)/\left(1 - \Psi(z_p^*)\right)$ in the support $z \in (z_p^*, \infty)$, as well as an initial stock of physical capital k_p; both z_p^* and k_p solve the steady state equilibrium conditions.

[16] These distortions may represent different forms of barriers to entry.

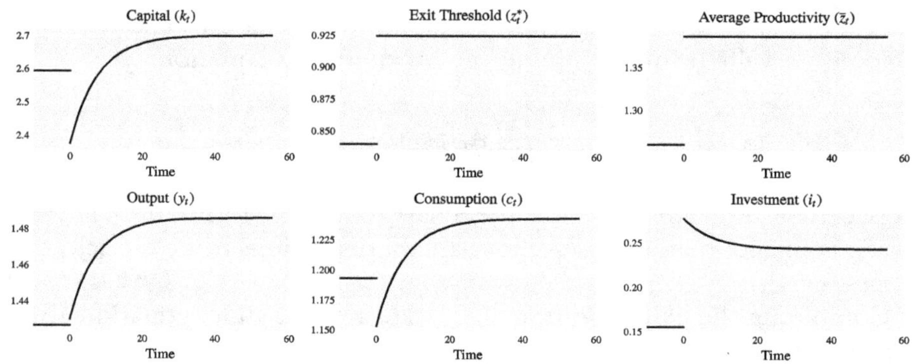

Fig. 3.1 Transition dynamics: permanent decline in investment distortions (η) (*Note* This figure was obtained setting $\sigma = 1$, $\rho = 0.05$, $\delta = 0.06$, $\alpha = 0.3$, $\kappa = 3$ and the initial investment distortion is $\eta = 1.2$. We then consider a 5% once for all reduction in η)

Let us also assume that from $t = 0$ a new policy permanently reduces investment distortions. For simplicity, let us refer to the new policy as η, with $\eta < \eta_p$. The cut-off productivity jumps then to a new steady state $z^* > z_p^*$ and the equilibrium distribution jumps to $\phi(z) = \psi(z)/(1 - \Psi(z^*))$.

Interestingly, the initial stock of capital is partially destroyed because of selection, implying that

$$k_0 = \left(1 - \frac{\eta - 1}{\eta - \Psi(z^*)}\Phi_p(z^*)\right)k_p < k_p.$$

Of course, the average productivity $\bar{z}$ jumps up at $t = 0$ making output to increase at the initial time. Similarly to the Neoclassical growth model, consumption at the initial time jumps down to the new saddle path solution converging monotonically with capital to the new higher steady state.

3.3.2 *Monopolistic Competition*

This section builds on a close economy of the Melitz (2003) type.

The Economy. Heterogeneous intermediary firms produce a continuum of intermediary inputs used in the manufacture of a sole final good. The final good is produced by a representative competitive firm under perfect competition; the final good is used as numeraire. Intermediary inputs, indeed, in line with Dixit and Stiglitz (1977), are produced under monopolistic competition. For comparability, we adopt a similar notation as in the previous section (Fig. 3.1).

There is a mass m_t of heterogeneous intermediary firms. Firms differ in their productivity z, producing each a differentiated intermediary input by the mean of the following linear technology

$$y_t(z) = Az\,\ell_t(z),$$

where $y_t(z)$ and $\ell_t(z)$ represent output and labor of a firm with productivity z, respectively; the state of technology $A > 0$ is assumed to be constant.[17] As in the previous sections, operative firms have productivity $z \geq z_t^*$.

The sole final good is allocated to consumption c_t only and it is produced by a mass unit of identical perfectly competitive final firms by the mean of the constant elasticity of substitution (CES) technology

$$c_t = \left(m_t \int_{z_t^*}^{\infty} y_t(z)^{\frac{\varrho-1}{\varrho}} \phi_t(z) \mathrm{d}z \right)^{\frac{\varrho}{\varrho-1}}$$

defined on a mass m_t of intermediary inputs, with constant elasticity of substitution $\varrho > 1$.

Final firms are price takers in both the final and the intermediary markets, optimally demanding of each intermediary input the quantity

$$y_t(z) = p_t(z)^{-\varrho} c_t.$$

The demand elasticity of any intermediary input is equal to the elasticity of substitution across varieties. More substitutable intermediary inputs are, more the final firm reacts to changes in input prices. Love-for-variety, in the sense of Dixit-Stiglitz, means that firms would like to use all available intermediary inputs, with relative quantities depending on relative prices.

Intermediary firms have monopoly power in the production of intermediary inputs. They maximize profits subject to the demand function

[17] It is easy to extend the Melitz model to an environment where the aggregate state of technology A_t grows at a constant exogenous rate, as assumed in the previous section.

above, optimally setting price

$$p_t(z) = \frac{\varrho}{\varrho - 1} \frac{w_t}{Az}.$$

Intermediary firms charge a markup $\frac{\varrho}{\varrho-1} > 1$ over marginal costs $\frac{w_t}{Az}$. More productive firms set a lower price, producing and selling more. The markup is inversely related to the demand elasticity.

An important property of the monopolistic competitive model is that all monopolistically competitive firms charge the same markup, implying that their relative prices are equal to their relative marginal productivities. The direct implication is that the allocation of production factors within a monopolistically competitive sector is efficient, since relative prices are equal to relative marginal productivities.[18] Of course, the allocation of production factors between the monopolistic competitive sector and other sectors of the economy may be distorted because of the markup. A recent literature stresses the role played by the dispersion of markups on the allocation of resources within an industry.[19]

Aggregating over intermediary firms, it can be shown that consumption per capita, the wage rate and total net revenues are

$$c_t = Am_t^{\frac{1}{\varrho-1}} \bar{z}_t L_t, \qquad w_t = \frac{\varrho - 1}{\varrho} Am_t^{\frac{1}{\varrho-1}} \bar{z}_t \quad \text{and} \quad \pi_t = \frac{1}{\varrho} c_t,$$

with average productivity defined as

$$\bar{z}_t = \left(\int_{z_t^*}^{\infty} z^{\varrho-1} \phi_t(z) \mathrm{d}z \right)^{\frac{1}{\varrho-1}},$$

where L_t represents the share of total labor allocated to production (excluded any fixed production costs). The mass of intermediary inputs m_t shows up in the aggregate technology as an externality, usually referred in this literature as love-for-variety. The more intermediary inputs are available for final production, the more efficient final production is. Moreover, selection positively affects output since it raises the average productivity of firms $\bar{z}_t$.

[18] See Koeninger and Licandro (2006) and Epifani and Gancia (2011).

[19] See Impullitti and Licandro (2018).

The production of the consumption good requires both labor and intermediary inputs, which mass is represented by m_t. Wages are the return to labor and profits the return to the investment required to create an intermediary input (the entry cost). It is possible to interpret the mass of intermediary inputs as the stock of intangible capital. In this framework, the distribution of income between intangible capital and labor critically depends on the elasticity of substitution across intermediary inputs. An increase in substitutability reallocates income from intangible capital to labor.

Net revenues of firm z are, indeed,

$$\pi_t(z) = \frac{1}{\varrho}\frac{c_t}{m_t}\left(\frac{z}{\bar{z}_t}\right)^{\varrho-1}.$$

Notice that net revenues of the average firm $\bar{z}_t$ are equal to average net revenues π_t/m_t. Firms with productivity larger than the mean make profits larger than the average profit.

Selection. Following Melitz (2003), let us assume intermediary firms have to pay a sunk entry cost $w_t f_e$ to enter, $f_e > 0$ being the amount of labor required to create a new intermediary input. After entry, firms draw a productivity$z$ from an entry distribution $\Psi(z)$ with support in the real line. Since new firms produce new varieties, the sunk entry cost may be interpreted as an R&D investment; i.e. the investment required to be able to produce the new input variety. Of course, if the technology producing the new intermediary input is not productive enough, the firm will close down making the value of this R&D investment to be zero ex-post.

At any time t, intermediary firms require a fixed amount of labor f, $f > 0$, to be operative, facing then a fixed production cost fw_t. At the steady state of the Melitz model, the marginal firm z^* is defined by the (zero-profit) exit condition

$$\pi(z^*) = \frac{1}{\varrho}\frac{c}{m}\left(\frac{z^*}{\bar{z}}\right)^{\varrho-1} = fw. \qquad (\mathrm{EC_M})$$

Any firm with productivity $z < z^*$ exits since net revenues are not large enough to cover the fixed production costs. Notice that, for any operative firm with $z \geq z^*$, profits can then be expressed in relation to the marginal firm as

$$\pi(z) - fw = \left(\left(\frac{z}{z^*}\right)^{\varrho-1} - 1\right) fw.$$

Any operative firm with productivity larger than z^* makes positive profits, equilibrium profits being proportional to the fixed production cost.

The value $v(z)$ of a firm with productivity z at steady state is the expected discounted flow of profits, which collapses to

$$v(z) = \frac{\left(\left(\frac{z}{z^*}\right)^{\varrho-1} - 1\right) fw}{r + \delta},$$

since expected profits are discounted at $r + \delta$, where $\delta > 0$ is the Poisson destruction rate of any operative firm.[20]

The free entry condition makes expected profits equal to the entry cost

$$\int_{z^*}^{\infty} v(z)\mathrm{d}\Psi(z) = f_e w. \qquad (\mathrm{FE_M})$$

Remember that a firm is assumed to invest in intangibles before knowing its productivity. Under the assumption that the entry distribution is Pareto, i.e., $\Psi(z) = 1 - \left(\frac{\zeta}{z}\right)^{\kappa}$, with $\kappa > 1$ and $\zeta > 0$, by combining the exit ($\mathrm{EC_M}$) and free entry ($\mathrm{FE_M}$) conditions, the steady state equilibrium cut-off becomes[21]

$$z^* = \left(\frac{f}{f_e}\frac{1}{r+\delta}\left(\left(\frac{\kappa}{\kappa-1}\right)^{\varrho-1} - 1\right)\right)^{\frac{1}{\kappa}} \zeta. \qquad (z^*_{\mathrm{M}})$$

Any policy addressed to reduce the entry cost f_e or the equilibrium interest rate r makes the economy more selective.

[20] Notice that the R&D entry cost, even if sunk, it has a value. We will interpret it as a form of intangible capital, which has different value depending on the productivity of the firm.

[21] At steady state, the interest rate $r = \rho$ is constant.

There is a stationary allocation of labor to production and R&D investments, such that at the stationary equilibrium the mass of new intermediary firms is equal to the mass of exiting firms and the labor market clears. At the stationary equilibrium of the Melitz model, the mass of intermediary firms is given by

$$m = \left(\varrho - 1 + \frac{\delta + r\left(\frac{\kappa - 1}{\kappa}\right)^{\varrho - 1}}{r + \delta} \right)^{-1} \frac{1}{f} \left(\frac{\kappa - 1}{\kappa} \right)^{\varrho - 1}.$$

In the Melitz model, the entry (R&D) cost depends on wages, which raises with selection. A more selective economy faces then a larger entry cost, which reduces the incentives to enter. This mechanism causes the economy to converge to a stationary mass of varieties and a stationary cut-off productivity. In Sect. 3.4, we analyze economies where both the cut-off productivity and the mass of intermediary inputs permanently increase, making the economy to be more innovative with growing productivity and output.

3.3.3 Oligopolistic Competition

In the monopolistic competitive framework, since intermediary firms share the same elasticity of substitution with each other, they all set the same time-invariant markup. As discussed by Koeninger and Licandro (2006), equal markups cause the monopolistic competitive allocation to be optimal. In this section, we discuss a close economy version of Impullitti and Licandro (2018), who develop an oligopolistic competitive framework allowing to understand the fundamental role of competition in shaping the relation between competition, selection and growth.[22]

The Economy. As in the monopolistic competitive model of Sect. 3.3.2, let us assume a sole consumption good is produced by a representative, perfectly competitive final firm by the mean of the constant elasticity of substitution (CES) technology with constant elasticity of substitution $\varrho > 1$. Final firms are price takers in both the final and the intermediary markets, and optimally demand

$$y_t(z) = p_t(z)^{-\varrho} c_t,$$

[22] See also Peretto (1996, 2003) and Navas and Licandro (2011).

where c_t is total production, $y_t(z)$ and $p_t(z)$ are, respectively, the demand and price of intermediary input *z*. As before, the final consumption good is used as numeraire.

Following Impullitti and Licandro (2018), intermediary inputs, indeed, instead of being produced under monopolistic competition as in Melitz (2003), are produced under Cournot competition. There are *n* firms, $n > 1$, producing variety *z* by the mean of technology

$$y_{i,t}(z) = Az\,\ell_{i,t}(z),$$

where $y_{i,t}(z)$ and $\ell_{i,t}(z)$ represent output and labor, respectively, of firm *i* sharing productivity *z* with other $n - 1$ firms, its direct competitors; the state of technology $A > 0$ is assumed to be constant. Of course, $y_t(z) = \sum_i y_{i,t}(z)$. As in the previous sections, operative intermediary inputs have productivity $z \geq z_t^*$.

The equilibrium price of the Cournot game, the same for all firms producing *z*, is

$$p_t(z) = \frac{1}{\theta}\frac{w_t}{Az},$$

where the inverse of the markup rate is $\theta = \frac{n-1/\varrho}{n}$, with the markup going from $\frac{\varrho}{\varrho-1}$ to one, as the economy moves from monopolistic competition ($n = 1$) to perfect competition, when the number of firms goes to infinity.

Aggregating over intermediary firms, it can be shown that consumption per capita, the wage rate and total net revenues are

$$c_t = Am_t^{\frac{1}{\varrho-1}}\bar{z}_t L_t, \quad w_t = \theta Am_t^{\frac{1}{\varrho-1}}\bar{z}_t \quad \text{and} \quad \pi_t = (1-\theta)c_t,$$

with average productivity defined as

$$\bar{z}_t = \left(\int_{z_t^*}^{\infty} z^{\varrho-1}\phi_t(z)\mathrm{d}z\right)^{\frac{1}{\varrho-1}},$$

where L_t represents the share of total labor allocated to production (excluded the fixed production costs). For a given cut-off productivity z^*, the Cournot and the monopolistic competitive economies produce the same output. However, the share of labor is larger in the Cournot equilibrium, increasing with competition. An increase in competition reallocates income from (intangible) capital to labor.

Selection. Interestingly, if the number of competitors n is given, and the entry decision were jointly taken by the n potential entrants, since profits of the marginal firm and expected profits of the potential entrant are both affected proportionally by θ, the equilibrium cut-off at steady state is equal to z^* in the equilibrium condition (z^*_M) of the Melitz model. An exogenous change in the number of competitors n does not affect selection. However, the fraction of labor allocated to production and the mass of intermediary inputs do. At steady state,

$$L = \left(1 + \frac{1-\theta}{\theta}\left(\frac{\delta + r\left(\frac{\kappa-1}{\kappa}\right)^{\varrho-1}}{r+\delta}\right)\right)^{-1}$$

and

$$m = \left(\frac{\theta}{1-\theta} + \frac{\delta + r\left(\frac{\kappa-1}{\kappa}\right)^{\varrho-1}}{r+\delta}\right)^{-1} \frac{1}{f}\left(\frac{\kappa-1}{\kappa}\right)^{\varrho-1}.$$

An increase in competition, measured by a raise in θ, renders the static allocation more efficient, which moves labor toward production, increasing L. As an implication, less labor has to be allocated to create new varieties and to cover the fixed production costs, which implies a reduction in the mass of varieties.

In fact, Impullitti and Licandro (2018) analyze the problem under a very different perspective. They assume that the entry condition determines endogenously n. They also assume that there is a mass one of potential varieties, m_t being the equilibrium mass. Potential entrants face a zero entry cost, but can only enter by producing a particular variety. At equilibrium, then, $1 - m_t$ varieties are introduced at any time t; from them a fraction $1 - \Psi(z^*)$ is produced, the others exit instantaneously. As a consequence, the equilibrium mass of varieties is determined by the stationary condition

$$(1-m)\big(1-\Psi(z^*)\big) = \delta m.$$

The free entry condition, instead, determines the number of competitor n that produce any intermediary input. Since n is determined before the productivity z is known, all varieties have the same number of competitors at a balanced growth path equilibrium.

3.3.4 Physical and Intangible Capital

An alternative way to Collard and Licandro (2018) of adding capital to the Hopenhayn model is in Hopenhayn (2014), which assumes that technology in (3.1) is defined in a composite production factor, such as,

$$y_t(z) = z^{\alpha} F(k_t(z), \ell_t(z))^{1-\alpha}$$

where $F(.)$ is a Neoclassical production function, $k_t(z)$ and $\ell_t(z)$ are physical capital and labor employed for firm z. Hopenhayn (2014) shows that at equilibrium the aggregate technology is

$$y_t = \left(\bar{z}_t m_t\right)^{\alpha} F(k_t, 1)^{1-\alpha}$$

where m_t is the mass of firms, k_t is physical capital per capita and, as before, total labor is assumed to be equal to one. Notice that in this economy there are two forms of capital: physical capital k_t and intangible capital $\bar{z}_t m_t$. The aggregate technology shows constant returns on labor, physical and intangible capital like in Corrado et al. (2009).

3.4 Firm Heterogeneity in Models with Innovation

3.4.1 Romer Model

Romer (1990) is based on the monopolistic competitive model developed by Dixit and Stiglitz (1977). Simplifying the model in Sect. 3.3.2, let us assume that identical intermediary firms (all with productivity $z = 1$) monopolistically compete in the intermediary goods market. In this framework, a typical intermediary firm sets price and produces quantity

$$p(z) = \frac{\varrho}{\varrho - 1} w_t \quad \text{and} \quad y(z) = \left(\frac{\varrho}{\varrho - 1} w_t\right)^{-\varrho} c_t,$$

respectively, where w_t is the equilibrium wage rate and c_t is aggregate consumption; $\varrho > 1$ is the elasticity of substitution between intermediary inputs in the production of the final (consumption) good. Since intermediary firms are symmetric, they all set the same price and produce the same quantity. At equilibrium, the technology producing the final consumption good is

$$c_t = A m_t^{\nu} L_t,$$

where the mass of intermediary inputs m_t shows up as an externality and L_t is the fraction of total labor allocated to the production of intermediary goods (there are no fixed productions costs in Romer). Aggregate technology shows the well-known love-for-variety externality: labor productivity in the final good sector raises with the mass of intermediary inputs m_t at the rate $\nu = \frac{1}{\varrho-1}$.[23]

Concerning innovation, let us assume that new intermediary varieties are produced by the mean of the R&D technology

$$\dot{m}_t = Bm_t(1 - L_t),$$

where R&D productivity B is normalized to $B = (\varrho - 1)A > 0$ in order to simplify notation. Since the total labor supply is normalized to one, $1 - L_t$ is the fraction of it allocated to research activities. The productivity of labor in the R&D sector is critically assumed to depend on the mass of varieties m_t.

Let us define the state of knowledge as $k_t = m_t^{\nu}$. This allows us to interpret the Romer model in line with the Arrow (1962) learning-by-doing model. The economy learns by producing new varieties of the intermediary input. By doing so, technology becomes more productive in both the final good sector and the R&D sector. Combining the two last equations, the feasibility condition becomes

$$\dot{k}_t = Ak_t - c_t.$$

With the state of knowledge k_t, the economy produces Ak_t, which can be consumed or allocated to the production of new knowledge—a form of intangible investment in the sense of Corrado et al. (2009). Notice that the normalization used to define k_t as a function of m_t, including that of B, is inconsequential since knowledge has no natural unit. Technology in the Romer model then collapses to a one-good AK technology like in Rebelo (1991), sharing with Rebelo (1991) the conditions for a constant endogenous growth rate.

The optimal allocation of output Ak_t to consumption and savings (adopting the form of intangible investment) is as usual governed by the

[23] Benassy (1996) adopts a more general framework, arguing that the love-for-variety externality ν may be any number between zero and infinity, independent of the elasticity of substitution ϱ.

Euler equation (EE). At equilibrium, the return on R&D is

$$r_t = \frac{1}{\varrho - 1} A L_t,$$

decreasing in the elasticity of substitution, but increasing in the final good productivity parameter A and the fraction of employment allocated to production. Notice that an increase in the degree of substitutability between intermediary goods raises the demand elasticity, reducing markups and profits and then decreasing the return on R&D.

Substituting the equilibrium interest rate r_t in the Euler equation (EE), it can be shown that the equilibrium growth rate is

$$g = \sigma\left(\frac{A-\rho}{\varrho} - \rho\right),$$

which negatively depends on the elasticity substitution ϱ, since it negatively affects the return on R&D.

Firm Heterogeneity. The Romer model can be combined with the Melitz model to generate endogenous growth with firm heterogeneity, where selection by affecting the productivity of the final good sector will have a direct effect on the growth rate. Aggregating over intermediary firms,

$$c_t = A\bar{z}_t k_t L_t.$$

By assuming that productivity B in the R&D technology also depends on the average productivity $\bar{z}_t$, knowledge evolves following

$$\dot{k}_t = A\bar{z}_t k_t (1 - L_t),$$

implying that the feasibility condition becomes

$$\dot{k}_t = A\bar{z}_t k_t - c_t.$$

Technology is AK with the marginal product of capital depending on selection through $\bar{z}_t$. The productivity gains through selection spillover to the consumption and R&D sectors.

Since new firms draw their productivity from a time-invariant distribution, the productivity cut-off is constant at a balanced growth path, as well as the average productivity $\bar{z}$. As in the Romer model, the return on R&D and the growth rate depend on the average productivity $\bar{z}$. At steady state

$$g = \sigma\left(\frac{A\bar{z} - \rho}{\varrho} - \rho\right).$$

Selection makes the average productivity of capital larger, positively affecting the stationary growth rate. Those parameters positively affecting selection in the Melitz model, have here also a positive effect on the growth rate.

3.4.2 *Selection and Imitation*

Following Luttmer (2007), selection by itself can generate endogenous growth through imitation, since selection raises the productivity of incumbents.[24] How do new firms react to this raise in productivity? Instead of drawing their productivity from a time-invariant distribution, the initial productivity of new firms is randomly drawn from an entry distribution that follows key moments of the incumbents equilibrium distribution. In this sense, new entrants learn from incumbents, imitating them, which causes productivity gains from selection to spillover innovators. A similar mechanism is used by Sampson (2016) to study the dynamic gains from trade.[25]

Let us follow the argument as developed by Sampson (2016), adapting his notation to be consistent with the notation in the previous sections. Sampson's model belongs to the family of monopolistic competitive models with labor as the sole production factor as developed by Melitz (2003) and reviewed in Sect. 3.3.2. Monopolistically competitive intermediary firms draw at entry a time-invariant labor productivity z from an entry productivity distribution $\tilde{\Psi}_t(z)$, which differently from Melitz is assumed to be time dependent. Firms productivity is time invariant. However, due to selection, learning spillovers cause the distribution from which they draw their productivity follow these improvements in technology. Intermediary firms require a variable and fixed (f) amount of labor to produce with w_t being the equilibrium wage rate.

24 See also Luttmer (2011, 2012).

25 Gabler and Licandro (1979) develop the same idea in a framework similar to the one in the Ramsey-Hopenhayn model.

As in Sect. 3.3.2, an intermediary firm with productivity z sets price

$$p_t(z) = \frac{\varrho}{\varrho - 1}\frac{w_t}{z}.$$

The zero profit condition implicitly defines the equilibrium cut-off productivity z_t^*,

$$\frac{1}{\varrho}\frac{c_t}{m_t}\left(\frac{z_t^*}{\bar{z}_t}\right)^{\varrho-1} = f w_t.$$

where c_t/m_t is total consumption per firm (reminds that final output is fully allocated to consumption in the Melitz model).

Entry and Spillovers. Like in Romer (1990), potential entrants undertake R&D activities to discover new varieties of intermediary inputs. They pay the R&D (entry) cost $f_e w_t$, where $f_e > 0$ is the amount of labor required to create a new intermediary input. R&D plays exactly the same role as an entry cost in the Melitz model. As usual in this literature, innovators are assumed to be protected by infinitely lived patents.

The critical assumption is the following: at any time t innovators (the entrants), after paying the R&D (entry) cost, draw a time-invariant productivity $z = \omega\bar{z}_t$, where $\bar{z}_t$ is the average productivity of incumbents and ω is a random variable distributed $\tilde{\Psi}(\omega)$. To fix ideas, let us assume that $\tilde{\Psi}(\omega)$ is Pareto with tail parameter $\kappa > 1$. The only difference with the Melitz model is that the entry distribution $\Psi_t(z) = \tilde{\Psi}(z/\bar{z}_t)$, from which innovators draw z, is time dependent. That is, it depends on the time varying average productivity of incumbents. Innovators learn from incumbents through this particular type of spillover.[26]

Let us define the firm-specific relative productivity $\tilde{z}_t$, $\tilde{z}_t = \frac{z}{z_t^*}$, relative to the cut-off productivity z_t^*. Since the domain of z is (z_t^*, ∞), the domain of $\tilde{z}$ is $(1, \infty)$. In a growing economy, z_t^* will be permanently moving to the right. Since firm's productivity is time invariant, the relative productivity of any firm will eventually converge to one on a finite time. When the lower bound is reached, the firm exits. Firms born at different moments in time belong to different technological cohorts, and since new cohorts are in average more productive, firms face a finite life,

[26] Imitation, since in this framework comes at a zero cost, can also be interpreted as diffusion.

i.e. firms are losing value over time since their technology becomes slowly obsolete.[27]

Despite the fact that firms have a finite life, under the assumption that the entry distribution $\tilde{\Psi}(\omega)$ is Pareto, with tail parameter $\kappa > 1$, the stationary productivity distribution is $\Phi_t(z) = 1 - \left(\frac{z_t^*}{z}\right)^{\kappa}$, for $z \geq z_t^*$. It is Pareto distributed, inheriting the tail parameter κ from the entry distribution. Since at a balanced growth path selection moves cut-off productivity z_t^* to the right, the equilibrium distribution $\Phi_t(z)$ is said to be a traveling wave.[28]

Combining the exit and entry conditions with the Euler equation, Sampson (2016) shows that the steady state endogenous rate of technical progress is

$$g = \frac{\sigma}{1 + \sigma(\kappa - 1)} \left(\frac{\varrho - 1}{\kappa + 1 - \varrho} \frac{f}{f_e} - \rho \right).$$

Output per capita and consumption also grow at the rate g. An increase in the variance of the entry distribution (a reduction in κ), which is equivalent to an increase in the probability of exceptionally good innovations, or a reduction in the R&D (entry) cost f_e both make the economy more selective. They increase the productivity of incumbent firms and through learning affects the productivity of innovators, inducing faster growth at steady state. An increase in the elasticity of substitution between intermediary inputs ϱ makes the economy more competitive, also inducing more selection and growth.

[27] In this sense, Sampson's model belongs to the vintage capital tradition. In Gilchrist and Williams (2000), for example, the productivity of new firms is drawn from a lognormal distribution, which mean has an exogenous trend. As shown by Boucekkine et al. (1997) and Boucekkine et al. (2005), vintage models involve (periodic) medium term movements which may be of relevance for the propagation of innovation. Bambi et al. (2014) extend this idea to vintage models with R&D, showing that the long delay that innovation takes to diffuse generates medium term cycles, which has to be considered when evaluating the performance of innovation policies.

[28] Even if not proved by Sampson (2016), under similar conditions as in Collard and Licandro (2018), the equilibrium distribution will likely be a truncated Pareto with cut-off productivity moving systematically to the right following the endogenous progress in technology.

3.4.3 *Schumpeterian Model*

In the Schumpeterian framework, the dynamics of firms is modeled through the fundamental concept of creative destruction, which takes two forms: business stealing and crowding-out (or obsolescence).

In Aghion and Howitt (1992), the final consumption good c_t is produced by the mean of technology

$$c_t = \left(\int_{z_t^*}^{\infty} \left(z\, x_t(z) \right)^{\frac{\varrho-1}{\varrho}} \phi_t(z)\, \mathrm{d}z \right)^{\frac{\varrho}{\varrho-1}},$$

where $x_t(z)$ represents the quantity of intermediary input z used in the production of the final consumption good c_t, $\varrho > 1$ is the elasticity of substitution between them, and $\phi_t(z)$ is the equilibrium (density) distribution. Differently from Romer (1990), the mass of varieties m_t is assumed to be time invariant and normalized to one, but the quality of goods z is assumed to be heterogeneous. In the Schumpeterian model, R&D activities are addressed to improve the quality of exiting varieties, which makes $\phi_t(z)$ time dependent, reflecting changes in technology induced by innovation.

Technology in the intermediary sector is assumed to be

$$x_t(z) = A\ell_t(z),$$

where parameter $A > 0$ and $\ell_t(z)$ is labor allocated to the production of the intermediary input z. Notice that the variable change $y_t(z) = zx_t(z)$ brings us back to the Melitz model, where $y_t(z)$ is measured in quality adjusted units.[29] Even if the Schumpeterian model is usually interpreted as a model of product innovation (addressed to improve the quality of intermediary goods), it can also be interpreted as a model of process innovation (addressed to reduce production costs).

Following the analysis in the previous sections, at equilibrium

$$c_t = A\bar{z}_t L_t,$$

[29] Price indexes are built with the objective of keeping quality constant, meaning that real quantities in national accounts are measured in quality adjusted units.

where

$$\bar{z}_t = \left(\int_{z_t^*}^{\infty} z^{\varrho-1} \phi_t(z) \mathrm{d}z \right)^{\frac{1}{\varrho-1}},$$

is the average product quality interpreted as in Aghion and Howitt (or average productivity as in Melitz) and L_t is labor allocated to the production of intermediary goods.

In the Schumpeterian model, an innovation is a new technology able to produce a better quality input, which is a perfect substitute of an already existing intermediary input (or a cheaper version of an intermediary input of the same quality). The particular input is randomly selected among the unit mass of existing intermediary inputs. When a new technology is discovered, the previous one becomes obsolete, making the previous producer to exit.[30] Creation of new technologies is then associated with the destruction of old ones. The probability that a new version arrives follows a Poisson process with arrival rate b for unit of labor allocated to R&D, $b > 0$.[31]

The productivity of the new version is assumed to be equal to the frontier, *leading-edge* technology ω_t, which given some $\omega_0 > 0$ at time $t = 0$, is assumed to follow

$$\frac{\dot{\omega}_t}{\omega_t} = b(1 - L_t), \tag{3.3}$$

where $1 - L_t$ represents the share of total labor allocated to R&D activities.[32] Individual research effort spills over into the whole economy by

[30] The distance in productivity between two consecutive innovations of a particular variety depends on the time interval between them. It may be that this distance is small enough to make the incumbent compete with the innovator. In this case, the innovation is said to be non-drastic. To avoid the associated complications of studying market structures with non-drastic innovations, it is assumed that the incumbent's technology is destroyed with the discovery of a new way of producing the same intermediary input.

[31] In this literature, an innovation is a random event. Let us denote by $F(T)$ the probability that this event occurs before a period of length T. A Poisson process assumes $F(T) = 1 - \mathrm{e}^{-\mu T}$, $\mu > 0$. The associated density function is $f(T) = \mu\, \mathrm{e}^{-\mu T}$, implying that the probability that the event occurs around $T = 0$ is μ. The probability that the event does not occur before T is $\mathrm{e}^{-\mu T}$.

[32] Note that technology has a vintage structure. Innovations introduced at time t have the frontier productivity ω_t, which will be growing at equilibrium.

moving the frontier of knowledge, mimicking a form of learning-by-doing.

Finally, let us assume that new varieties receive infinitely lived patents, giving to the innovator the exclusivity on the use of this technology to produce the corresponding intermediary input.

Let us denote by $a_t = \frac{z}{\omega_t}$ the productivity of z relative to the frontier technology and by $H(a)$, $a \in [0, 1]$, the cumulative distribution of firms across technologies. It can be easily shown that at steady state the distribution $H(a)$ is uniform in $(0, 1)$.[33] It can also be shown that

$$\bar{z}_t = \mu\, \omega_t \quad \text{with} \quad \mu = \varrho^{\frac{1}{1-\varrho}} < 1.$$

The average technology $\bar{z}_t$ is at a distance μ from the frontier technology ω_t. The ***distance to the frontier technology*** is increasing in ϱ, for $\varrho > 1$, with $\lim_{\varrho \to \infty} \mu = 1$, meaning that the average distance to the technological frontier approaches unity when intermediary inputs are close to perfect substitutes. On the other extreme, it goes to e^{-1} when ϱ goes to one.

At the balanced growth path, at any time t, the return to a patent aged s is

$$r = \underbrace{\frac{\pi_{st}}{v_{st}}}_{\text{dividend-to-value}} + \underbrace{\frac{\dot{v}_{st}}{v_{st}}}_{\text{capital gains}} - \underbrace{b(1-L)}_{\text{business-stealing}} - \underbrace{(\rho-1)b(1-L)}_{\text{obsolescence}}.$$

As usual, the return to assets adds capital gains to the dividend-to-value ratio. The remaining terms represent the negative effect that technical progress has on the patent protecting existing intermediary inputs. The third term is the so-called ***business-stealing effect***. It measures the Poisson rate at which the patent will eventually die, when the associated intermediary input is substituted by a subsequent innovation. The last term represents the ***obsolescence cost*** produced by the emergency of cheaper (better quality) versions of other intermediary inputs, reducing the demand for the input produced by the patent.[34] As time passes, other varieties become more and more productive, reducing the demand and

[33] The distribution of firms across relative productivities is uniform because, by assumption, the rate at which innovations arrive is the same as the rate at which the frontier technology grows. Otherwise, the distribution is Pareto, as it is usually assumed in this literature.

[34] Aghion and Howitt (1992) refer to it as the *crowding-out effect*.

profits of the variety we are evaluating. The obsolescence cost depends on the velocity at which the frontier technology moves, $b(1-L)$, and the elasticity of substitution across varieties. When varieties become perfect substitutes, old varieties are substituted out by new varieties fully, making the crowding-out effect infinity.

3.4.4 Innovation and the Life Cycle of Firms

Klette and Kortum (2004) extends the Melitz model in line with the literature on endogenous growth with the aim of describing better the life cycle of firms. In this framework, the productivity of firms does not depend on their own intrinsic characteristics, but it is randomly assigned.[35]

Firms and Products. In the Klette and Kortum (2004) framework, a continuum of firms produces a continuum of measure of one of intermediary inputs, with each firm producing an integer number n_t of them, $n_t \in \{1, 2, 3, ...\}$. The integer number of intermediary inputs produced is heterogeneous and endogenously determined at equilibrium.

As in the Schumpeterian model, producing one unity of any intermediary input requires one unit of labor; labor productivity is normalized to one, and the same holds for all inputs. However, intermediary inputs are heterogeneous in their quality. The quality frontier of an intermediary input is denoted by z_t.

Innovation. Technical progress in each intermediary input is represented by a quality ladder model as in Grossman and Helpman (1991). The dynamics of the frontier technology for the different intermediary inputs is governed by two types of innovations: innovation by incumbent firms and innovation by potential entrants. When a discovery takes place, it is randomly assigned to a single intermediary input moving its quality frontier one step in the quality ladder. The gain in quality is given by a firm-specific factor $q > 1$, which is specific to the firm that makes the discovery.

The firm-specific factor q maps one-to-one to a firm-specific profit per intermediary input π, $\pi \in (0, 1)$, and it is the same for all intermediary inputs produced by the same firm; π and q are positively related and time invariant. In the following, it is assumed that firms draw π from

[35] See also Acemoglu and Cao (2015).

the continuous distribution function $\Phi(\pi)$, which is equivalent to draw factor q from a known distribution. An operative intermediary firm is then characterized by a duple $\{n_t, \pi\}$, with n_t evolving over time.

Innovation by Incumbents. A firm that exercises intensity λ, when undertaking R&D activities, has a Poisson rate λn of making a discovery, where n is the number of intermediary inputs being currently produced by the firm. This discovery allows the firm to move one step in the quality ladder of the frontier technology of a randomly selected intermediary input. The particular input is unknown to the firm at the time the firm undertakes the R&D activities. The R&D cost function of a firm $\{n, \pi\}$ is

$$\frac{\pi}{\bar{\pi}}\, c(\lambda)\, n.$$

Function $c(\lambda)$ is increasing and strictly convex (some other technical assumptions s.t. $c(\lambda) > \lambda c'(\lambda)$ are also required). The cost function depends on the firm-specific innovation factor q through π; more innovative firms, those with larger q, face larger innovation costs. The optimal (interior) innovation policy requires

$$c'(\lambda) = v$$

$$(r + \mu - \lambda)v = \bar{\pi} - c(\lambda),$$

where v represents the expected value of a product produced by a firm of average type $\bar{\pi}$, r is the equilibrium interest rate and μ is the rate of creative destruction (measuring the rate at which the firm may lose a product line because another firm has just innovated in this particular product line). The first condition states that the marginal cost of innovation has to be equal to its marginal value. The second condition states that the expected return on innovation has to be equal to its opportunity cost. Irrespective of the firm-specific duple $\{n, \pi\}$, all firms optimally chose the same innovation intensity λ, the Poison rate of innovation of a firm with n products being λn. Indeed, more profitable firms face larger R&D costs and have larger per product value.

Innovation by Potential Entrants. There is a mass of potential entrants investing at the rate F, $F > 0$, in return for a unit Poisson rate of entering the economy with a single product. Potential entrants, after entering, draw a firm-specific profit π from $\Phi(\pi)$. The firm-specific profit

π and the associated innovation factor q apply to the first and any subsequent discovery of the firm. As in the case of incumbents, a new entrant randomly chose an intermediary input.

Equilibrium Innovation. Notice first that at equilibrium $\mu = \lambda + \eta$, where η is the Poisson rate of innovation by potential entrants. Free entry requires $F = v$, since in expected terms the potential entrant covers the entry cost F with the value of the innovation. Combining the free entry condition and the optimal innovation policy of incumbents, the equilibrium innovation intensity of incumbents is determined by the condition

$$c'(\lambda) = F,$$

and the equilibrium innovation intensity of potential entrants by

$$\eta = \frac{\bar{\pi} - c(\lambda)}{F} - \rho,$$

where the interest rate $r = \rho$ at the balanced growth path.

These two equations are fundamental to understand the incentives to innovation in the Klette-Kortum model, and hence the potential effects of innovation policies. An increase in the entry cost F reduces the R&D activity of potential entrants η, but raises the incumbents' innovation intensity λ. An increase in average profits $\bar{\pi}$ raises the innovation intensity of new entrants but has no effect on incumbents. A raise in the innovation cost of incumbents (affecting both average and marginal costs) will have negative incentives for both incumbents and potential entrants. In this model, innovation policy affects innovation only through these channels, Of course, any policy that reduces the financial costs of firms, as reflected by ρ, also promotes innovation by potential entrants.

Limit Pricing. From the point of view of the final firm, the quality frontier version of any intermediary input is a perfect substitute of any previous version of the same input, with all versions weighted by their respective qualities. Under Bertrand competition, the firm producing the frontier quality optimally charges a markup q to its marginal cost in order to deter any competitor. Consequently, at equilibrium only the frontier quality is produced with the last innovator charging a markup equal to its specific factor q.

Intermediary inputs aggregate into the final output through the Cobb-Douglas technology

$$y_t = \int_z \log\left(z\,x(z)\right)\phi(z)\mathrm{d}z,$$

where $\phi(z)$ is the equilibrium distribution of the frontier quality across intermediary inputs. It is easy to see that the optimal demand implies $p(z)x(z) = 1$. A firm with quality improvement factor q yields then the same constant profit flow $\pi = 1 - q^{-1}$, $\pi \in (0, 1)$, for each intermediary input it produces irrespective of its quality z, since $p(z)x(z) = 1$ for all z.

3.5 Further Contributions

This survey does not review other important dimensions of the innovation process that may also be relevant for policy analysis, which should be considered when designing macro models for the evaluation of innovation policies.

First, there is a large literature analyzing the role of financial frictions shaping market selection and innovation.[36] The evaluation of policies addressed to reduce financial frictions in order to promote innovation and productivity growth requires a rigorous modeling of the financial sector and the associated frictions.

Second, innovation policy needs also to be evaluated by its redistributive effects on the labor market, with regard to the correction of the negative effects that technical progress has in the evolution of employment and wages across industries and occupations. The recent literature on job polarization, automatization and skill obsolescence is addressed to study the labor market effects of innovation and technical progress. Technical progress develops differently in different sectors, affecting unevenly the dynamics of jobs and occupations. One of the most striking implications of these diverse sectorial evolutions of technology is stressed by the literature on structural transformation.[37] This literature looks at replicating the evidence of non-balanced patterns of the three main

[36] See Cooley and Quadrini (2001), Buera et al. (2011), and Midrigan and Yi Xu (2014), among others.

[37] See Duarte and Restuccia (2010), as well as Herrendorf et al. (2014) for a survey on this literature.

sectors of modern economies: agriculture, manufacturing and services. An appropriate modeling of this dimension, likely in line with Kongsamut et al. (2001), Ngai and Pissarides (2007), and Acemoglu and Guerrieri (2008), will be of great importance in order to evaluate industrial policies addressed to promote innovation.

The unbalanced evolution of industries is mimicked by an unbalanced evolution of occupations (see Duernecker & Herrendorf, 2017), which is reflected in the polarization of wages and employment observed in the data (see Autor & Dorn, 2013). Modeling the joint evolution of technology and occupations, in line with the skill obsolescence hypothesis in Licandro and Poschke (2017), is of fundamental importance to evaluate the labor market effect of innovation policies.

Third, trade, although omitted in this chapter, is fundamental to understand the impact of innovation policies. This is particularly important for the evaluation of innovation policies in the European Union, where policies are expected and frequently addressed to affect regions and countries differently (See Atkeson and Burstein [2010], Aw et al. [2011], Baldwin and Robert-Nicoud [2008], and Broda and Weinstein [2006], among others). A model of this nature is needed to evaluate the trade-off between promoting excellence, by addressing resources toward the most efficient regions, and regional convergence or catching-up.

References

Acemoglu, D., & Cao, D. V. (2015). Innovation by entrants and incumbents. *Journal of Economic Theory*, *157*, 255–294.

Acemoglu, D., & Guerrieri, V. (2008). Capital deepening and nonbalanced economic growth. *Journal of Political Economy*, *116*(3), 467–498.

Adams, J. (1990). Fundamental stocks of knowledge and productivity growth. *Journal of Political Economy*, *98*(4), 673–702.

Aghion, P., & Howitt, P. (1992). A model of growth through creative destruction. *Econometrica*, *60*, 323–351.

Akcigit, U., & Kerr, W. R. (2017). Growth through heterogeneous innovations. *Journal of Political Economy*.

Arrow, K. (1962). The economic implications of learning-by-doing. *Review of Economic Studies*, *29*(1), 155–173.

Atkeson, A., & Burstein, A. T. (2008). Pricing-to-market, trade costs, and international relative prices. *American Economic Review*, *98*(5), 1998–2031.

Atkeson, A., & Burstein, A. T. (2010). Innovation, firm dynamics, and international trade. *Journal of Political Economy*, *118*(3), 433–484.

Autor, D. H., & Dorn, D. (2013). The growth of low-skill service jobs and the polarization of the US labor market. *American Economic Review, 103*(5), 1553–1597.

Aw, B. Y., Roberts, M. J., & Yi Xu, D. (2011). R&D investment, exporting, and productivity dynamics. *American Economic Review, 101*(4), 1312–1344.

Baldwin, R., & Robert-Nicoud, F. (2008). Trade and growth with heterogeneous firms. *Journal of International Economics, 74*(1), 21–34.

Bambi, M., Gozzi, F., & Licandro, O. (2014). Endogenous growth and wave-like business fluctuations. *Journal of Economic Theory, 154*, 68–111.

Benassy, J.-P. (1996). Taste for intermediary input and optimum production patterns in monopolistic competition. *Economics Letters, 52*(1), 41–47.

Boucekkine, R., Del Rio, F., Licandro, O., & Puch, L. (2005). Vintage capital and the dynamics of The AK model. *Journal of Economic Theory, 120*(1), 39–72.

Boucekkine, R., Germain, M., & Licandro, O. (1997). Replacement echoes in the vintage capital growth model. *Journal of Economic Theory, 74*(2), 333–348.

Broda, C., & Weinstein, D. (2006). Globalization and the gains from variety. *Quarterly Journal of Economics, 121*(2), 541–585.

Buera, F., Kaboski, J., & Shin, Y. (2011). Finance and development: A tale of two sectors. *American Economic Review, 101*(5), 1964–2002.

Collard, F., & Licandro, O. (2018). *The neoclassical model and the welfare cost of selection*. Mimeo.

Comin, D., & Hobijn, B. (2010). An exploration of technology diffusion. *American Economic Review, 100*(5), 2031–2059.

Comin, D., Hobijn, B., & Rovito, E. (2008). Technology usage lags. *Journal of Economic Growth, 13*(4), 237–256.

Cooley, T., & Quadrini, V. (2001). Financial markets and firm dynamics. *American Economic Review, 91*(5), 1286–1310.

Corrado, C., Hulten, C., & Sichel, D. (2009). Intangible capital and US economic growth. *Review of Income and Wealth, 3*(55), 661–685.

Dixit, A. K., & Stiglitz, J. E. (1977). Monopolistic competition and optimum product diversity. *American Economic Review, 67*(3), 297–308.

Duarte, M., & Restuccia, D. (2010). The role of structural transformation in aggregate productivity. *The Quarterly Journal of Economics, 125*(1), 129–173.

Duernecker, G., & Herrendorf, B. (2017). *Structural transformation of occupation employment*. mimeo.

Epifani, P., & Gancia, G. (2011). Trade, markup heterogeneity and misallocations. *Journal of International Economics, 83*(1), 1–13.

Felbermayr, G., & Licandro, O. (2005). *The underestimated virtues of the two-sector AK model*. Contributions to Macroeconomics, The B: E. Journal.

Gabler, A., & Licandro, O. (1979).*Endogenous growth through selection and imitation*. European University Institute WP 2007/26.

Gilchrist, S., & Williams, J. (2000). Putty-Clay and investment: A business cycle analysis. *Journal of Political Economy*, *108*(5), 928–960.

Greenwood, J., Hercowitz, Z., & Krusell, P. (1997). Long-run implications of investment-specific technological change. *American Economic Review*, *87* 342–362.

Grossman, G. M., & Helpman, E. (1991). Quality ladders in the theory of growth. *Review of Economic Studies*, *68*, 43–61.

Herrendorf, B., Rogerson, R., & Valentinyi, A. (2014). Growth and structural transformation. *Handbook of Economic Growth*, *2*, 855–941.

Hopenhayn, H. (1992). Entry, exit and frim dynamics in long run equilibrium. *Econometrica*, *70*, 1127–1150.

Hopenhayn, H. (2014). Firms, misallocation, and aggregate productivity: A review. *Annual Review of Economics*, *6*, 735–770.

Hsieh, C.-T., & Klenow, P. (2009). Misallocation and manufacturing TFP in China and India. *Quarterly Journal of Economics*, *124*(4), 1403–1448.

Impullitti, G., & Licandro, O. (2018). Trade, firm selection, and innovation; The competition channel. *Economic Journal*, *128*, 189–229.

Jovanovic, B. (1982). Selection and the evolution of industry. *Econometrica*, *50* 640–670.

Jovanovic, B., & Lach, S. (1997). Product innovation and the business cycle. *International Economic Review*, *38*(1), 3–22.

Klette, T. J., & Kortum, S. (2004). Innovating firms and aggregate innovation. *Journal of Political Economy*, *112*(5), 986–1018.

Koeninger, W., & Licandro, O. (2006). On the use of substitutability as a measure of competition. *The B.E. Journal of Macroeconomics*, *6*(1).

Kongsamut, P., Rebelo, S., & Xie, D. (2001). Beyond balanced growth. *Review of Economic Studies*, *68*(4), 869–882.

Licandro, O. & Poschke, M. (2017). *Skill obsolescence*. mimeo.

Lucas, R. (1978). On the size distribution of business firms. *Bell Journal of Economics*, *9*(2), 508–523.

Luttmer, E. G. J. (2007). Selection and growth, and the size distribution of firms. *Quarterly Journal of Economics*, *122*(3), 1103–1144.

Luttmer, E. G. J. (2011). On the mechanics of firm growth. *Review of Economic Studies*, *78*(3), 1042–1068.

Luttmer, E. G. J. (2012). Technology diffusion and growth. *Journal of Economic Theory*, *147*, 602–622.

Mansfield, E. (1989). The diffusion of industrial robots in Japan and the United States. *Research Policy*, *18*, 183–192.

Melitz, M. (2003). The impact of trade on intra-Industry reallocations and aggregate industry productivity. *Econometrica*, *71*, 1695–1725.

Melitz, M., & Redding, S. (2015). New trade models, new welfare implications. *American Economic Review*, *105*(3), 1105–1146.

Midrigan, V., & Yi Xu, D. (2014). Finance and misallocation: Evidence from plant-level data. *American Economic Review, 104*(2), 422–458.

Navas, A., & Licandro, O. (2011). Trade liberalization, competition and growth. *The B.E. Journal of Macroeconomics, 11*(1).

Ngai, R., & Pissarides, C. (2007). Structural change in a multisector model of growth. *American Economic Review, 97*(1), 429–443.

Peretto, P. (1996). *Industrialization, technological change and long-run growth.* Department of Economics, Working Papers 96-22.

Peretto, P. (2003). Endogenous market structure and the growth and welfare effects of economic integration. *Journal of International Economics, 60*(1), 177–201.

Rebelo, S. (1991). Long-run policy analysis and long-run growth. *Journal of Political Economy, 99*, 500–521.

Restuccia, D., & Rogerson, R. (2017). The causes and costs of misallocation. *Journal of Economic Perspectives, 31*(3), 151–174.

Romer, P. M. (1990). Endogenous technological change. *Journal of Political Economy, 98*, 71–102.

Sampson, T. (2016). Dynamic selection: An idea flows theory of entry, trade, and growth. *Quarterly Journal of Economics, 131*(1), 315–380.

Solow, R. (1962). Substitution and fixed proportions in the theory of capital. *Review of Economic Studies, 29*, 207–218.

Solow, R., Tobin, J., Von Weizsacker, C., & Yaari, M. (1966). Neoclassical growth with fixed factor proportions. *Review of Economic Studies, 33*, 79–115.

4

Economic Growth, Innovation and Alternative Modeling Strategies

Omar Licandro

4.1 Introduction

The JRC-IEA Roundtable on Macroeconomic Modelling for R&D and Innovation was jointly organized by the DG Joint Research Centre (JRC) of the European Commission and the International Economic Association (IEA). The design and development of macroeconomic models addressed to study the impact of innovation policies is critical for the European Union, for which innovation policies are one of the highest priorities. The Roundtable aimed to discuss, in the framework of the recent development of the literature on economic growth and innovation, alternative modelling strategies for innovation and medium/long-term productivity and economic growth. The debate was organized having in mind the need for new ideas that may help the design of economic models addressed to evaluate the impact of innovation and related policies.

During the Roundtable, top researchers, including Philippe Aghion (Harvard), among others, presented some key new developments in the

O. Licandro (✉)
University of Nottingham, Nottingham, UK
e-mail: Omar.Licandro@nottingham.ac.uk

field of innovation and growth. The Roundtable aimed to better understand where the frontier of knowledge in the field of innovation and growth is to, and in a second stage, figure out the key elements a macro model designed to evaluate innovation policies should include. In particular, Ufuk Akcigit (Chicago) presented a survey on his views on the current academic research agenda on R&D and innovation. The session was closed by a panel composed mainly of practitioners, and a few academics, with the object of giving the perspective of those more directly involved in the evaluation of innovation policies or in the development of those models designed to evaluate these policies. A short summary of each contribution and my reading of the debate that followed are provided in Section 2. Section 3 discusses the proposed alternative lines of modelling that emerged from the Roundtable. It reflects the views of the author on a highly fruitful, sometimes controversial, debate that took place during the Roundtable.

4.2 Macroeconomic Modelling of Innovation

This section contains some of the lessons from the papers presented at the JRC-IEA Roundtable on Macroeconomic Modelling for R&D and Innovation.

- **Missing Growth from Creative Destruction** by Philippe Aghion, Antonin Bergeaud, Timo Boppart, Peter J. Klenow and Huiyu Li (Aghion et al., 2019).

  Statistical agencies aim to compute price indexes for representative baskets of constant quality products. However, in practice, some products disappear being displaced by better quality ones. The authors point out that, in these cases, statistical agencies typically impute inflation for disappearing products from the inflation for surviving products, when likely its inflation may be lower because of quality improvements embodied in the substituting product. As a result, creative destruction may result in overstated inflation and understated growth. The authors use a simple model to relate this missing growth to the frequency and size of various kinds of innovations. Using US Census data, they assess the magnitude of missing growth for all private non-farm businesses from 1983 to 2013. They find: (i) missing growth from imputation is substantial, between 0.5

and 1 percentage points per year; and (ii) almost all of the missing growth is due to creative destruction (as opposed to new varieties).

The paper points to a key issue on evaluating the macroeconomic impact of innovation policies: the critical problem of measuring real output and productivity in a world where technical progress is embodied in new, better quality versions of existing products. The measurement strategy suggested by the authors is model-based. However, statistical agencies are reluctant to explicitly use models to measure price changes and strongly prefer well-designed methods based on data collection, which depend much less on highly specific modelling assumptions. Of course, there is no measurement without theory. Hence, data collection and statistical methods used to aggregate individual data are both based on theory. However, the theory behind these methods is usually quite general and does not depend on specific functional forms and parameter values.

In the same direction, Broda and Weinstein (2006) suggest a different strategy, based on love-for-variety theories, to measure gains associated with new products. Contrary to Aghion et al. (2019)' s findings reported above, Broda and Weinstein (2006) conclude that the US missing growth from increasing the product variety is of around 1.2 yearly percentage points for the period 1972–2001. Indeed, this estimation strongly depends on some strong assumptions about the extent of utility gains coming from love-for-variety.

The measurement of productivity at the firm level raises also some important measurement problems. It is generally accepted now that productivity at the firm level has at least two components: product value (or demand shock) and technical efficiency (generally referred as TFPQ) whose estimation faces some important issues. Indeed, the propagation of productivity gains in a network, by reducing the cost of inputs of upstream firms, calls for a third dimension of productivity: the quality and price of production inputs.

The main lesson to retain from the Aghion et al. (2019) paper is that a careful analysis of the way GDP growth is measured in the data is needed to make a correct evaluation of innovation policies. This problem has to be seriously taken into account when comparing model simulations used to evaluate innovation policy with the data. If gains from innovation are not in the statistics, we will never find them in the data and it will be difficult to find them in model's simulations.

- **The Dynamics of Development: Innovation and Reallocation** by Francisco Buera and Roberto Fattal-Jaef (Fattal Jaef & Buera, 2015).

  Buera and Fattal-Jaef study the aggregate and firm-level properties of the dynamics of economic development, by investigating the macro and micro features of successful growth take-offs in the data and find that, while every episode exhibits sustained growth in TFP and investment rates, there are substantial differences in the evolution of the firm size distribution between the experiences of post-communist economies and the rest of the successful take-offs. The pattern is that firms tend to get larger on average during a typical acceleration, while the average size of a firm is declining along a post-communist transition. To understand this behaviour, the authors provide a quantitative theory of transitions featuring endogenous innovation, entry and exit, and the dismantling of idiosyncratic distortions. They evaluate hypothetical reforms in which the rate of progress in the reversal of distortions is calibrated to the experiences of China and Chile, to find that the mechanisms in the model are able to capture the salient features that they document in the data. The approach may be relevant for economies undergoing a similar transition or catching-up.

- **Fewer but Better: Sudden Stops, Firm Entry, and Financial Selection** by Sina Ates and Felipe Saffie (Ates & Saffie, 2021).

  In a dynamic stochastic general equilibrium (DSGE) model with firm heterogeneity and innovation, Ates and Saffie incorporate endogenous technical change into a real business cycle small open economy framework to study the productivity costs of sudden stops. In this economy, productivity growth is determined by the entry of new firms and the decision by incumbent firms to expand. New firms are created after the implementation of business ideas, yet the quality of ideas is heterogeneous and good ideas are scarce. Selection of the most promising ideas gives rise to a trade-off between mass (quantity) and composition (quality) in the entrant cohort. Chilean plant-level data from the sudden stop triggered by the Russian sovereign default in 1998 confirm the main mechanism of the model, as firms born during the credit shortage are fewer, but better. The quantitative analysis shows that four years after the crisis, 12.5% of the output deviation from trend is due to permanent productivity losses. Distortions in the entry margin account for 40% of the loss, and the remaining is due to distortions in the expansion decisions of incumbents.

Many of the elements suggested by Ates and Saffie (2021) in their DSGE model with heterogeneous innovative firms are of high value for the design of macro models addressed to evaluate innovation policy. Moreover, they also suggest a methodology that facilitates solving this family of models. Innovation policies are expected to have long-lasting effects that show up slowly during long transition periods. However, when evaluating the effects of policies, institutions cannot wait until all their effects have realized. Then, being able to characterize the transition from a balanced growth path to another is critical for policy evaluation. When equilibrium depends on the endogenous productivity distribution of heterogeneous firms and innovation makes firms' productivity endogenous, solving the dynamics of a general equilibrium model becomes a non-trivial object. Having this in mind, the methodology suggested by Ates and Saffie (2021) is consequently of first importance. Their theory features firm heterogeneity and innovation in a way that can be easily added to a DSGE model, to which standard algorithms may be applied to solve for transitional dynamics. On top of that, such an approach is likely to be useful to understand the differential effects of innovation policies during booms and recessions, since, during the latter, projects are likely to become more risky, thus they are being financed by the private market less likely.

- **Creative Destruction and Uncertainty** by Petr Sedlacek (Sedlacek, 2020).

Sedlacek (2020) develops a dynamic stochastic general equilibrium model with heterogeneous innovative firms highly related to the literature on Schumpeterian creative destruction (Aghion and Howitt (1994), and Caballero and Mohammed (1996)) and documents how firm dynamics and firm-level uncertainty respond to technology shocks. He argues that even if there is agreement on the fact that uncertainty rises during recessions, it is less clear whether uncertainty causes downturns or vice versa. He shows that faster technology growth raises uncertainty through a growth option channel: firms face larger productivity gains if they innovate and relatively larger productivity losses if they do not. In addition, faster growth spurs a process of creative destruction generating a temporary downturn and rendering uncertainty countercyclical. Estimates from structural VARs on the US data confirm the model's predictions. Growth explains 1/4 of the cyclical variation in uncertainty on average, and up to 2/3 around the dot-com bubble.

The contribution of Sedlacek (2020)'s paper is of the same nature as the Ates and Saffie (2021) paper and should be considered as a cornerstone approach to modelling innovation in a framework designed to evaluate innovation policies. The model can also be easily embodied into a DSGE model for whose solution standard algorithms can be used. The link between growth and business cycles with innovation uncertainty being the driver of both long-term growth and the business cycle, the model can be used to study the transitional dynamics of innovation policies.

- **How much Keynes and how much Schumpeter? An Estimated Macromodel of the US Economy** by Guido Cozzi, Beatrice Pataracchia, Philipp Pfeiffer and Marco Ratto (Cozzi et al., 2017).

  The macroeconomic experience of the last decade clearly shows that long-term growth and business cycle fluctuations need to be studied in the same framework. To analyse this issue, the authors embed a Schumpeterian growth model into an estimated medium-scale DSGE model. Results from a Bayesian estimation suggest that investment risk premia are a key driver of the slump following the Great Recession. Endogenous innovation dynamics amplify financial crises and help explain the slow recovery. Moreover, financial conditions also account for a substantial share of R&D investment dynamics. Cozzi et al. (2017) estimate for the US a DSGE model with Schumpeterian (semi-endogenous) growth. They document that the recent financial crisis seems to show a clear change in the pattern of GDP growth. Up to 2007, the US was clearly behaving as predicted by Neoclassical growth theory, with GDP systematically reverting towards the same trend. By contrast, after the financial crisis, GDP seems to have moved down to a lower trend. To match the data, Cozzi et al. (2017) suggest a semi-endogenous growth model that converges to the same balanced growth path, but only after a very long transition.

- **Innovation and Trade Policy in a Globalized World** by Ufuk Akcigit, Sina Ates and Giammario Impullitti (Akcigit et al., 2018).

Akcigit et al. (2018) assess the role of import tariffs and R&D subsidies as policy responses to foreign technological competition. To this end, they build a dynamic general equilibrium growth model where firm innovation shapes endogenously the dynamics of technology, and, therefore, market leadership and trade flows in a world with countries at different stages of development. The model accounts for competitive pressures exerted by both entrant and incumbent firms. Firms R&D decisions are driven by (i) the size of the market, (ii) the effort to escape international competition, (iii) domestic and international business stealing and (iv) technology spillovers. This theoretical investigation finds that, in a static context, globalization, proxied by reduced trade barriers, benefits domestic workers, while it has an ambiguous effect on business owners. In a dynamic context, globalization is shown to boost domestic innovation through an escape-competition effect. A calibrated version of the model reproduces the foreign technological catch-up the US experienced during the 1970s and early 1980s. Accounting for transitional dynamics, they show that foreign technological acceleration hurts US welfare in the short and medium run through business stealing, but generates long-run benefits via higher quality of imported goods and higher domestic innovation induced by the escape-competition effect. The model suggests that the introduction of the Research and Experimentation Tax Credit in 1981 proves to be an effective policy response to foreign competition, generating substantial welfare gains in the long run. A counterfactual exercise shows that increasing trade barriers, as an alternative policy response, produce gains only in the very short run, leading to large losses in the medium and long run. Protectionist measures generate large dynamic losses from trade, distorting the impact of openness on innovation incentives and productivity growth. Finally, the counterfactual exercise shows that less government intervention is needed when trade barriers are reduced as a result of globalization.

4.3 Modelling the Macroeconomic Effects of Innovation Policies

The JRC-IEA Roundtable between academics, policymakers and practitioners was animated by a lively discussion. Some of the more general issues related to the modelling and impact assessment of European innovation policies will be presented in subsequent sections of the book. The remainder of this chapter will instead focus on more specific, albeit not less important, modelling issues:

- There is a well-known debate on the nature of economic growth in macroeconomics: *Is growth exogenous, endogenous or semi-endogenous?* Yet, no agreement has been reached, with empirical and theoretical arguments pointing in different directions. There is no doubt that relevant variables should be part of the analysis, with GDP and its growth rate being among the most important variables economists would like to understand. Hence, models of endogenous growth should be at the top of the agenda. However, the debate is not about the nature of growth (endogenous or not), but about the empirical pertinence of existing endogenous growth models.
- *Should predictions cover the short, medium or long run?* Of course, growth is about the long term, but innovation policies need to be regularly evaluated. In this sense, intermediary effects, those taking place during the transition from a balanced growth path to another, are critical for the evaluation of innovation policies.
- Since a model has to be understood as a lab for policy simulations, the fit of the model to the data is a fundamental criterion in model selection. In this regard, the large availability of microdata at present permits adding more *micro heterogeneity in macro models.*
- *Firm heterogeneity, the dynamics of firms (entry and exit) and innovation.* The last decade witnessed the emergence of a sizeable literature on the dynamics of heterogeneous firms, with most contributions assuming exogenous productivity processes. The Schumpeterian model is a model of innovation with heterogeneous firms, governed by entry and exit (creation and destruction). When innovation is at centre stage, the question that emerges is: what are the main differences between the Schumpeterian model and the Hopenhayn-Melitz model?[1] A new literature developed in recent years attempts to shed light in this respect.
- It is important to identify the *trade-offs between promoting excellence and/or promoting convergence*, which relates to the trade-offs

[1] The Hopenhayn-Melitz model refers to Hopenhayn (1992) and Melitz (2003)

between growth and inequality. At the national/regional level, European innovation policies may be addressed to give incentives to the most developed regions to deepen their innovation process or alternatively to promote the development of those regions that need to catch-up with the frontier technology.

R&D subsidies aimed to promote innovation and growth affect the variance of the productivity distribution across firms and regions. A better understanding of this effect is important to improve our comprehension of the distributive consequences of innovation policies.

Models must be able to clearly specify why excellence and convergence matter in order to quantitatively evaluate what is the right balance between them. This issue is highly connected to the related problem of inter-regional migration.

- It is important to analyse the differential behaviour of *small, medium and large firms*. The theory of firm dynamics is a good framework to study the dynamics of firm size.
- Should models distinguish between *innovation and adoption*? The success of an innovation policy depends not only on the number and degree of innovation of new technologies/ideas that it helps to create, but on the extent of their diffusion through a long process of adoption by others.

  This is related to the nature of technical progress: radical innovation and general-purpose technologies (GPT). Is innovation policy aimed at diffusing existing technological paradigms or, rather, at promoting the emergence of new ones? Should we, for example, invest in the diffusion of IT technologies or bid on the emergence of robotics?
- There is an important debate in the theoretical and empirical growth literature about the nature and extent of *technological spillovers*, in particular those related to trade. The impact of innovation policy and its regional effects critically depends on these spillovers.
- *Macro models must be disciplined by macro and micro data.* The decline of the endogenous growth literature in the first decade of the twenty-first century was due to the inability for the models belonging to this family to replicate by existing data. Its recent resurgence is attributable to the appropriate use of macro and microdata. In this sense, modelling microheterogeneity is important for macro

models in order to be able to capture the observed microeconomic data.

- As a general *modelling strategy*, one needs to first identify the policy-relevant question, second, investigate what the profession already knows (i.e, the relevant literature) as well as look for the available macro and microdata and, third, develop a model that is able to answer the policymakers' questions while fitting the data to the best degree possible. The overarching fundamental principle underlying this step-wise approach to modelling is that models are question and data dependent.
- In the process of identifying a good model, the dialogue between policy and economic analysts in policymaking institutions, on one hand, and academia, on the other, is crucial. This helps to identify and design the most appropriate models to answer the most relevant questions in the policy arena at a given point in time.
- Until now, the big absent in the innovation debate, primarily on the academic side but also on the policy debate, has been the *welfare and distributional consequences of innovation policy*. Creative destruction leads to new jobs often requiring new skills, but it also leads to job losses with associated distributional and welfare consequences, which may be unevenly distributed across sectors, regions and generations.
- A fundamental principle of Italian cooking is: *the least ingredients, the better*. One of the key questions that emerged during the workshop presentations was how one can implement this principle when modelling innovation policies aimed at very different objectives and likely operating through very different channels. This necessitates a thoughtful exchange between all the parties involved.

References

Aghion, P., Bergeaud, A., Boppart, T., Klenow, P. J., & Li, H. (2019). Missing growth from creative destruction. *American Economic Review, 109*(8), 2795–2822.

Aghion, P., & Howitt, P. (1994). Growth and unemployment. *The Review of Economic Studies, 61*, 477–494.

Akcigit, U., Sina, A., & Impullitti, G. (2018). *Innovation and Trade Policy in a Globalized World*. NBER Working Paper, No. 24543.

Ates, S. T., & Saffie, F. E. (2021). Fewer but better: Sudden stops, firm entry, and financial selection. *American Economic Journal: Macroeconomics, 13*(3), 304–56.

Broda, C., & Weinstein, D. (2006). Globalization and the gains from variety. *Quarterly Journal of Economics, 121*(2), 541–585.

Caballero, R., & Mohammed, H. (1996). On the timing and efficiency of creative destruction. *The Review of Economic Studies, 446*(3), 805–852.

Cozzi, G., Pataracchia, B., Pfeiffer, P., & Ratto, M. (2017). How much Keynes and how much Schumpeter? An estimated macromodel of the US economy. MPRA Paper No. 7777.

Fattal Jaef, R., & Buera, F. (2015). The dynamics of development: Entrepreneurship, innovation and reallocation. 2015 Meeting Papers 274, Society for Economic Dynamics.

Hopenhayn, H. (1992). Entry, exit and frim dynamics in long run equilibrium. *Econometrica, 70*, 1127–1150.

Melitz, M. (2003). The impact of trade on intra-industry reallocations and aggregate industry productivity. *Econometrica, 71*, 1695–1725.

Sedlacek, P. (2020). Creative destruction and uncertainty. *Journal of the European Economic Association, 18*(4), 1814–1843.

PART II

Innovation Policy Evaluations: Diverse Macroeconomic Models

5

European Commission and RHOMOLO Spatial CGE Model

Martin Aarøe Christensen

5.1 Introduction

RHOMOLO is the dynamic Spatial Computable General Equilibrium (CGE) model of the European Commission. It is developed and maintained by the Joint Research Centre (JRC) and used for policy impact assessment and for sector-, region- and time-specific model-based support to EU policymakers on structural reforms, growth and cohesion policies, including R&D support programmes.

The objective of RHOMOLO is to allow for the analysis of EU policies at the regional NUTS 2 level. Given the regional focus of RHOMOLO, a particular attention is devoted to the explicit modelling of spatial linkages, interactions and spillovers between regional economies. The model aims to account for local specificities which may affect the dynamics of

The views expressed are purely those of the author and may not in any circumstances be regarded as stating an official position of the European Commission.

M. A. Christensen (✉)
European Commission, DG JRC, Seville, Spain
e-mail: Martin.Christensen@ec.europe.eu

the regional economies such as factor endowment and local geography. In addition, European regions are very open, small economies, well integrated within and across national borders. Therefore, socio-economic developments in each region may be significantly affected by policy developments in their neighbouring regions and this dimension needs to be taken into account when analysing policy scenarios. The socio-economic conditions of European territories vary substantially at a sub-national level. Figure 5.1 illustrates the divergent economic conditions across EU regions. The figure shows the regional Gross Value Added (GVA) per capita for regions at the NUTS 2 level for the year 2013 which is the reference year of the most recent version of RHOMOLO. The figure shows that substantial deviation in per capital GVA can be observed across the EU and even within the EU Member States. Across the EU a number of metropolitan regions are characterized by per capita GVA which are considerable higher than the EU average. For example the 8 regions with the highest per capita value added all have per capita GVA that are more than twice the EU average.[1] Per capita GVA in Inner London is about 3.5 times the EU average and 26 times higher than in the EU region with the lowest per capita GVA which is the Bulgarian Region Severozapaden. In contrast, the 25 regions with the lowest per capita value added all have per capita GVA which is less than a third of the EU average.[2] Most Member States host one or more metropolitan areas where per capita GVA is considerable higher than the national average. The eight regions which have the highest per capita value added relatively to their national average, all have per capita GVA which is more than 1.6 times their national average.[3]

Given the variations in socio-economic conditions across EU regions, the economic impact of EU policies in support for R&D may also vary substantially across regions. The RHOMOLO model has been used in an attempt to capture deviations in regional outcomes of R&D polices. This chapter is organized as follows. The next section provides a short introduction to the current version of RHOMOLO with special emphasis

[1] The 8 regions are: Inner London, Luxembourg, Stockholm, the Region of Brussels, Hamburg, Groningen, Copenhagen and Île-de-France.

[2] The 25 regions mentioned are located in Poland, Romania, Hungary and Bulgaria.

[3] The 8 regions are: Inner London, Bratislava, Bucharest, Prague, the Region of Brussels, Hamburg, Île-de-France, Yugozapaden (incl. Sofia).

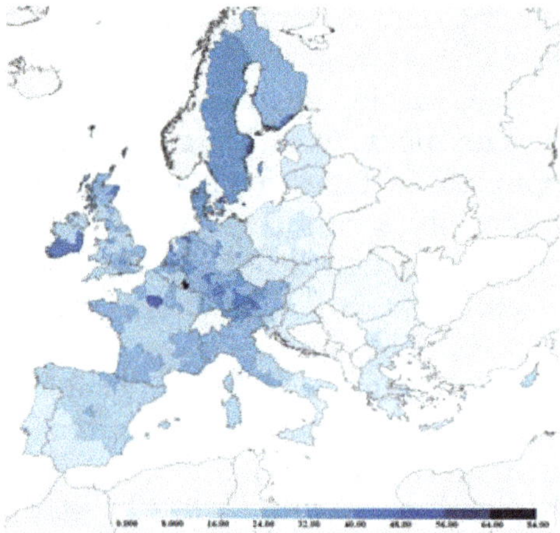

Fig. 5.1 Gross value added per capita across EU regions (1000 euro)

on how R&D enters the model. It also discusses the main limitations to the treatments of R&D in the model and highlights some requirements which future developments of R&D modelling in RHOMOLO should address. The last section contains a discussion of scenarios and findings following the economic impact assessment exercise of the Horizon Europe Framework Programme for Research and Innovation.

5.2 The Model

RHOMOLO is a Spatial Dynamic General Equilibrium model with new economic geography features.[4] The model contains a detailed specification of 267 regional economies and their spatial interactions.

Each region contains 10 economic sectors: Agriculture, Forestry and Fishing; Mining, Quarrying and Utilities[5]; Manufacturing; Construction; Whole and Retail Trade; Information and Communication; Financial, Insurance and Real Estate Activities; Professional, Scientific and Technical Activities; Public administration, Education, Health and Social Services; Other Services. A subset of these operates under monopolistic competition. The rest of the sectors operate under perfect competition. In the

[4] A detailed description of the latest available version of RHOMOLO can be found in Lecca et al. (2018).

[5] Here the term utilities refer to the sectors: Electricity, Gas, Steam and Air Conditioning Supply, Water Supply, waste Management and Remediation Activities.

imperfectly competitive sectors, each firm produces a given variety of the good which is an imperfect substitute for other varieties. The variety is produced with constant returns to scale technology. In addition, the firm faces fixed costs *FC* in the form of a fixed amount of its production which is not sold on the market. This introduces increasing returns to scale. To survive firms, in the imperfectly competitive sectors, have to charge positive mark-ups over marginal costs. These mark-ups are determined by the properties of the demand curve these firms face. We assume that there are free entry and exit of firm. Hence, given fixed costs and substitutability between goods the number of firms operating within a sector in a region are endogenously given to ensure that the zero profit condition holds. Firms in the perfectly competitive sectors have constant returns to scale technologies, minimize costs and are constrained to marginal costs pricing.

In all regional production sectors, goods are produced by combining labour and capital with domestic and imported intermediates, creating vertical linkages between firms. The production structure is given by a nested CES production function as shown in Fig. 5.2.

For a firm in sector i in region r, the demand for intermediate input $V_{r,i}$ and value added $Y_{r,i}$ in the upper nest of the production function is

Fig. 5.2 Production structure

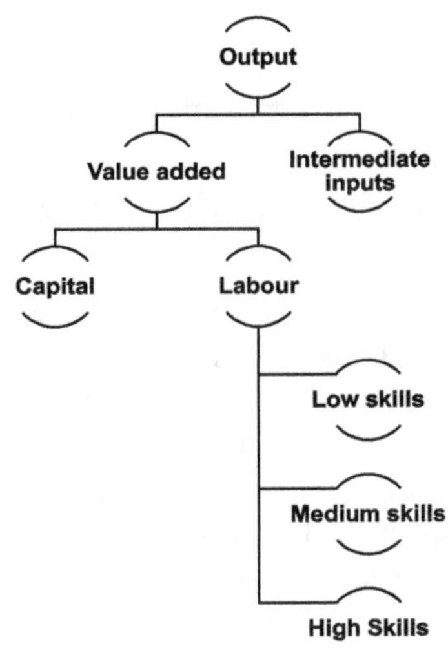

given by

$$V_{r,i} = \frac{\alpha^z_{r,i}}{(Ax_{r,i})^{1-\sigma^z}} \left[\frac{P^v_{r,i}}{P^z_{r,i}} \right]^{-\sigma^z} (Z_{r,i} + FC_{r,i}) \tag{5.1}$$

$$Y_{r,i} = \frac{(1-\alpha^z_{r,i})}{(Ax_{r,i})^{1-\sigma^z}} \left[\frac{P^y_{r,i}}{P^z_{r,i}} \right]^{-\sigma^z} (Z_{r,i} + FC_{r,i}) \tag{5.2}$$

where $\alpha^z_{r,i}$ is the calibrated share of intermediate inputs in total production, $Ax_{r,i}$ is a scale parameter and σ^z is the elasticity of substitution. The prices $P^z_{r,i}$, $P^v_{r,i}$ and $P^y_{r,i}$ is respectively the marginal production cost, the composite price index for intermediate inputs and the composite price index for value added. The marginal production cost $P^z_{r,i}$ is given by

$$P^z_{r,i} = \frac{1}{Ax_{r,i}} \left(\alpha^z_{r,i} \left(P^v_{r,i}\right)^{1-\sigma^z} + (1-\alpha^z_{r,i}) \left(P^y_{r,i}\right)^{1-\sigma^z} \right)^{\frac{1}{1-\sigma^z}} \tag{5.3}$$

whereas the composite price indices are given by

$$P^v_{r,i} = \left(\sum_j \alpha^v_{r,j,i} \left(P_{r,j}\right)^{1-\sigma^v} \right)^{\frac{1}{1-\sigma^v}} \tag{5.4}$$

$$P^y_r = \frac{1}{\left(\varphi_{r,i}(K^{g,d}_r)^{\xi}\right)} \left(\alpha^y_{r,i} \left(rk_{r,i}\right)^{1-\sigma^y} + (1-\alpha^y_{r,i}) \left(W_{r,i}\right)^{1-\sigma^y} \right)^{\frac{1}{1-\sigma^y}} \tag{5.5}$$

where $P_{r,j}$ is the price of the intermediate input from sector j, $rk_{r,i}$ is the return on capital, $W_{r,i}$ is a composite wage index, $\alpha^v_{r,j,i}$ and $\alpha^y_{r,i}$ are share parameters, and σ^v and σ^y are the elasticities of substitution for intermediate inputs and capital-labour respectively. Public capital services $K^{g,d}_r$ enters the production function as an unpaid factor of production meaning that all firms, in all sectors, enjoy the same level of public capital at no cost. The parameter $\varphi_{r,i}$ captures changes in total factor productivity. As discussed below, this is a key parameter for introducing long-term impacts of R&D in the model. Demand for capital and labour is given by

$$KD_{r,i} = \frac{\alpha^y_{r,i}}{\left(\varphi_{r,i}(K^{g,d}_r)^{\xi}\right)^{1-\sigma^y}} \left[\frac{rk_{r,i}}{P^y_{r,i}} \right]^{-\sigma^y} Y_{r,i} \tag{5.6}$$

$$LD_{r,i} = \frac{(1-\alpha^{y}_{r,i})}{\left(\varphi_{r,i}(K^{g,d}_{r})^{\xi}\right)^{1-\sigma^{y}}} \left[\frac{W_{r,i}}{P^{y}_{r,i}}\right]^{-\sigma^{y}} Y_{r,i} \tag{5.7}$$

The composite wage index $W_{r,i}$ is given by

$$W_{r,i} = \frac{1}{Al_{r,i,e}} \left(\sum_{e} \alpha^{ld}_{r,i} \left(W_{r,i,e}\right)^{1-\sigma^{ld}}\right)^{\frac{1}{1-\sigma^{ld}}} \tag{5.8}$$

where $Al_{r,i,e}$ is a scale parameter that captures labour productivity, $W_{r,i,e}$ is the wage for labour of skills type e and σ^{ld} is the elasticity of substitution between labour of different skills types. The firms demand for labour of skills type e is

$$LD_{r,i,e} = \frac{\alpha^{ld}_{r,i,e}}{\left(Al_{r,i,e}\right)^{1-\sigma^{ld}}} \left[\frac{W_{r,i,e}}{W_{r,i}}\right]^{-\sigma^{ld}} LD_{r,i} \tag{5.9}$$

Final goods are consumed by households, government and investors. Each region is inhabited by a representative household which supplies labour of three skills type (high, medium and low), consume and save. The composite of household consumption is described by CES preferences. Household's demand for the composite good from sector i is given by

$$C_{r,i} = \alpha_{r,i} \left[\frac{P_{r,i}}{P^{c}_{r}}\right]^{-\sigma^{c}} C_{r} \tag{5.10}$$

where C_r is the aggregate composite consumption good, $\alpha_{r,i}$ is a share parameter and σ^c is the elasticity of substitution. The associated consumption price index P^c_r is defined in terms of prices $P_{r,i}$ of the different sector i composite goods.

$$P^{c}_{r} = \left(\sum_{i=1} \alpha_{r,i} \left(P_{r,i}\right)^{1-\sigma^{c}}\right)^{\frac{1}{1-\sigma^{c}}} \tag{5.11}$$

The household saves a fixed share s_r of disposable income.

$$S_r = s_r YD_r \tag{5.12}$$

The government levies taxes, purchases public consumption goods, conducts public investments and allocates transfers to the various agents in the economy. Public consumption, public investments and transfers in real terms are exogenous to the model.

The RHOMOLO model incorporates imperfect competition in the labour market which allows for unemployment. The model allows one to switch from a wage curve assumption to a Phillips curve assumption in wage formation.

The model contains two types of capital, sector-specific private capital and public capital available to firm in all sectors within the region. Sector-specific private capital is accumulated by private investors. The optimal path of private investments $I^{p}_{r,i}$ is defined as

$$I^{p}_{r,i} = \delta_r K^{p}_{r,i}\left(\frac{rk_{r,i}}{uck_r}\right)^{\nu} \tag{5.13}$$

where ν is the accelerator parameter and δ is the depreciation rate. The investment-capital ratio is a function of the rate of return to capital and the user cost of capital uck_r allowing the capital stock to reach its desired level in a smooth fashion over time. The user cost of capital is derived from a no arbitrage condition and is given by

$$uck_r = (r + \delta_r)P^{I}_{EU} + \Delta P^{I}_{EU} + rp_r \tag{5.14}$$

where r is the interest rate, rp is an exogenous risk premium and P^{I}_{EU} is the price index for investments at the EU level. The demand for investment $I^{p}_{r,i}$ by sector i is translated into demand for investments goods through a capital matrix

$$I^{s}_{r,j} = \sum_i KM_{r,i,j} I^{p}_{r,i} \tag{5.15}$$

where $I^{s}_{r,j}$ is the demand for the investment good produced by sector j.

Public capital is accumulated by the government. Public capital in the model is not treated as a pure public good but is characterized by some degree of congestion. Hence, the public capital services available from the public capital stock $K^{g,s}$ are adjusted for congestion by aggregate production. Therefore an increase in production reduces the effective quantity of public capital stock enjoyable by all firms.

$$K_r^{g,d} = K_r^{g,s}\left(\sum_i N_{r,i} Y_{r,i}\right)^{\gamma} \quad \gamma \in (0, -\infty) \tag{5.16}$$

where γ is the congestion parameter.

Goods and services can be sold in the domestic economy or exported to other regions. Trade between regions is associated with a set of bilateral regional transportation costs. In each region aggregate demand, $X_{r,i}$, for the composite good from sector i is determined by the sum of intermediate demand by all firms and all components of final demand. In perfectly competitive sectors, the composite good i is based on an Armington assumption and takes the form of a CES aggregate of domestically produced goods and imported goods. In imperfectly competitive sectors, the composite good i is based on a Dixit-Stiglitz specification capturing the product differentiation at the individual firm level. Normalizing the number of firms in the competitive sector to 1 then the demand by region r for sector i good from an individual firm in region r' under the two assumptions can be formulated identically as

$$\frac{X_{r',i,r}}{(1+\tau^{tr}_{r',i,r})} = \alpha^{x}_{r',i,r}\left[\frac{(1+\tau^{tr}_{r',i,r})(1+\tau^{p}_{r,i})P^{x}_{r',i,r}}{P_{r,i}}\right]^{-\sigma^x} X_{r,i} \tag{5.17}$$

with the price index

$$P_{r,i} = \left(\sum_{r'} N_{r',i}\alpha^{x}_{r',i,r}\left((1+\tau^{tr}_{r',i,r})(1+\tau^{p}_{r,i})P^{x}_{r',i,r}\right)^{1-\sigma^x}\right)^{\frac{1}{1-\sigma^x}} \tag{5.18}$$

where $P^{x}_{r',i,r}$ is the price set by a firm in region r' (net of product taxes $\tau^{p}_{r,i}$ and transport costs at the net rate $\tau^{tr}_{r',i,r}$) selling to region r.

Due to its high dimensionality, RHOMOLO is solved following a recursively dynamic approach. It contains a sequence of short-run equilibria that are related to each other through the build-up of physical and intangible capital stocks.

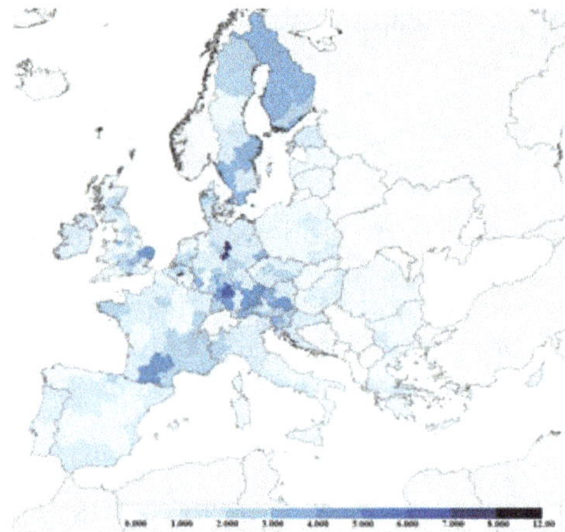

Fig. 5.3 R&D intensity across EU regions

5.2.1 R&D in RHOMOLO

The objective of the RHOMOLO model is to address regional deviations in policy impacts. The model is calibrated to the regional levels of R&D investments observed in the reference year. Hence, the model captures the large regional differences in R&D expenditures across the EU. Figure 5.3 shows the geographical variations in regional R&D intensity in the model's reference year. The highest R&D intensities can be observed in the Belgian region Brabant Wallon and the German regions Braunschweig and Stuttgart. R&D intensity is, respectively, 5.6, 3.6 and 3.0 times higher than the EU average.[6] The figure also reveals that deviation in R&D intensity exists within EU Member States. Most Member States contains one or several regions which are considerable more R&D intensive relatively to the national average.

RHOMOLO captures in detail regional deviations in R&D spending in the reference year whereas the modeling of dynamic R&D impacts are specified in a relatively simple setup. Any changes in the R&D investment level are introduced into the model as an exogenous shock.[7] The impact of a change in R&D expenditures enters into the model through two

[6] For more perspective on regional disparities, R&D intensity in Brabant Wallon is 19 times higher than in the regions with the lowest R&D intensity, namely the Romanian region Sud-Est and the Autonomous Spanish region of Ceuta.

[7] The current version of RHOMOLO does not include any endogenous respond to R&D spending in response to changes in economic activity. Hence, a change in say

channels; a channel with temporary demand effects and a channel with permanent structural effects.

First, consider the temporary demand effects. The way this is introduced into the model depends on whether the R&D expenditure is undertaken as a public R&D activity or as a R&D expenditure conducted by the private sector. A change in public R&D spending is associated with a change in public expenditures introduced as an exogenous public expenditure shock. Hence, a change in public R&D expenditure affects the demand for public final consumption goods. A change in private R&D spending is associated with a change in private investments introduced as a change in the risk premium faced by firms. A change in risk premium affects the firms' user cost of capital and hence the desired level of investments. A change in private R&D expenditure thus affects the demand for investment goods.

Second, consider the permanent, structural effect. It is assumed that regional R&D spending leads to an increase in the intangible knowledge capital stock which in turn spills into an increase in TFP for all firms in the region. In the model, the impact of R&D expenditure on TFP through the accumulated knowledge capital stock is captured by a regional R&D elasticity σ^{rd} defined as

$$\sigma_r^{RD} = \frac{\partial \varphi_{r,t}}{\partial RDexp_{r,t}} \frac{RDexp_{r,t0}}{\varphi_{r,t0}} \tag{5.19}$$

where $RDexp_r$ is R&D expenditure in region r, the subscript $t0$ denotes value in the reference year. The R&D elasticity is conditional on R&D intensity within the region. Hence, the model allows for spatial variations in the economic impact from R&D spending across EU regions. Higher regional R&D intensity is associated with higher spillover from R&D expenditure to TFP. The intuition is that firms in regions that are already spending much on R&D signal their pre-existing capacity to generate value from innovation activities. The deviation of TFP from the reference scenario evolves according to

$$\varphi_{r,t} = \varphi_{r,t0}\left(1 + \sigma_r^{RD} \sum_i \frac{RDexp_{r,t-i} - RDexp_{r,t0}}{RDexp_{r,t0}} \left(\frac{1}{1+\delta^{rd}}\right)^i\right) \tag{5.20}$$

public investments for transport infrastructure will not lead to an endogenous change in regional R&D spending.

where δ^{rd} is the depreciation rate of TFP for firms in region r.

The R&D elasticities used in RHOMOLO are based on estimates by Kancs and Siliverstovs (2016). They estimate the relationship between R&D investment and firm productivity growth by explicitly modelling non-linearities in the R&D-productivity relationship. They find that the impact of R&D investment on firm productivity is different at different levels of R&D intensity with the relationship between R&D expenditures and productivity growth being highly non-linear. Only after a certain critical mass of knowledge accumulates productivity growth becomes significantly positive. Based on the estimates by Kancs and Siliverstovs, we assign values to the R&D elasticities for all the regions in the model. The geographical distribution is shown in Fig. 5.4. The R&D elasticities vary from 0.008 to 0.152. More than half of the EU regions have R&D elasticities below 0.01. The assumption of the non-linear nature of R&D impact means that regions with high R&D intensity in the reference year also has substantial higher R&D elasticities. Therefore a policy of R&D support would yield different returns across regions. However, the economic impact of R&D support not only depends on the regional R&D elasticity but also on the structural composition of the regional economy, factor endowments and trade patterns. Given the recursive dynamics of RHOMOLO, the parameter capturing changes in TFP for all firms in a region is updated before each model iteration.

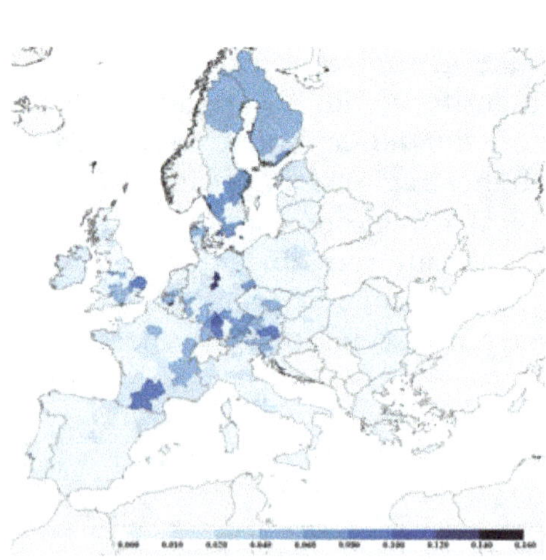

Fig. 5.4 Regional R&D elasticities in RHOMOLO

5.2.2 *Limitations*

The way R&D impacts the economy in the current version of RHOMOLO has limitations. Firstly, changes in R&D spending are exogenous. Hence, firms do not endogenously decide on the optimal level of R&D investments in the model based on expected future returns.

Secondly, R&D expenditures enter the model at a regional level with all firms benefiting equally from an improvement in TFP. Estimates from Kancs and Siliverstovs (2016) suggest that R&D elasticities could vary substantially across sectors. The current specification of R&D does not capture that policies targeting different sectors may impact TFP differently. Furthermore, sector-specific R&D investments may result in improvements in TFP which mainly benefit firms in the sector conducting the R&D activity with more limited TFP impact on firms in other sectors.[8]

Thirdly, the current specification does not explicitly address diffusion of technologies across regions. In the current model setting an increase in TFP in a region would benefit firms in neighbouring regions through trade due to cheaper imported intermediate inputs. Furthermore, in sectors characterized by monopoly power, a fraction of firms would real-locate to the region experiencing TFP growth. However, TFP of firms in neighbouring regions does not increase due to technology absorption. This reduces the benefit of R&D investments across the EU.

Fourthly, the impact of public R&D investments and private R&D investments is assumed to result in identical increases in TFP for firms within a region. Ideally, one would assign different R&D elasticities to these two types of R&D investments.

5.2.3 *Addressing the Limitations for R&D Modelling in RHOMOLO*

The need for assessing the regional economic impacts of R&D policies in RHOMOLO means that the way R&D enters into the model is continuously updated and improved. Some key challenges have been identified which the modelling of R&D in RHOMOLO should address. First, a specification that endogenizes decisions on R&D investments by private

[8] Although some multi-purpose technologies may improve TFP across all sectors.

firms could be introduced into the model. This would allow public policies to affect R&D decisions in other regions. A challenge for such a specification is that the model is solved by recursive dynamics. Hence, agents current behaviour is not influenced by expectations about the economic conditions in future periods. A possible solution could be to introduce a specification which capture agents' expectations based on current or past states of the economy.

Second, to allow for sectoral differences in R&D impact one could introduce sector-specific R&D spending into the model. Furthermore, one could distinguish between public sector and private sector R&D expenditure. Allowing for sector-specific R&D spending would also allow for varying spillover effects within and across sectors. However, introducing sector-specific R&D investments to the model significantly increase the data requirements as one would need sectoral R&D investments at the regional level and estimated sectoral R&D's own and cross elasticities capturing the impact of R&D investments on TFP.

Third, a formal modelling of R&D production, which puts a higher emphasis on high-skilled labour input and high tech intermediate inputs, could be introduced. Currently, the cost of R&D production is defined as, respectively, the price of the public consumption composite or the price of the capital goods composite. A more formal treatment of R&D production would also allow policies targeting education or improved labour skills to impact the cost of R&D production.

Fourth, a formal modelling of the linkages through which R&D production impacts the economy could be incorporated into the model. This could be through a combination of the mechanism found in the expanding variety model originally proposed by Romer (1990) and the Schumpeterian endogenous growth model focusing on innovation-led growth and creative destruction originally proposed by Aghion et al. (1998) and Aghion and Howitt (1992).

Fifth, the model should address how technology and innovation diffuse into other sectors and regions. Several models of diffusion have been proposed in the literature (see e.g. Barro & Sala-I-Martin, 1997; Grossman & Helpman, 1993). One possibility would be to add the modelling of a costly process through which firms may adopt existing technologies as for example proposed by Comin and Gertler (2006). This would allow one to distinguish between the impact from policies targeting R&D production and policies concerned with technology adoption in regions. Clearly any modelling of technology diffusion and R&D

spillovers across sectors and regions would need to rest on stylized facts identified in empirical studies covering data at the level of firms, regions or countries.

5.2.4 *Model Summary*

The spatial dynamic general equilibrium model RHOMOLO contains a detailed specification of regional economies and their spatial interactions. The model allows for a regional assessment of economic impacts of R&D expenditures by the use of a relatively simple treatment of R&D. An exogenously determined level of R&D expenditures impacts the economy through a temporary demand channel that either raises public consumption or private investments through a permanent structural channel that leads to changes in TFP for all firms in a region. The impact of R&D spending varies across regions as a result of variations in the composition of input demand and regional variations in the R&D elasticity which is assumed to rise with higher R&D intensity. However, the impact of R&D spending also depends on regional variations in factor endowments and trade linkages. The specification of R&D in RHOMOLO has a number of limitations including the lack of endogenous adjustment of R&D spending and no formal modelling of technology diffusion across regions and sectors. These limitations could be addressed in future developments of the model.

5.3 An Example: Simulating the Ex-Ante Macroeconomic Impact of Horizon Europe

Macroeconomic modelling is used by the European Commission for policy impact assessments including assessments of policies in support to Research and Innovation (R&I). The aim of such assessments is to assist policymakers by providing an ex-ante assessment of potential outcomes of the suggested policy proposals. This section provides an example of how the dynamic Spatial Computable General Equilibrium model RHOMOLO is used to examine the economic impact of R&I support policies. More specifically we present some of the findings of the economic impact assessment accompanying the proposal for the Horizon Europe Framework Programme. Horizon Europe is the European Commission proposal for the EU research and Innovation programme for 2021–2027.[9] The programme aims to support the provision of European R&I investments. Through EU-wide competition and cooperation, the programme supports training and mobility for scientists, creates transnational cross-sectoral and multidisciplinary collaborations and leverages additional public and private investments. The objective is to strengthen the scientific and technological bases of the EU and foster its competitiveness, including for its industry. The programme seeks to address particular R&I challenges faced by the EU and to contribute to tackling global challenges, including the Sustainable Development Goals.

Substantial variations in industrial structures, infrastructure and socio-economic conditions exist across the EU Member States at the national level and even more so at the sub-national level. Likewise, R&I activities vary largely at the sub-national level with R&I activities clustering in some areas leaving other areas with more modest R&I activities. Reflecting such regional differences, the allocation of resources under Horizon Europe is likely to vary across regions. Horizon Europe may shift resources across EU regions and impact differently the various regional economies. Furthermore, structural socio-economic differences across EU regions may result in heterogeneous regional responses to public R&I support. This calls for an impact assessment of the European R&I support programme to also consider the sub-national level.

This section exemplifies the use of RHOMOLO for the ex-ante impact evaluation of the Horizon Europe policy scenario. A discussion of its economic impacts at both the aggregate EU level and at the regional level is provided.

5.3.1 Scenarios and Method

Our example is taken from the economic impact assessment accompanying the proposal for the Horizon Europe Framework Programme (see Christensen, 2018; European Commission, 2018). The proposal concerns EU support to R&I for the period 2021–2027. More specifically, we examine the outcome of a policy scenario describing the introduction of Horizon Europe. The budget size of the Horizon Europe scenario is assumed to be identical to the programme it replaces (Horizon 2020) in constant prices, minus the contribution from the UK (assumed to be 15%

[9] It replaces the current Framework Programme Horizon 2020 which will expire by the end of 2020.

of the budget). The impact assessment thus considers total cumulative spending of approximately 70 billion which is equivalent to 0.5% of GDP in 2017 for the EU excluding the UK.[10] In the Horizon Europe scenario, we assume that public support to R&I generates a further rise in private R&I spending through a direct leverage effect. In the impact assessment we assume a direct leverage effect of 9.75% which is a weighted average of the direct leverage effect of respectively basic research and applied research suggested by Boitier et al. (2018). Their suggested leverage effects take outset in a survey on research units involved in the 7th Framework Programme and empirical estimates in the literature.

The outcome of the Horizon Europe scenario is compared to a reference scenario without Horizon Europe. Instead, the EU Member States spend an amount identical to their Horizon Europe contribution on public investments including national R&I support programmes. Spending by the Member States is financed by lump sum taxes. We assume that the regional allocation of the additional public investments follows the regional allocation of current public investments within the Member States. Public spending for national R&I support is assumed to follow the same regional allocation within each Member State as of the current EU R&I support programme (Horizon 2020). Given these assumptions, substantial variations exist in the regional allocation of respectively public investments and public R&I support in the reference scenario. While public investments are spread out across regions within the Member States, the regional allocation of public R&I support is concentrated in R&I intensive metropolitan regions (Figs. 5.5 and 5.6). We assume that the introduction of Horizon Europe involves a reduction in public investments and in national public support to R&I which is paid as contribution to Horizon Europe and distributed across EU regions as public support to R&I. The regional allocation of EU-wide support to R&I is assumed to be identical to the regional allocation of Horizon 2020.

Given these assumptions, large regional variations in EU R&I support can be observed. The largest recipient of accumulated public spending

[10] After the impact assessment was carried out the proposed budget by the European Commission for Horizon Europe has been increased to 94.1 billion. In addition to the Horizon Europe's 2021–2027 Framework Programme the proposed European Commission R&I support programme also includes the 2021–2025 Research and Training programme of the European Atomic Energy Community (the Euratom Programme) with a proposed budget of 2.4 billion and 3.5 billion allocated under the InvestEU fund.

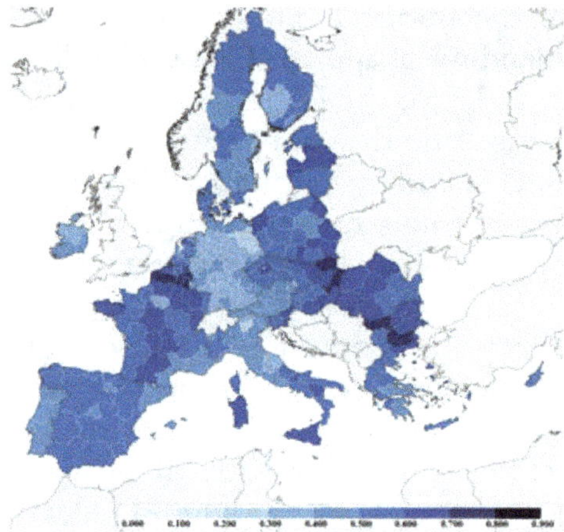

Fig. 5.5 Additional public investments in reference scenario (% of GDP)

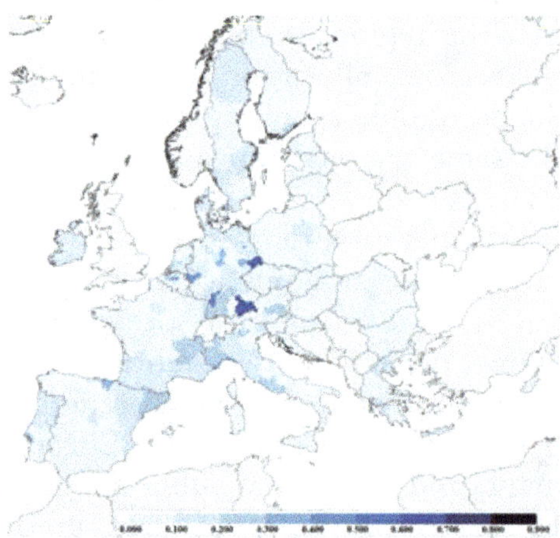

Fig. 5.6 Additional national public R&I support in reference scenario (% of GDP)

for R&I support during the programme period is Île-de-France (5,900 million) followed by Oberbayern (3,600 million). Other large recipients of public spending are Rhône-Alpes (2,300 million), Cataluña (2,000 million), Lombardia (2,000 million) and Lazio (2,000 million) as illustrated in Fig. 5.7.

Considering the regional allocation of cumulative EU spending in support for R&I relative to the size of the regional economy also reveals that R&I support is concentrated in metropolitan regions. In percent of GDP in the RHOMOLO model's base year (2013) the largest recipients

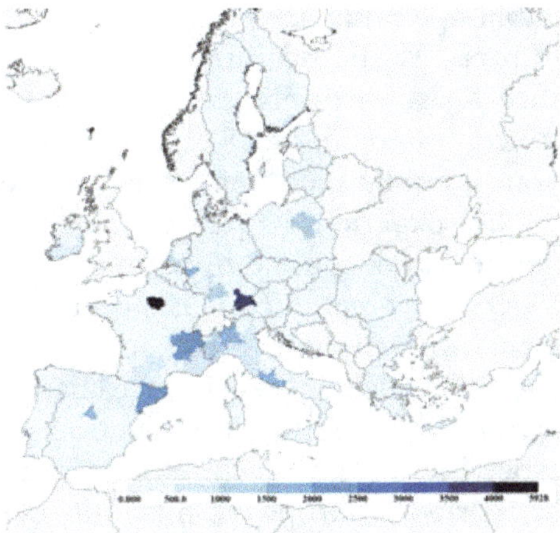

Fig. 5.7 EU support for R&I in Horizon Europe scenario (million euro)

of cumulative public spending in support to R&I over the programme period is assumed to be the Belgian regions of Brussels (1.9% of base year GDP) and Vlaams-Brabant (1.7% of base year GDP). This is followed by Dresden (1.7% of base year GDP), Oberbayern (1.6% of base year GDP), País Vasco (1.5% of base year GDP), Bucharest (1.5% of base year GDP) and Bratislava (1.5% of base year GDP). The geographical allocation is illustrated in Fig. 5.8.

Differences in regional allocation of respectively public investments and public expenditures for R&I support change the net allocation of

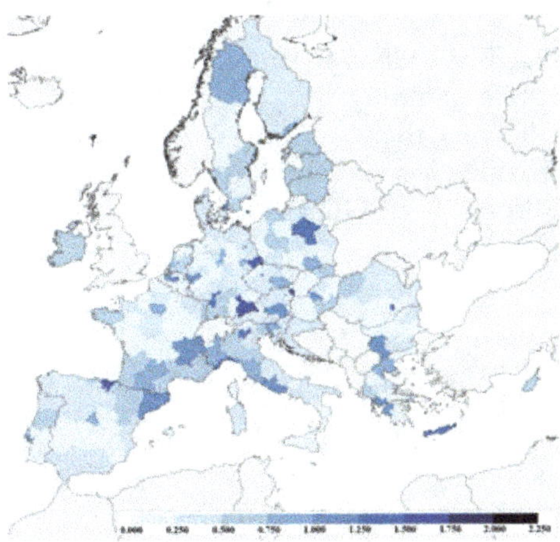

Fig. 5.8 EU support for R&I in Horizon Europe scenario (% of GDP)

public spending across EU regions following the introduction of Horizon Europe. With the introduction of Horizon Europe all regions experience a rise in public R&I support, however, the bulk of the increase is concentrated in the R&I intensive regions. As a result, the net allocation of public spending received by each region varies. The R&I intensive regions experience a net gain as the rise in public R&I support outweighs the decline in public investments whereas the less R&I intensive regions experience a net decline in public spending as the decline in public investments outweighs the rise in public R&I support. This is illustrated in Fig. 5.9 which shows the net change in public spending received by each region following the introduction of Horizon Europe. Although a region experiences a net decline in public spending following the introduction of Horizon Europe, it may still benefit from the EU R&I programme through trade linkages with neighbouring regions and from improved productivity resulting from higher R&I investments.

The reference scenario and the Horizon Europe policy scenario are simulated on the most recent version of RHOMOLO described in Lecca et al. (2018), with the R&D sector as described in the previous section. R&I expenditure is modelled as private investments. Public expenditure in support for R&I is introduced into the model as a reduction in user cost of capital which, in turn, generates an increase in private sector R&I investments. Hence, public spending in support to R&I generates demand for capital goods. In addition, R&I expenditure leads to accumulation of an intangible knowledge capital stock which, in turn, spills

Fig. 5.9 Change in public spending following the introduction of Horizon Europe (% of GDP)

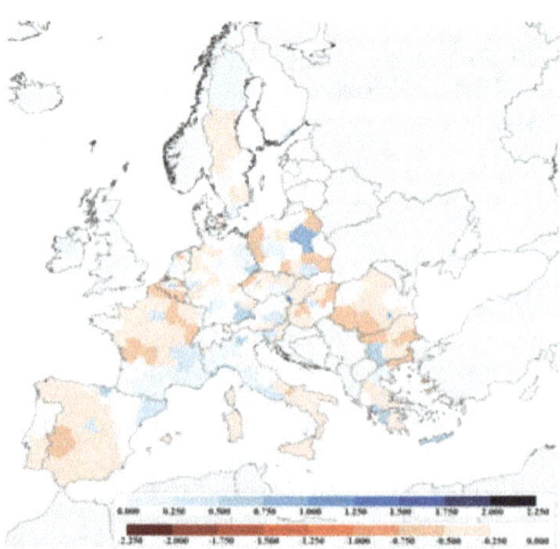

into an increase in TFP. The impact of R&I expenditure on TFP through the accumulated knowledge capital stock is captured by a set of regional spillover elasticities which are conditional on R&D intensity within the region. Higher regional R&D intensity is associated with higher spillover from knowledge capital to TFP. The intuition is that firms in regions that are already spending much on R&D signal their pre-existing capacity to generate value from innovation activities. The R&D spillover elasticities are based on estimates by Kancs and Siliverstovs (2016). The model is solved by recursive dynamics.

5.3.2 *Economic Impact at Aggregate EU Level*

We begin by considering the aggregate economic impact for the EU excluding the UK (for simplicity we will refer to this as EU). Results are presented as deviations from the reference scenario.

It is assumed that the EU R&I programme is financed by a reallocation of public spending by each Member State from domestic public investments and national public R&I support towards contributions to Horizon Europe. In RHOMOLO such a shift in policy would mainly affect the economy through two channels; a demand channel and a productivity channel. First, consider the demand channel. Introducing Horizon Europe leads to a rise in EU public spending for R&I support which is partly offset by a decline in national public spending for R&I support. The net effect is an increase in private R&I investments which raises private demand for capital goods. Resources are being reallocated from public investments within the regions which reduce the public demand for capital goods. How this shift in spending strategy effects the aggregate demand in a region depends on the combined net effects from the decline in regional public investment and the rise in R&I investments. Aggregate demand is also affected by the composition of inputs (material inputs and factor inputs) used in the production of the composite capital good demanded by respectively the private R&I investors and the government. This would depend on the sectors from which the material inputs are sourced, how much of these sectors' input that is produced domestically and how much that is imported, and on the share of the various domestic production factors used in the production of the capital goods. For example, a shift in investment demand towards capital goods with a higher domestic input share and a higher share of factor inputs would, all else equal, increase domestic production and household income. Second, consider the productivity channel. A rise in private R&I investments leads to higher knowledge accumulation which, in turn, generates a rise in TFP. In contrast, a lower public capital accumulation is assumed to generate a negative productivity effect through which public capital services bring reduced efficiency to the private production sectors in the region.

Figure 5.10 shows the change in EU GDP relative to the reference scenario. The introduction of Horizon Europe leads to a gradual rise in EU GDP. This is mainly determined by higher TFP growth which outweighs the lower productivity growth caused by the reduction in public investments. The largest deviation in EU GDP occurs in 2029 where EU GDP is 0.2% higher than the reference scenario. The long-run GDP impact of introducing the EU R&I support programme is more modest. Horizon Europe runs until 2027 after which it is assumed that EU R&I support stops. In the RHOMOLO model, an efficiency gain from the accumulated knowledge stock is assumed to depreciate. Hence, TFP gains from R&I investments made in the past gradually die out.

Table 5.1 shows the cumulative EU GDP deviation relative to the reference scenario. The introduction of Horizon Europe results in cumulative EU GDP in 2040 to become 0.1% higher than in the reference scenario. The increase in cumulative EU GDP in 2050 is slightly less due to the depreciation of TFP gains.

The deviation of EU GDP relative to the reference scenario can be decomposed into macroeconomic aggregates. This is shown in Fig. 5.11. The introduction of the EU R&I support programme causes a temporary

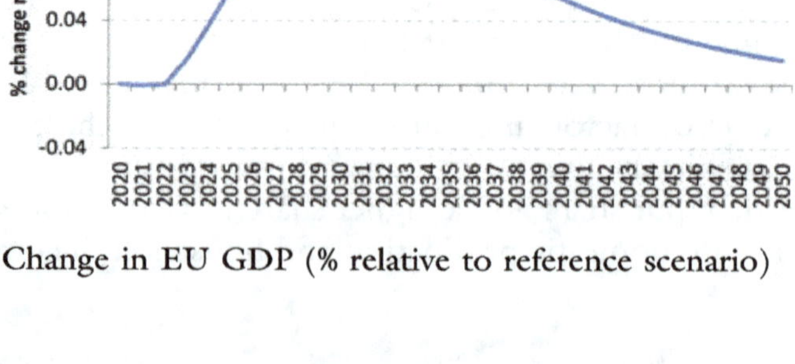

Fig. 5.10 Change in EU GDP (% relative to reference scenario)

Table 5.1 Deviation of EU GDP (% relative to reference scenario)

	Impact of EU R&I programme
Cumulative EU GDP deviation in 2030	0.063
Cumulative EU GDP deviation in 2040	0.071
Cumulative EU GDP deviation in 2050	0.056

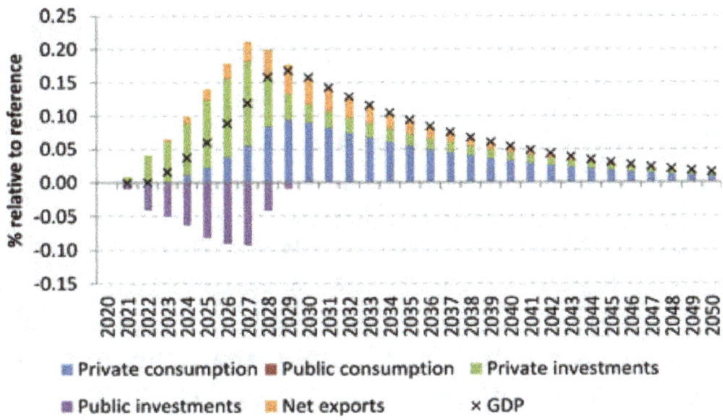

Fig. 5.11 Contribution to change in EU GDP (% relative to reference scenario)

decline in public investments in the EU Member States in the period 2021–2029. Private R&I investments rise and this contributes the most to the overall increase in EU GDP relative to the reference scenario. The introduction of the EU R&I support programme also leads to a rise in private household consumption and a rise in net exports. From 2030 the rise in private household consumption contributes the most to the change in EU GDP. Higher productivity growth results in an improvement of the EU trade balance, private investments and consumption opportunities for EU households.

The introduction of Horizon Europe stimulates EU medium to long term employment. This is illustrated by Fig. 5.12 that shows the change in EU employment relative to the reference scenario. At first the shift in spending from public investments towards R&I support leads to a small decline in employment as the production of public capital goods is more labour intensive. The initial decline in EU employment peaks in 2022

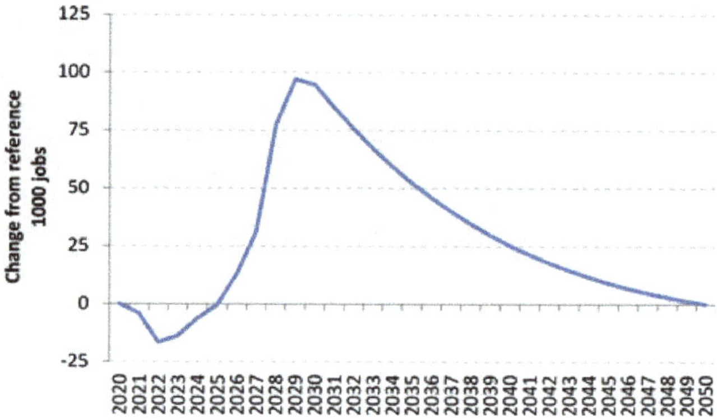

Fig. 5.12 Change in EU employment

where it is 17,000 jobs lower than in the reference scenario. However, gradually EU employment increases as a result of higher TFP growth which improves competitiveness. EU employment is at its highest in 2029 where employment is 97,000 jobs higher than the reference scenario. Long-term EU employment returns to the level of the reference scenario.

Table 5.2 shows the average EU employment deviation in 1000 jobs. Horizon Europe results in a rise in average EU employment for the period 2021–2040 of 40,000 jobs per year. The introduction of the EU R&I support programme has a persistent impact on EU employment. For the period 2021–2050, the rise in average EU employment is 30,000 jobs per year.

Table 5.2 Average EU employment deviation

	Impact of EU R&I programme
Average EU GDP deviation 2020–2030	27.9
Average EU GDP deviation 2020–2040	40.1
Average EU GDP deviation 2020–2050	29.9

5.3.3 Economic Impact at Regional Level

The results discussed so far have considered changes in EU aggregates. However, RHOMOLO further allows for an assessment of the economic impact at the regional level. The allocation of spending for R&I support varies across regions. Furthermore, regions vary in industrial structure, trade patterns and composition of production factors. Hence, regions may be impacted differently by the introduction of Horizon Europe. We, therefore, also consider the regional impact of Horizon Europe.

The regional impact on GDP and Employment from the introduction of Horizon Europe can be examined in a box plot as shown in Fig. 5.13. The box plot provides a display of the distribution of the regional deviation in respectively cumulative GDP in 2040 and cumulative employment in 2040. The central rectangle spans the first quartile to the third quartile with the small horizontal line inside the rectangle showing the median. The vertical line that extends from the top of the rectangle indicates the maximum value of regional impact, and the vertical line that extends from the bottom of the rectangle indicates the minimum value of regional impact.

The introduction of the EU R&I support programme results in a rise in cumulative EU GDP in 2040. However, as shown in the box plot, considerable divergence exists in regional GDP impact. Less than half of the regions experience a rise in cumulative GDP in 2040. The span from the third quartile to the maximum value is higher than the span from the minimum value to the first quartile. This is due to a small

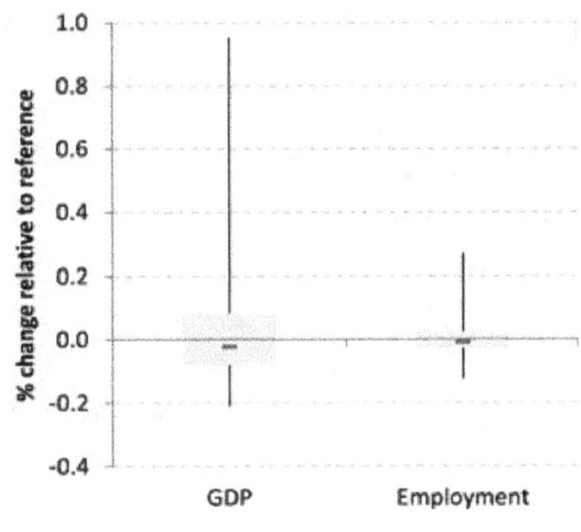

Fig. 5.13 Change in regional GDP and employment (% relative to reference scenario)

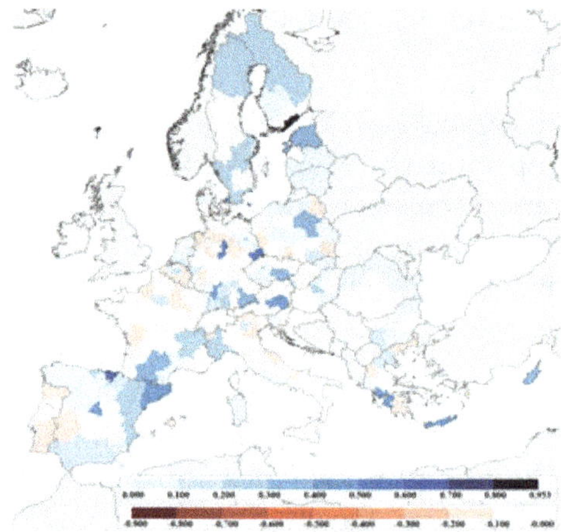

Fig. 5.14 Change in regional GDP (% relative to reference scenario)

number of regions which experience relatively large increases in cumulative GDP. Horizon Europe causes a shift from public investments to private R&I investments. This results in a rise in regional TFP growth and a decline in public capital services. However, the changes in spending are not evenly distributed across regions. Some regions experience large increases in public expenditures in support to R&I others suffer from decline in public investments that are allocated to the regions. The shift in demand and productivity gains across regions lads to changes in relative prices. Therefore, as a result of the shift in spending strategy, some regions experience a decline in GDP while other regions gain. Horizon Europe also results in considerable regional variations in employment impact. As illustrated in the box plot the number of regions that suffer from a decline in employment outnumber the regions benefitting from an improvement in employment. More specifically, Horizon Europe results in a rise in cumulative employment in 2040 for 90 regions and a reduction in employment for 140 regions.[11] As can be seen in the box plot, a small number of regions experience relatively large increases in cumulative employment due to the introduction of the EU R&I support programme.

Figure 5.14 shows the geographical distribution of cumulative regional GDP deviation in 2040 following the introduction of Horizon Europe. We observe that the rise in cumulative GDP is more prominently in regions that are large recipient of public spending in support for

[11] Excluding the UK reduces the number of EU regions in the model to 230.

R&I. Generally, these regions would experience higher TFP growth and improved competitiveness leading to a rise in GDP. The largest increase in GDP is found in the Finnish region of Helsinki-Uusimaa where cumulative GDP in 2040 is 1.0% higher than in the reference scenario. Other regions that experience some of the largest increases in GDP are the Spanish region of País Vasco (0.6%) and the German region of Dresden (0.5%). In contrast, other regions attract less of the public R&I support spending and suffer from the decline in public investments which results in a decline in cumulative GDP. The largest decline in cumulative GDP occurs in the autonomous Spanish regions Ceuta (−0.2%) and Melilla (−0.2%). The introduction of Horizon Europe results in a rise in GDP in 97 regions and a decline in GDP in 133 regions relative to the reference scenario.

In Fig. 5.15 we explore the relationship between the cumulative deviation in public spending in support to R&I and the cumulative deviation in GDP in 2040 for all EU regions. The figure reveals a positive relationship between public spending in support to R&I and the change in cumulative GDP. The higher the rise in public spending in support to R&I the higher the rise in GDP. However, the change in GDP also depends on other regional characteristics such as differences in industry structures, the mix of factor inputs and trade patterns which affects the relative change in competitiveness relative to main trading partners. The figure shows that regions which experience a small increase in public support

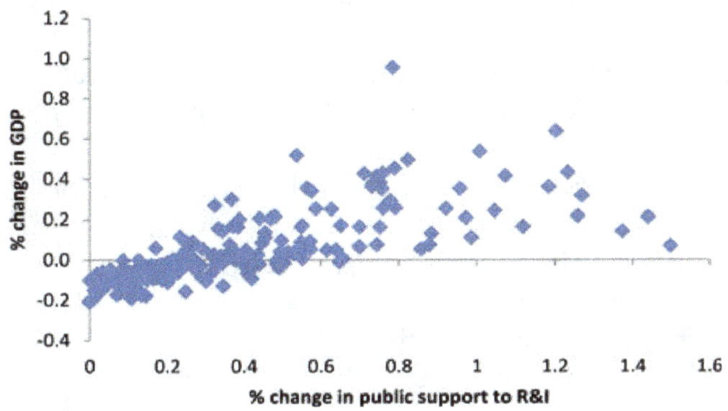

Fig. 5.15 Relationship between the deviation of cumulative public support (EU and national) to R&I and cumulative regional GDP deviation in 2040 (% change from reference scenario)

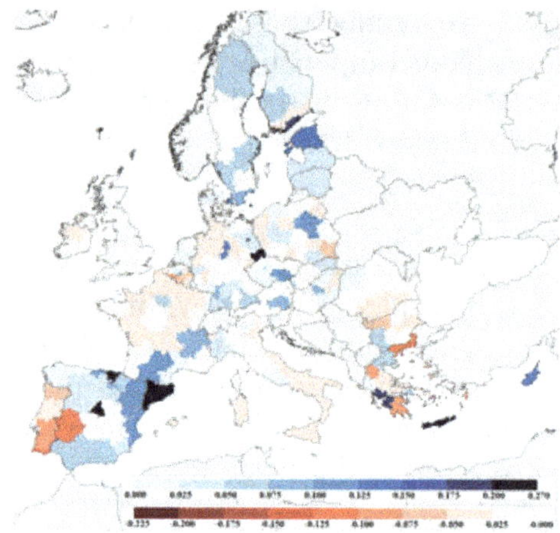

Fig. 5.16 Change in regional employment (% relative to reference scenario)

to R&I generally suffer a small decline in cumulative GDP relative to the reference scenario. In the analysis, Horizon Europe is assumed to be financed by Member States' contributions taken from public investments and national R&I programmes. Within each Member State, resources for public investments are allocated differently than the regional allocation of public R&I support. Hence, regions which are allocated small shares of the public spending in support to R&I may suffer from a decline in public spending allocated to the region. For these regions, the impact from a decline in public investments outweighs the impact from a rise in public spending for R&I support. In contrast, regions receiving a large share of public support to R&I are associated with higher cumulative GDP relative to the reference scenario. For these regions, the impact from a rise in public spending to R&I support outweighs the impact from lower public investments.

Figure 5.16 shows the geographical distribution of the regional changes in cumulative employment in 2040 relative to the reference scenario. The largest rise in employment can be found in regions which are among the largest recipients of EU spending in support to R&I and, at the same time, also have relatively high unemployment rates, which gives potential for employment growth.[12] The largest rise in employment

[12] The impact assessment is conducted on a version of RHOMOLO in which net migration between regions is held constant and household labour supply is exogenous. Hence, a rise in employment can only arise from a reduction in the unemployment rate.

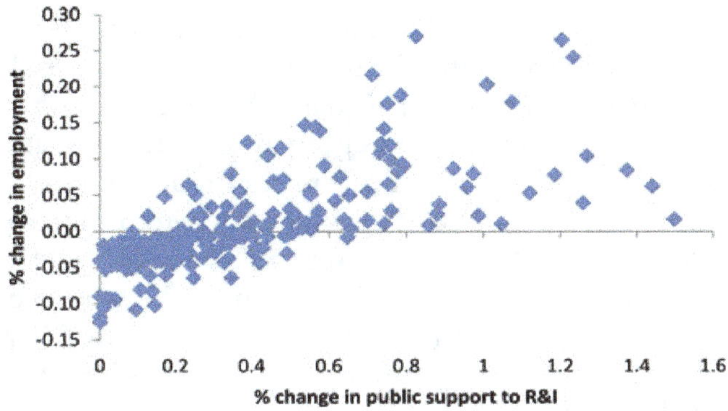

Fig. 5.17 Relationship between the deviation of cumulative public support (EU and National) to R&I and cumulative regional employment deviation in 2040 (% change from reference scenario)

occurs in the Spanish region of Cataluña where cumulative employment in 2040 is 0.3% higher than in the reference scenario. The largest decline in cumulative employment can be found in the two autonomous Spanish regions Ceuta (−0.1%) and Melilla (−0.1%) who suffers from the decline in national public investments.

In Fig. 5.17 we explore the relationship between the cumulative deviation in public spending in support to R&I and the cumulative deviation in Employment in 2040 for all the EU regions. The figure reveals a positive relationship between public spending in support to R&I and the change in cumulative employment. However, the change in employment also depends on other regional characteristics which affect the demand for labour such as differences in labour intensity in production, skills composition, regional unemployment rates, industry structures and trade patterns which affect the relative change in competitiveness relative to main trading partners. For example, the regions benefiting from the largest rise in public support to R&I are not the regions with the largest rise in employment.

5.3.4 *Summary*

This section presents findings from the economic impact assessment accompanying the European Commission proposal for the Horizon Europe Framework Programme. The impact assessment compares the outcome of a policy scenario with Horizon Europe to a reference scenario in which an identical amount of resources are spent by the Member States on public investments and national R&I support programmes. The economic impact is evaluated at the aggregate EU level and at the regional level. Results show that the EU R&I programme contributes to GDP growth and employment in the EU. In 2040 the cumulative EU GDP would be 0.1% higher than in the reference scenario. The deviation of total EU employment is at its maximum in 2029 where employment would be 97,000 jobs higher than the reference scenario. For the period 2021–2040, EU employment would on average be 40,000 jobs per year higher than in the reference scenario.

However, considerable regional variations in economic impact emerge. Shifting resources from public investments and national R&I support programmes to the EU R&I support programme mainly benefits the most R&I intensive regions in the EU who are the large receivers of EU spending in support to R&I. These regions experience an increase in TFP growth and an improvement in competitiveness leading to a rise in GDP and employment. We find that cumulative GDP in 2040 increases up to 1.0% and cumulative employment in 2040 rises up to 0.3% relative to the reference scenario. However, the regional impact on GDP and unemployment is unevenly distributed across EU regions. About 60% of all regions experience a decline in cumulative GDP and employment following the change in policy. These regions suffer from the reallocation of public spending from public investments and national R&I support to EU-wide R&I support. The declines in cumulative GDP in 2040 are up to 0.2% relative to the reference scenario while the declines in cumulative employment are up to 0.1% relative to the reference scenario.

The variations in regional economic impacts are largely resulting from assumptions concerning allocations of R&I support across regions. In addition, regional impacts are influenced by regional variations in R&D elasticities which in RHOMOLO are conditional on regional R&D intensity, on trade linkages and on the regional economic conditions such as the sectoral composition and labour market characteristics. Horizon Europe aims to support the provision of European R&I investments through EU-wide competition and cooperation programme support. In the impact assessment, it is assumed that the R&I intensive regions are able to attract an identical share of funds as in the previous EU R&I support programme. A large proportion of funding is, therefore, allocated to the most R&I intensive regions.

Although our results show that about 60% of the regions experience a decline in GDP and employment following the implementation of Horizon Europe, it may still be the case that these regions potentially could benefit from the higher growth in their R&I intensive neighbouring regions. Firstly, Member States may use public policies and fiscal transfers to redistribute the higher income in R&I intensive regions across all domestic regions. This could compensate households in the regions suffering from the decline in public investments. Secondly, diffusion of technologies may ensure that TFP increases in R&I intensive regions benefits neighbouring regions. In the simulation analysis, productivity gains from higher knowledge creation in the R&I intensive regions spills into other regions through trade linkages. However, the model simulation does not explicitly address the effects from diffusion of technologies across regions. Hence, interregional spillovers from productivity increases in a region may be underestimated. Thirdly, Horizon Europe is supplemented by other EU programmes which aim to strengthen economic and social cohesion. Programmes such as the European Regional Development Fund, the Cohesion fund and the European Social fund may help address regional imbalances and promote faster dissemination and uptake of R&I results across regions. Such synergies are not examined in the impact assessment.

References

Aghion, P., Harris, C., & Vickers, J. (1998). *Endogenous Growth Theory.* Cambridge, MA: MIT Press.

Aghion, P., & Howitt, P. (1992). A model of growth through creative destruction. *Econometrica, 60*, 323–351.

Barro, R. J., & Sala-I-Martin, X. (1997). Technological Diffusion, Convergence, and Growth. *Journal of Economic Growth, 2*, 1–27.

Boitier, B., P. Le Mouël, P. Zagamé, R. Winjes, P. Mohnen, A. Ricci, H. Brozaitis, J. Espasa, and V. Stanciauskas (2018). Support for the assessment of socio-economic and environmental impacts (SEEI) of European R&I programmes: the case of Horizon Europe. Technical report, European Commission. Luxembourg: Publications Office of the European Union. ISBN 978-92-79-92736-2.

Christensen, M. (2018). Assessing the regional socio-economic impact of the European R&I programme. JRC Working Papers on Territorial Modelling and Analysis No. 05/2018, European Commission, Seville, 2018, JRC114347.

Comin, D., & Gertler, M. (2006). Medium-Term Business Cycles. *American Economic Review, 96*, 523–551.

European Commission (2018). Commission Staff Working Document: Impact Assessment. SWD(2018) 307 final, Part 2/3 . Brussels, 7.6.2018.

Grossman, G. M., & Helpman, E. (1993). *Innovation and Growth In the Global Economy*. MIT press.

Kancs, D., & Siliverstovs, B. (2016). R&D and Non-linear Productivity Growth. *Research Policy, 45*, 634–646.

Lecca, P., J. Barbero-Jimenez, M. Christensen, A. Conte, F. Di Comite, J. Diaz Lanchas, O. Diukanova, G. Mandras, D. Persyn, and S. Sakkas (2018). *RHOMOLO V3: A Spatial Modelling Framework*. JRC Technical Reports 111861, Publications Office of the European Union, Luxembourg.

Romer, P. M. (1990). Endogenous Technological Change. *Journal of Political Economy, 98*, 71–102.

6

The Description and Applications of QUEST III Model

Werner Roeger, Janos Varga and Jan in't Veld

6.1 Introduction

The QUEST III model is a global DSGE model from the Directorate-General Economic and Financial Affairs (DG ECFIN) of the European Commission employed for the quantitative analysis of various types of policies. More specifically the model has been used by DG ECFIN to analyse reforms such as the increase of the employment of low-skilled workers, the change in the skill composition of the labour force, fiscal measures for increasing investment in knowledge, the removal of entry barriers and administrative burdens in certain markets, and the effects of financial market imperfections.[1] QUEST III is a useful and robust

[1] For more information about the different applications of QUEST III, visit https://ec.europa.eu/info/business-economy-euro/economic-and-fiscal-policy-coordination/economic-research/macroeconomic-models_en.

W. Roeger
DIW Berlin and VIVES KU Leuven, Leuven, Belgium
e-mail: w.roeger@web.de

J. Varga (✉) · J. in't Veld
European Commission, DG ECFIN, Brussels, Belgium
e-mail: janos.varga@ec.europa.eu

tool to (i) explicitly model the reforms in terms of concrete and quantifiable policy measures, such as taxes, benefits, subsidies and education expenditures, administrative costs faced by firms (for both entrants and incumbents) and regulatory indices; (ii) assess the impact of each policy measure on a comprehensive set of macroeconomic indicators such as GDP growth, employment, the composition of investment and skill premia in the short, medium and long run; and (iii) provide insights into the transmission mechanisms of various structural and fiscal measures.

6.2 The model

The version of QUEST III presented in this book captures both investment in tangibles and intangibles (R&D), while also disaggregating employment into various skill categories.[2] The framework adopted is the Jones (1995, 2005) extension of the Romer (1990) model, augmented with mark-ups for the final goods sector and entry costs for the intermediate sector. The equations in the model are explicitly derived from intertemporal optimisation under technological, institutional and budgetary constraints, while the model incorporates nominal, real and financial frictions in order to fit the data. In the model, there are two types of households, namely liquidity and non-liquidity constrained, a feature which has become standard in Dynamic Stochastic General Equilibrium modelling. Three types of labour skills, low, medium and high, are considered that allow to conduct more detailed human capital reforms. The model also includes a fiscal and monetary authority with the appropriate decision rules. Importantly, the model is multi-country, with individual country blocks interlinked via international trade and knowledge spillovers.[3] While Jones (1995, 2005) were theoretical, illustrative models, QUEST III is brought to the data and calibrated on actual data of the countries of interest.

The model economy is populated by households, final and intermediate goods producing firms, a research industry, a monetary and a fiscal authority. In the final goods sector firms produce differentiated

[2] This section draws heavily from the description contained in Roeger et al. (2014).

[3] The model can be used in a one-country, open-economy version and it can also be extended to more regions (e.g. Euro Area and non-Euro Area blocks of the EU, US, Asia, major oil-exporters). Individual European Union member states can also be modelled separately in interaction with the rest of the EU.

goods which are imperfect substitutes for goods produced abroad. Final good producers use a composite of intermediate goods and three types of labour - low-, medium-, and high-skilled. Non-liquidity constrained households buy the patents of designs produced by the R&D sector and license them to the intermediate goods producing firms. The intermediate sector is composed of monopolistically competitive firms which produce intermediate products from rented capital input using the designs licensed from the household sector. The production of new designs takes place in research labs, employing high-skilled labour and making use of the commonly available domestic and foreign stock of knowledge. Technological change is modelled as increasing product variety in the tradition of Dixit and Stiglitz (1977).

6.2.1 Households

The household sector consists of a continuum of households $h \in [0, 1]$. A share $(1-\epsilon)$ of these households are not liquidity constrained and indexed by $i \in [0, 1-\epsilon]$. They have access to financial markets where they can buy and sell domestic and foreign assets (government bonds), accumulate physical capital which they rent out to the intermediate sector, and they also buy the patents of designs produced by the R&D sector and license them to the intermediate goods producing firms.[4] The remaining share ϵ of households is liquidity constrained and indexed by $k \in [1-\epsilon, 1]$. These households cannot trade in financial and physical assets and consume their disposable income each period. The members of both types of households offer low-, medium- and high-skilled labour services indexed by $s \in \{L, M, H\}$. For each skill group, we assume that both types of households supply differentiated labour services to unions which act as wage setters in monopolistically competitive labour markets. The unions pool wage income and distribute it in equal proportions among their members. Nominal rigidity in wage setting is introduced by assuming that households face adjustment costs for changing wages.

[4] It is important to note that in a semi-endogenous model, the number of intermediate good varieties (A_t) can be interpreted in multiple ways. It corresponds to the total number of designs (or patents) invented by the R&D sector but at the same time, it can be interpreted as the stock of ideas or as the stock of knowledge (or intangible) capital in the economy. Also, it can be considered as an endogenous total factor productivity element.

Non-liquidity constrained households

Non-liquidity constrained households maximise an intertemporal utility function in consumption and leisure subject to a budget constraint. These households make decisions about consumption $C_{i,t}$, labour supply $L_{i,t}$, purchases of investment good $J_{i,t}$ and government bonds $B_{i,t}$, the renting of physical capital stock $K_{i,t}$, the purchases of new patents from the R&D sector $J_{A,i,t}$, and the licensing of existing patents $A_{i,t}$, and receives wage income $W_{s,t}$, unemployment benefits $bW_{s,t}$, transfer income from the government $TR_{i,t}$, and interest income, i_t, $i_{K,t}$ and $i_{A,t}$.[5] Hence, non-liquidity constrained households face the following Lagrangian

$$
\begin{aligned}
\max_{\left\{\begin{matrix} C_{i,t},\, L_{i,s,t},\, B_{i,t},\, J_{i,t}, \\ K_{i,t},\, J_{A,i,t},\, A_{i,t} \end{matrix}\right\}_{t=0}^{\infty}} \quad V_{i,0} = {} & E_0 \sum_{t=0}^{\infty} \left(U(C_{i,t}) + \sum_{s\in\{L,M,H\}} V(1-L_{i,s,t}) \right) \\
& - E_0 \sum_{t=0}^{\infty} \lambda_{i,t} \frac{\beta^t}{P_t} \Bigg((1+t_{C,t}) P_{C,t} C_{i,t} + B_{i,t} \\
& + P_{i,t}\Big(J_{i,t} + \Gamma_J(J_{i,t})\Big) P_{A,t} J_{A,i,t} \\
& - (1+i_{t-1}) B_{i,t-1} \\
& - \sum_s \big((1-t_{w,s,t}) W_{s,t} L_{i,s,t} \\
& + bW_{s,t}(1 - NPART_{i,s,t} - L_{i,s,t})\big) \\
& - (1-t_K)\big(i_{K,t-1} - rp_K\big) P_{I,t-1} K_{i,t-1} \\
& - t_K \delta_K P_{I,t-1} K_{i,t-1} - \tau_K P_{I,t} J_{i,t} \\
& - (1-t_K)\big(i_{A,t-1} - rp_A\big) P_{A,t-1} A_{i,t-1} \\
& - t_K \delta_K P_{A,t-1} K_{i,t-1} - \tau_K P_{A,t} J_{A,i,t} \\
& - TR_{i,t} - \int_0^N PR_{fin,j,i,t}\, dj
\end{aligned}
$$

[5] Households only make a decision about the level of employment but there is no distinction on the part of households between unemployment and non-participation. It is assumed that the government makes a decision on how to classify the non-working part of the population into unemployed and non-participants. The non-participation rate (NPART) must therefore be seen as a policy variable characterising the generosity of the benefit system.

$$
\begin{aligned}
&- \int_0^{A_t} PR_{int,m,i,t}\, dm \Big) \\
&- E_0 \sum_{t=0}^{\infty} \lambda_{i,t} \xi_{i,t} \beta^t \Big(K_{i,t} - J_{i,t} \\
&- (1 - \delta_K) K_{i,t-1} \Big) \\
&- E_0 \sum_{t=0}^{\infty} \lambda_{i,t} \psi_{i,t}, \beta^t \Big(A_{i,t} - J_{A,i,t} \\
&- (1 - \delta_A) A_{i,t-1} \Big)
\end{aligned} \tag{6.1}
$$

where s is the index for the corresponding low- (L), medium- (M) and high-skilled (H) labour type respectively ($s \in \{L, M, H\}$). The budget constraints are written in real terms with prices for consumption, investment and patents ($P_{C,t}$, $P_{I,t}$, $P_{A,t}$) and wages ($W_{s,t}$) divided by the GDP deflator (P_t). All firms of the economy are owned by non-liquidity constrained households who share the total profit of the final and intermediate sector firms, $\int_0^N PR_{fin,j,i,t}\, dj$ and $\int_0^{A_t} PR_{int,m,i,t}\, dm$, where N and A_t denote the number of firms in the final and intermediate sector, respectively. As shown by the budget constraints, all households pay wage income taxes ($t_{w,s,t}$), consumption taxes ($t_{C,t}$) and t_K capital income taxes less tax credits (τ_K and τ_A) and depreciation allowances ($t_K \delta_K$ and $t_K \delta A$) after their earnings on physical capital and patents. When investing into tangible and intangible capital, households demand risk premia rp_K and rp_A in order to cover the risk inherent to the return related to these assets.

The utility function is additively separable in consumption $C_{i,t}$ and leisure $1 - L_{i,s,t}$. Log-utility for consumption as well as the presence of habit persistence is assumed.

$$U(C_{i,t}) = (1 - habc) \log(C_{i,t} - habcC_{i,t-1}). \tag{6.2}$$

CES preferences with common labour supply elasticity are assumed for leisure, but a skill-specific weight ω_s on leisure. This is necessary in order to capture differences in employment levels across skill groups. Thus preferences for leisure are given by

$$V(1 - L_{i,s,t}) = \frac{\omega}{1 - \kappa}(1 - L_{i,s,t})^{1-\kappa}, \quad \text{with} \quad \kappa > 0 \tag{6.3}$$

For the sake of brevity, the following derivations of the optimality equations focus only on the ones related to the R&D investments made by non-liquidity constrained households. These households buy new patents of designs produced by the R&D sector $I_{A,t}$ and rent their total stock of designs A_t at rental rate $i_{A,t}$ to intermediate goods producers in period t. Households pay income tax at a rate t_K on the period return of intangibles and receive tax subsidies at rate τ_A.[6] Hence, the first-order conditions with respect to R&D investments are given by:

$$\frac{\partial V_0}{\partial A_{i,t}} : \quad -\lambda_{i,t}\psi_{i,t} + E_t\Bigg(\lambda^i_{t+1}\psi^i_{t+1}\beta(1-\delta_A) + \lambda_{i,t+1}\beta\frac{P_{A,t}}{P_{t+1}}\big((1-t_K)(i_{A,t}-rp_A)+t_K\delta A\big)\Bigg) = 0 \tag{6.4}$$

$$\frac{\partial V_0}{\partial J_{A,i,t}} : \quad -\frac{P_{A,t}}{P_t}(1-\tau_A) + \psi_{i,t} = 0 \tag{6.5}$$

Neglecting second-order terms, it can be shown that the rental rate of intangible capital is:

$$i_{A,t} \approx E_t\frac{(1-\tau_A)\big(i_t - \pi_{A,t+1} + \delta_A(1+\pi_{A,t+1})\big) - t_K\delta_A}{1-t_K} + rp_A \tag{6.6}$$

where $1+\pi_{A,t+1} = \frac{P_{A,t+1}}{P_{A,t}}$.

Hence, households require a rate of return on intangible capital which is equal to the nominal interest rate minus the rate of change of the value of intangible assets and also covers the cost of economic depreciation plus a risk premium. Governments can affect investment decisions in intangible capital by giving tax incentives in the form of tax credits and depreciation allowances or by lowering the tax on the return from patents.

Liquidity constrained households

Liquidity constrained households do not optimise but simply consume their current income at each date. Real consumption of household k is

[6] For a more detailed description of all the optimality conditions, the reader is again referred to Roeger et al. (2014).

thus determined by the net wage income plus net transfers

$$(1+t_{C,t})P_{C,t}C_{k,t} = \sum_{s\in L,M,H}\left(\left(1-t_{w,s,t}\right)W_{s,t}L_{k,s,t} + bW_{s,t}(1-NPART_{k,s,t}-L_{k,s,t})\right) + TR_{k,t}. \quad (6.7)$$

Wage setting

Within each skill group, a variety of labour services are supplied which are imperfect substitutes to each other. Thus trade unions can charge a wage mark-up $\frac{1}{\eta_{s,t}}$ over the reservation wage.[7] The reservation wage is equal to the marginal utility of leisure divided by the corresponding marginal utility of consumption. The relevant net real wage to which the mark-up adjusted reservation wage is equated is the gross wage adjusted for labour taxes, consumption taxes and unemployment benefits, which act as a subsidy to leisure. Thus the wage equation reads

$$\frac{U_{1-L,h,st}}{U_{C,h,s,t}}\frac{1}{\eta_{s,t}} = \frac{W_{s,t}(1-t_{w,s,t}-b)}{P_{C,t}(1+t_{C,t})} \quad \text{for} \quad h\in\{i,k\} \text{ and } s\in\{L,M,H\}. \quad (6.8)$$

Aggregation

The aggregate of any household-specific variable $X_{h,t}$ in per capita terms is given by

$$X_t = \int_0^1 X_{h,t}\,dh = (1-\epsilon)X_{i,t} + \epsilon X_{k,t}, \quad (6.9)$$

Hence, aggregate consumption and employment is given by

$$C_t = (1-\epsilon)C_{i,t} + \epsilon C_{k,t} \text{ and } L_t = (1-\epsilon)L_{i,t} + \epsilon L_{k,t}. \quad (6.10)$$

[7] The mark-up depends on the intratemporal elasticity of substitution between different types of labour σ_s and fluctuations in the mark-up arise because of wage adjustment costs and the fact that a fraction $(1-sfw)$ of workers indexes the growth rate of wages π_W to wage inflation in the previous period $\eta_{s,t} = 1 - \frac{1}{\sigma_s} - \frac{\gamma_W}{\sigma_s}\left(\beta(sfw\pi^{w}_{W,t+1} - (1-sfw)\pi_{W,t-1}) - \pi_{W,t}\right)$.

6.2.2 Firms

Final output producers

Since each firm j produces a variety of the domestic good which is an imperfect substitute for the varieties produced by other firms, it acts as a monopolistic competitor facing a demand function with a price elasticity given by σ_d.[8] Final output Y_t is produced using A_t varieties of intermediate inputs $x_{m,t}$ with an elasticity of substitution $\frac{1}{1-\theta} > 1$. The final good sector uses labour aggregate $L_{Y,t}$ and intermediate goods with Cobb-Douglas technology, subject to a fixed cost FC_Y and overhead labour FC_L

$$Y_t = \left(L_{Y,t} - FC_L\right)^{\alpha}\left(\int_0^{A_t} \left(x_{m,t}\right)^{\theta} dm\right)^{\frac{1-\alpha}{\theta}} KG_t^{\alpha_G} - FC_Y, \quad 0 < \theta < 1 \tag{6.11}$$

with

$$L_{Y,t} = \left(\Lambda_L^{\frac{1}{\mu}}\left(\chi_L L_{L,t}\right)^{\frac{\mu-1}{\mu}} + \Lambda_M^{\frac{1}{\mu}}\left(\chi_M L_{M,t}\right)^{\frac{\mu-1}{\mu}} + \Lambda_{HY}^{\frac{1}{\mu}}\left(\chi_{HY} L_{HY,t}\right)^{\frac{\mu-1}{\mu}}\right)^{\frac{\mu}{\mu-1}} \tag{6.12}$$

where $L_{L,t}$, $L_{M,t}$ and $L_{HY,t}$ denote the employment of low, medium and high-skilled in final goods production, respectively. Parameter Λ_z is the corresponding share parameter of every skill group, χ_z is the corresponding efficiency unit and μ is the elasticity of substitution between different labour types. Note that high-skilled labour can be allocated to both the final goods and the R&D sector, therefore the total number of high-skilled workers is equal to the high-skilled employed in the final goods and the R&D sector. The employment aggregates L_t^s combine varieties of differentiated labour services supplied by individual household

$$L_t^s = \left(\int_0^1 L_t^{s,h\,\frac{\sigma_s-1}{\sigma_s}} dh\right)^{\frac{\sigma_s}{\sigma_s-1}} \tag{6.13}$$

[8] From this point onwards, notation is slightly simplified by removing the j subscript, as in equilibrium production is symmetrical across all firms.

The parameter $\sigma_s > 1$ determines the degree of substitutability among different types of labour.[9]

The production function above is based on the product variety framework proposed by Dixit and Stiglitz (1977), widely applied in the literature of international trade and R&D diffusion.[10] The underlying structure of R&D is explicitly modelled through the semi-endogenous framework of Jones (1995, 2005).[11]

The objective of the firm is to maximise profits

$$PR_t = P_t Y_t - \left(W_{L,t} L_{L,t} + W_{M,t} L_{M,t} + W_{H,t} L_{HY,t}\right) - \int_0^{A_t} (px_{m,t} x_{m,t}\, dm), \tag{6.14}$$

where px is the price of intermediate inputs, $W_{s,t}$ is a wage index corresponding to the CES aggregate $L_{s,t}$ and P_t is the price of domestic final goods.

Intermediate good producers

The intermediate sector consists of monopolistically competitive firms which enter the market by licensing a design from domestic households and by making an initial payment FC_A to overcome administrative entry barriers. Capital inputs are also rented from the household sector for a rental rate of $i_{K,t}$. Firms which have acquired a design can transform each unit of capital into a single unit of an intermediate input. In a symmetric equilibrium, intermediate producers face the following inverse demand function from final good producers

$$px_{m,t} = \eta(1-\alpha)(Y_t + FC_Y)\left(\int_0^{A_t} (x_{m,t})^{\theta} dm\right)^{-1} (x_{m,t})^{\theta-1}$$
$$\text{where } \eta = 1 - \frac{1}{\sigma_d}. \tag{6.15}$$

[9] The productivity-enhancing effects of public infrastructure investment are accounted in the production function where the public capital stock ($K_{G,t}$) and its elasticity (α_G) enters externally.

[10] See Grossman and Helpman (1991) and Aghion et al. (1998).

[11] Butler and Pakko (1998) also applied Jones (1995)'s semi-endogenous growth framework to examine the effect of endogenous technological change on the properties of a real business cycle model without skill disaggregation.

Taking demand as given, each domestic intermediate firm solves the following profit-maximisation problem

$$PR^x_{m,t} = \max_{x_{m,t}} \left(px_{m,t} x_{m,t} - i_{K,t} P_{C,t} k_{m,t} - i_A P_{A,t} - FC_A \right) \tag{6.16}$$

subject to a linear technology which allows to transform one unit of capital k_m into one unit of an intermediate good $x_{m,t} = k_{m,t}$. As a standard result of these types of models, intermediate good producers set prices as a mark-up over marginal cost, i.e. $px_{m,t} = \frac{i_{K,t}}{\theta}$.

The no-arbitrage condition requires that entry into the intermediate goods producing sector takes place until the present discounted value of profits is equated to the fixed entry costs plus the net value of patents, or

$$PR_{int,m,t} = i_{A,t} P_{A,t} + \left(i_{A,t} + \pi_{A,t+1} \right) FC_A, \quad \forall m. \tag{6.17}$$

For an intermediate producer, entry costs consist of the licensing fee $i_{A,t} P_{A,t}$ for the design or patent which is a prerequisite of production of innovative intermediate goods and a fixed entry cost FC_A.

R & D sector

Innovation corresponds to the discovery of a new variety of producer durables that provides an alternative way of producing the final good. The R&D sector hires high-skilled labour L_A and generates new designs according to the following knowledge production function:

$$\Delta A_t = \nu A^{*\varpi}_{t-1} A^{\phi}_{t-1} L^{\lambda}_{A,t}. \tag{6.18}$$

International R&D spillovers are present, following Bottazzi and Peri (2007). Parameters ϖ and ϕ measure the foreign and domestic spillover effects from the aggregate international and domestic stock of knowledge, A^*_t and A_t, respectively. Negative value for these parameters can be interpreted as the *fishing out* effect, implying negative research spillovers, while positive values refer to the *standing on the shoulders of giants* effect, implying positive research spillovers. Note that $\phi = 1$ would yield the strong scale effect feature of fully endogenous growth models with respect to the domestic level of knowledge. Parameter ν can be interpreted as total factor efficiency of R&D production, while λ measures the elasticity of R&D production to the number of researchers L_A. The international stock of knowledge grows exogenously at rate g_{A^*}. It is assumed that the R&D sector is operated by a research institute which employs high-skilled labour at their market wage rate, $W_{H,t}$. It is also assumed that the research institute faces an adjustment cost γ_A for hiring new employees and maximises the following discounted profit-stream

$$\max_{L_{A,t}} \sum_{t=0}^{\infty} d^t \left(P_{A,t} \Delta A_t - W_{H,t} L_{A,t} - \frac{\gamma_A}{2} W_{H,t} (\Delta L_{A,t}^2) \right) \tag{6.19}$$

where d^t is the discount factor.[12] The first-order condition of this problem reads

$$\lambda P_{A,t} \frac{\Delta A_t}{L_{A,t}} = W_{H,t} + \gamma_A \left(W_{H,t} \Delta L_{A,t} - d_t W_{H,t+1} \Delta L_{A,t+1} \right)$$

6.2.3 *Policy*

On the expenditure side, it is assumed that consumptionG_t, investment IG_t and transfers TR_t from the government are proportional to GDP, while unemployment benefits BEN_t are indexed to wages as follows

$$BEN_t = \sum_{s \in L,M,H} b W_{s,t} (1 - NPART_{s,t} - L_{s,t}),$$

where b is the replacement rate.

The government provides subsidies SUB_t on physical capital and R&D investments to firms in the form of tax credit and depreciation allowances

$$SUB_t = t_K \left(\delta_K P_{I,t-1} K_{i,t-1} + \delta_A P_{A,t-1} A_{i,t-1} \right) + \tau_K P_{I,t} J_{i,t} + \tau_A P_{A,t} J_{A,i,t}.$$

Government revenues R_t^G are made up of taxes on consumption as well as capital and labour income. Government debt B_t evolves according to

$$B_t = (1 + i_t) B_{t-1} + G_t + IG_t + TR_t + BEN_t + SUB_t - R_t^G.$$

[12] Note that, in equilibrium, high-skilled workers are paid the same wages across sectors: $W_{H,t} = W_{HY,t}$.

The labour tax $t_{w,t}$ adjusts to the debt to GDP ratio according to the following rule

$$\Delta t_{w,t} = \tau_B \left(\frac{B_{t-1}}{Y_{t-1}} - b^T \right) + \tau_{DEF} \Delta \left(\frac{B_t}{Y_t} \right)$$

where τ_B captures the sensitivity of the labour tax with respect to deviations from the government debt target, b^T, and τ_{DEF} controls the response of the tax to changes in the debt-to-output ratio.

Monetary policy is modelled via the following Taylor rule, which allows for a degree of smoothness of the interest rate response to the inflation and output gap,

$$i_t = \gamma_{ilag} i_{t-1} + (1 - \gamma_{ilag})(r_{EQ} + \pi_{TAR} + \gamma_{inf}(\pi_{C,t} - \pi_{TAR}) + \gamma_{ygap} \hat{y}_t) \tag{6.20}$$

The central bank has a constant inflation target π_{TAR} and adjusts interest rates whenever actual consumer price inflation $\pi_{C,t}$ deviates from the target. It also responds to the output gap $\hat{y}_t$ via the corresponding γ_{inf} and γ_{ygap} coefficients.[13] There is also some inertia in the nominal interest rate determined by γ_{ilag}, both with respect to its past and the equilibrium real interest rate (r_{EQ}).[14]

6.2.4 *Trade*

In order to facilitate aggregation, it is assumed that households, the government and the final goods sector have identical preferences across goods used for private consumption, investment and public expenditure. Let $Z_t =\in \{C_t, I_t, G_t, IG_t\}$ be the demand of households, investors or the government as defined in the previous section, then their preferences

[13] The output gap is defined as deviation of capital and labour utilisation from their long-run trends.

[14] In QUEST's III multi-country setting, members of the euro area do not conduct independent monetary policy, and it is assumed that the European Central Bank sets the nominal interest rate by taking into account euro area wide aggregate inflation and output gap changes.

are given by the following utility function:

$$Z_t = \left(\left(1 - \rho\right)^{\frac{1}{\sigma_{im}}} Z_{d,t}^{\frac{\sigma_{im}-1}{\sigma_{im}}} + \rho^{\frac{1}{\sigma_{im}}} Z_{f,t}^{\frac{\sigma_{im}-1}{\sigma_{im}}} \right)^{\frac{\sigma_{im}}{\sigma_{im}-1}} \tag{6.21}$$

where ρ is the share parameter and σ_{im} is the elasticity of substitution between domestic ($Z_{d,t}$) and foreign produced goods ($Z_{m,t}$).

6.2.5 *Calibration*

Behavioural and technological parameters are calibrated so that the model can replicate important empirical ratios such as labour productivity, investment, consumption to GDP ratios, the wage share, the employment rate and the R&D share, given a set of structural indicators describing market frictions in goods and labour markets, tax wedges and skill endowments. The specific approaches to calibration for each of the main parts of the model are:

- **Goods market**: the calibration of mark-ups is based on the method suggested by Roeger (1995). Concerning entry barriers, estimates provided by the *Doing Business Database* are used. In particular, entry costs are directly calibrated following the methodology developed by Djankov et al. (2002), who estimate the costs that new firms need to incur before starting to operate.[15]
- **Knowledge production technology**: the two main sources of empirical evidence on elasticities are Bottazzi and Peri (2007) and Pessoa (2005). In particular, estimates from the former are used to calibrate the knowledge elasticity parameters with respect to domestic and foreign knowledge capital. The authors estimate the ratios of $\lambda/(1-\phi)$ and $\omega/(1-\phi)$ where λ in the QUEST model corresponds to the wage cost share in total R&D spending.[16] Pessoa (2005) is used for obtaining the growth rate of ideas, with the

[15] The authors carry out a very thorough data work to construct a measure of the regulation of entry (expressed in GDP per capita terms) across a very large number of countries based on costed measures of the total number of procedures and the time it takes to complete them as well as the actual administrative costs incurred (e.g., registration fees). For a detailed discussion, please see Djankov et al. (2002).

[16] Country-specific elasticities are, however, not available.

assumption of a 5% obsolescence rate. The Bottazzi and Peri (2007) estimate, together with the long-run growth rate of intangible capital and λ, pin down the knowledge elasticity parameters. Specifically, λ is obtained from available data on the wage share of R&D labour in total R&D spending whereas ν is directly derived from the knowledge production function after estimating the other elasticities, normalising the initial stock of domestic and international knowledge, calibrating the growth rate of ideas and initialising the share of research labour. Likewise, the calibration of φ relies on both econometric estimations carried out in the literature and the theoretical restrictions/equations of the model in equilibrium. Hence, its final value will partly depend on the observed long-run growth rate of population and patents as well as on the relationship between other related parameters estimated in the literature.[17]

- **Labour market and the skill composition of the labour force**: Estimations in Ratto et al. (2009) are used to calibrate the adjustment parameters of the labour market. The labour force is disaggregated into three skill-groups: low-, medium- and high-skilled labour. High-skilled workers are defined as that segment of labour force that can potentially be employed in the R&D sector, namely engineers and natural scientists. The definition of low-skilled corresponds to the standard classification of ISCED 0-2 education levels and the rest of the labour force is considered as medium-skilled. Data on skill-specific population shares, participation rates and wages are obtained from the Labour Force Survey, SES, and the Science and Technology databases of EUROSTAT. The elasticity of substitution between different labour types μ is one of the major parameters addressed in the labour economics literature. Precise values are taken from Acemoglu and Autor (2011), who updated the seminal reference for this elasticity parameter by Katz and Murphy (1992). In the baseline calibration, low-skilled wages are obtained from the annual earnings of employees with low educational attainment (ISCED 0-2) irrespective of their occupation. High-skilled wages are approximated by the annual earnings of scientists and engineers with tertiary

[17] For a more detailed explanation of the parameter calibration and estimation procedure, see D'Auria et al. (2009). It is to be noted that at the time of writing, the elasticities of the knowledge production function are being revisited with updated datasets.

educational attainment employed as professionals or associate professionals in physical, mathematical, engineering, life science or health occupations (ISCO-08 occupations 21, 22, 31, 32). Earnings data of employees with tertiary educational attainment not working as scientists and engineers and employees with medium educational attainment (ISCED 3-4) irrespective of their occupation are taken to calculate wages for medium-skilled workers in the model.
- **Fiscal, monetary and trade variables**: EUROSTAT data are used for the breakdown of government spending into consumption, investment and transfers, whereas effective tax rates on labour, capital and consumption are used to determine government revenues. Estimates of R&D tax credits are taken from Warda (2009) and OECD (2014). Monetary policy parameters are adopted from Ratto et al. (2009), while bilateral trade data is obtained from the EUROSTAT/COMEXT database.

6.3 An Example: Simulating the Ex-ante Macroeconomic Impact of Horizon Europe

QUEST III has been recently used by the European Commission to assist policy makers with an ex-ante impact assessment of Horizon Europe Framework Programme 2021–2027.[18] This represents the continuation of the current Framework Programme Horizon 2020 and consists of a large set of interventions encompassing the allocation of R&D and innovation investments with the aim of harnessing the EU scientific and technological community increasing competitiveness, productivity and economic welfare.

The simulations of Horizon Europe are carried out assuming a continuation of Horizon 2020 budget with the same size, allocation and in constant prices but without UK contributions.[19] The cross-country spillovers, represented by international trade and knowledge spillovers, are based on trade statistics and elasticities taken from the relevant literature. Moreover, it has been assumed that both EU and nationally funded R&I have the same leverage and performance effects. In other words, EU-level

[18] Horizon Europe 2021–2027 is also known as Framework Programme FP9.

[19] For more details on Horizon Europe and the scenarios simulated the reader can refer to Chapter 5.

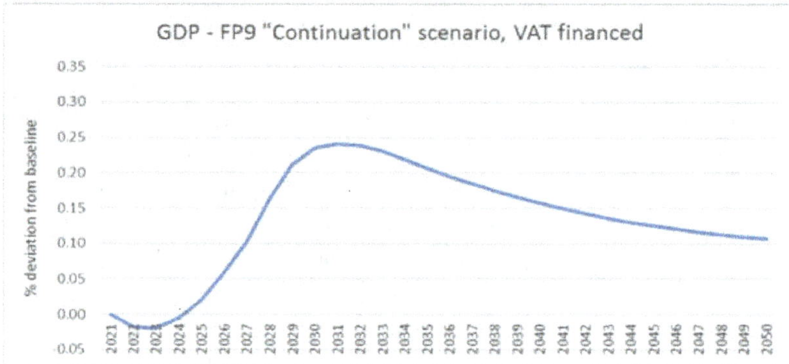

Fig. 6.1 GDP - VAT financed

coordination and optimisation of the funding across Member States is not taken into account in the simulation results, which may underestimate the impact of Horizon Europe.[20]

Based on different financing structures, two scenarios are simulated. In the first scenario, it is assumed that the financing of Horizon Europe relies on additionally raised Value Added Tax (VAT) revenues in the Member States (see Fig. 6.1). Instead, the second scenario assumes that the interventions are financed at the expense of lowering national public investment (see Fig. 6.2). Comparing the two figures, the results highlight the importance of the underlying financing assumptions. As VATs are some of the least distortive taxes, financing productivity enhancing R&D investments from these resources is unambiguously beneficial at the EU level in the medium and long run. GDP is up by 0.25% relative to the no-FP9 baseline towards the end of the Programme and gradually decreasing afterwards. Note that there is a small short-run output loss due to crowding-out effects in the beginning of the intervention period. This is because R&D subsidies stimulate innovation by helping R&D intensive companies to attract more high-skilled labour from traditional production into research with higher wages. In the second scenario, the expected GDP effects are less beneficial at the EU level. Similar to R&D investments, public investment is also productivity enhancing, therefore,

[20] This assumption is somewhat different to what has been assumed in similar impact assessment performed by RHOMOLO and NEMESIS models that are discussed in the other two chapters.

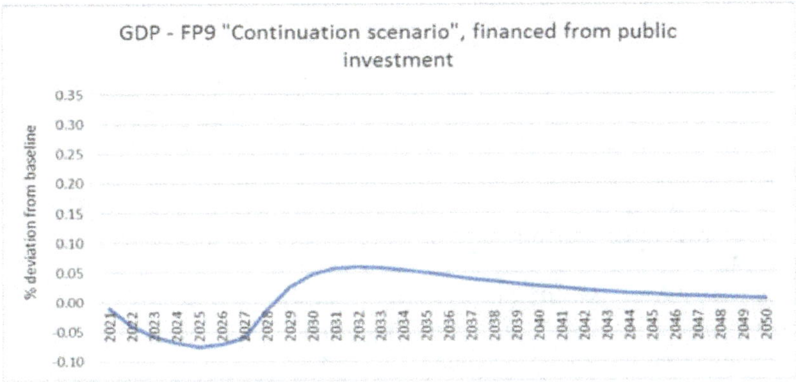

Fig. 6.2 GDP - Financed through public investment cuts

this type of financing is more costly for the Member States. As expected, changing from VAT financing to public investment cuts (e.g. roads, buildings), the Members States loose the potential productivity effects of these investments and the GDP results are much lower both in the short and long run. It also takes longer to compensate the short-run output loss; GDP is only about 0.05% higher relative to the no-FP9 scenario by the end of the Programming period. In both scenarios, the GDP gains gradually decrease after the Programming period due to the depreciation of tangible and intangible capital. Note that in the QUEST simulations EU and nationally funded R&I have the same leverage and performance effects.

The simulation obtained with QUEST III has been compared to the ones obtained with other two models widely used by the European Commission, RHOMOLO and NEMESIS. Nevertheless, as R&D investment decisions require a forward-looking dynamic approach, Di Comite and D'Artis (2015) consider the QUEST-R&D model to be the most suitable model for assessing the impact of R&D and innovation policies over time compared to the other macroeconomic models. However, as a main caveat, it does not distinguish between research undertaken by private or public R&I entities, and being an aggregate macroeconomic model, QUEST also misses the extensive regional details present in RHOMOLO.

References

Acemoglu, D., & Autor, D. (2011). Skills, tasks and technologies: Implications for employment and earnings. In *Handbook of labour economics* (Vol. 4b).

Aghion, P., Harris, C., & Vickers, J. (1998). *Endogenous growth theory*. MIT Press.

Bottazzi, L., & Peri, G. (2007). The international dynamics of R&D and innovation in the long run and in the short run. *The Economic Journal*, *117*, 486–511.

Butler, A., & Pakko, M. R. (1998). *R&D spending and cyclical fluctuations: Putting the "technology" in technology shocks* (Working paper No. 020A). Federal Reserve Bank of St. Louis.

D'Auria, F., Pagano, A., Ratto, M., & Varga, J. (2009). *A comparison of structural reform scenarios across the EU Member States: Simulation-based analysis using the QUEST model with endogenous growth DG ECFIN, European Economy* (Economic Papers 392).

Di Comite, F., & D'Artis, K. (2015). *Macroeconomic models for R&D and innovation policies* (IPTS Working Papers on Corporate R&D and Innovation).

Dixit, A. K., & Stiglitz, J. E. (1977). Monopolistic competition and optimum product diversity. *American Economic Review*, *67*(3), 297–308.

Djankov, S., La Porta, R., Lopez De Silanes, F., & Shleifer, A. (2002). The regulation of entry. *The Quarterly Journal of Economics*, *117*(1), 1–37.

Grossman, G. M., & Helpman, E. (1991). Quality ladders in the theory of growth. *Review of Economic Studies*, *68*, 43–61.

Jones, C. I. (1995). R&D-based models of economic growth. *Journal of Political Economy*, *103*(4), 759–84.

Jones, C. I. (2005). Growth and ideas. *Handbook of Economic Growth*, *1*, 1063–1111.

Katz, L. F., & Murphy, K. M. (1992). Changes in relative wages, 1963–1987: Supply and demand factors. *Quarterly Journal of Economics*, *107*(1), 35–78.

OECD. (2014). *Science and Technology Scoreboard 2013* (Technical report, OECD). Innovation for Growth. OECD Publishing.

Pessoa, A. (2005). Ideas driven growth: The OECD evidence. *The Portuguese Economic Journal*, *4*(1), 46–67.

Ratto, M., Roeger, W., & in't Veld, J. (2009). QUEST III: An estimated DSGE model of the euro area with fiscal and monetary policy. *Economic Modelling*, *26*(1), 222–233.

Roeger, W. (1995). Can imperfect competition explain the difference between primal and dual productivity? *Journal of Political Economy*, *26*(1), 222–233.

Roeger, W., Varga, J., & in't Veld, J. (2014). Growth effects of structural reforms in Southern Europe: The case of Greece, Italy, Spain and Portugal. *Empirica*, *41*(2), 323–363.

Romer, P. M. (1990). Endogenous technological change. *Journal of Political Economy*, *98*, 71–102.

Warda, J. (2009). *An update of R&D tax treatment in OECD countries and selected emerging economies*, 2008–2009, mimeo.

7

The NEMESIS Model and its Implementation

Baptiste Boitier, Pierre Le Mouël, Julien Ravet and Paul Zagamé

7.1 Introduction

The NEMESIS model was first used to analyse the impact of the 3% R&D objective envisaged in the Lisbon Strategy (Brécard et al., 2004, 2006). This first study was followed by the assessment of the European Commission's National Action Plans related to the Barcelona Objective (Chevallier et al., 2006).

After several other contributions revolving around EU innovation policy strategies, the NEMESIS model has been mainly used for *ex-ante* impact assessments of the European Research and Innovation Framework Programmes (FPs). In 2005, the NEMESIS model was implemented

---

Julien Ravet is co-author for section 7.3 on the ex-ante impact of Horizon Europe

---

B. Boitier · P. Le Mouël · P. Zagamé
SEURECO/ERASME, Paris, France

J. Ravet (✉)
European Commission, DG RTD, Brussels, Belgium
e-mail: julien.ravet@ec.europa.eu

for the *ex-ante* assessment of the 7th FP (Delanghe & Muldur, (2007; European Commission, 2005) and thereafter for the Horizon 2020 Programme (European Commission, 2012). From 2010 to 2013, the NEMESIS model supported the annual *ex-ante* assessment of the 7th FP calls for proposals (Fougeyrollas et al., 2010, 2011; Zagamé, 2010; Zagamé et al., 2012).

More recently, NEMESIS has been significantly improved by enlarging the innovation mechanisms captured besides R&D investments. In particular, investments in Information and Communication Technologies (ICT) and in intangible assets other than R&D (mainly software and training) have been incorporated. This enhances the assessment of R&I policies, by including some of the most up-to-date theoretical as well as empirical findings in the field (Le Mouël et al., 2016). This new version of NEMESIS has been used for the *ex-post* assessment of the 7th FP and the interim assessment of the Horizon 2020 programme (European Commission, 2017b; PPMI, 2017). It has also been used to simulate the socioeconomic and environmental impact assessment of the future 2021–2027 EU R&I Programme, Horizon Europe (Boitier et al., 2018).

The chapter is divided in two parts. The first provides a description of the NEMESIS model with a strong focus on its innovation mechanisms. The second part provides an example of the implementation of the model, by summarising the results of the recent work carried out with the model in the context of the impact assessment of the Horizon Europe programme (European Commission, 2018).

7.2 The Model

The NEMESIS model differs from the rest of the models presented in this book, in which behavioral equations are directly derived from optimality condition. Being a macro-econometric model, in NEMESIS the short to medium term dynamics are influenced by several factors that keep the economic agents out of the optimal paths. These include adjustment costs, sticky prices, and adaptive expectations, governed by error correction mechanisms for ensuring convergence to the long term equilibrium. Furthermore, the capital market is not explicitly modeled in NEMESIS, which precludes the attainment of a general equilibrium, even in the long term. The notion of equilibrium in this type of models refers instead to a stable state where some of the markets modelled can permanently be out of equilibrium.

Regarding innovation, the model features the following important properties to analyse innovation policy:

- Heterogeneity of economic sectors in many dimensions, including: investments in innovative assets, energy consumption, environmental externalities, capital-labour ratios, qualification requirements.
- Sectoral dynamics and related interdependencies, including knowledge spillovers that allow knowledge to be diffused across sectors and countries.
- Long-term economic growth properties as in the seminal theoretical formulation of the fully endogenous approach initiated by Aghion and Howitt (1998). Under this formulation, the long-term rate of economic growth is an increasing function of R&D intensity, and can thus be influenced by policy.
- Distinction between process and product innovation, with dissimilar impacts on the economy.
- Presence of intangible assets other than R&D (training and software) and ICT assets, which allow a more realistic representation of the innovation mechanisms, particularly in the services sectors.

In what follows, we first present the general characteristics of the model, and then its innovation and endogenous growth properties. We finish by presenting an application of the model to the ex-ante socio-economic impact assessment of the future EU R&I programme: Horizon Europe.

7.2.1 General Overview of NEMESIS

The NEMESIS model is a detailed sectoral macro-econometric model estimated for every country of the EU.[1] It distinguishes between 30 sectors operating within five-level nested-CES functions. The model covers both the supply and demand sides of the economy, and incorporates endogenous technical change. The conversion matrices of the model for final consumption, investment goods, intermediate consumption,

[1] The model's development has been financed by different European Framework Programmes and has been coordinated by the ERASME team that became SEURECO.

energy/environment and technological transfers, capture the interdependencies between production sectors (with one representative firm per sector) and between producers and other agents in the economy, namely households, the government and foreign countries. Every country model includes an *economic core* that can be simulated in interaction with a detailed energy/environment module. Simulation of policy effects can be carried out for an individual country or for all countries simultaneously.

7.2.1.1 Model's Structure

The NEMESIS model uses several datasets that are compiled, harmonized and complemented to feed the model in a manner that fits its structure.[2]

Two types of equations are at play in NEMESIS: (i) the accounting equations, reflecting the system of national accounts, and (ii), the behavioral equations, which capture, based on both theoretical and empirical grounds, how economic agents operate. The latter include long-term structural equations featuring an error correction mechanism that captures convergence towards the variables' long term values. The key elasticity parameters of behavioral equations are either estimated using panel data techniques, or calibrated based on consensus values arising from the relevant literature.

On the supply side, each sector is modeled with a representative firm that makes decisions regarding output and the use of factors, given expectations on demand and input prices. Firms produce output according to five-level nested-CES production functions, employing the following inputs: low-skilled labour, high-skilled labour, capital, energy and intermediate consumption. In addition, firms include innovation in their invesment decisions to improve their productivity and/or their products, implying that technical progress is endogenously determined in the model. Innovation is the result of investments in three types of assets: R&D, ICT and Other Intangibles (including software and training). The specification of the innovation process in the model allows to account for a large range of innovative activities, including ICT, which are considered a general purpose technology (GPT). Furthermore, while R&D

[2] The data sources include National Accounts (Eurostat, 2018a), Labour Force Surveys (Eurostat, 2018c), Annual Sectors Accounts (Eurostat, 2018b), WIOD (Timmer et al., 2015), statistics on research and development (Eurostat, 2018d) and OECD (2017) statistics on intangible investments and assets (Corrado et al., 2014) and statistics on taxation (European Comission, 2017).

investments are central in industrial sectors, the other types of innovation assets capture more appropriately the process of innovation in the service sectors. Finally, interdependencies between sectors and countries are captured by a collection of matrices describing the exchanges of intermediary goods and capital goods as well as the flows of knowledge spillovers.

Firms are monopolistically competitive, so that in the long-term markups are constant, albeit different between sectors. Wages are determined via an augmented Phillips curve in which the growth rate of wages is a function of the unemployment rate, labour productivity and consumption prices. Since the model features two types of labour (low-skilled and high-skilled), there exist two such equations for wage determination.

On the demand side, the representative household determines its aggregate consumption as a function of its disposable income arising from wages, capital income and social transfers. Child and old-age dependency rates are also included to capture changes in consumption patterns caused by changes in the structure of the population. The unemployment rate is used, in the short term, as a proxy for the perceived degree of uncertainty in the economy. Total aggregate household consumption is split into 27 different consumption sub-functions capturing relative prices, substitution elasticities and the specific nature of the products (e.g., durable/non durable).

The are two type of trade flows in NEMESIS: intra-EU and trade with the rest of the world. Exports are driven by both an *income effect*, which captures demand arising from other regions, and a *price effect*, which captures relative competitiveness with respect to other EU-countries and the rest of the world. Exports are also influenced by structural competitiveness due to quality-adjusted prices, on which all the demand functions are based. For imports, the drivers are similar: the income effect is captured by internal demand, and the price effect by the ratio between the import price and the price of domestic producers.

7.2.1.2 Model's Main Mechanisms

The general functioning of the model is shown in Figure 7.1.

As most macro-econometric models, which are based on national accounting, NEMESIS is by construction governed by aggregate demand in the short to medium term. Feedback effects, however, exist between demand and supply conditions that finally determine prices and quality of products. As illustrated in the next section later, the link between R&D

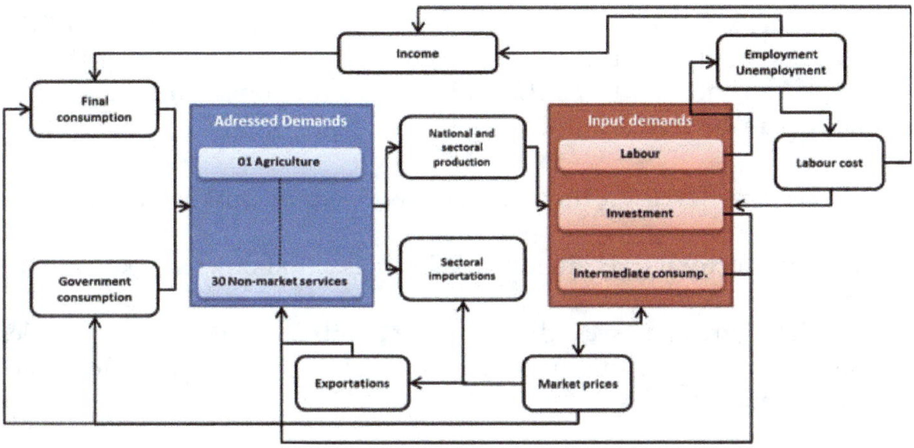

Fig. 7.1 NEMESIS basic structure

investments and economic growth is based in the model on the new endogenous growth theory, where it is possible to increase productivity growth by increasing R&D intensity. The implication of this is that the long term economic growth rate can be modified, bringing the model away from its core Keynesian features and closer to the Schumpeterian paradigm.

The starting point of the economic dynamics in NEMESIS arises from a shock to some of the exogenous variables: demographic, world demand, exchange and interest rates, world commodity prices (including fossil fuels prices) and internal policy rules. The dynamics are recursive and based on three main elements: (i) state variables (stocks), (ii) adaptive expectations and adjustment lags, and (iii) adjustment processes to each variable's optimal level.

There are two types of stock variables, namely physical capital and knowledge. Regarding the former, there is a maturation lag of one year to transform investments into operational capital. On the other hand, knowledge is generated through investment flows in R&D, ICT and other intangibles (OI), with maturation lags of two years for public R&D and one year for private R&D, ICT and OI. The transformation of knowledge into innovation is also progressive and affected by sector-specific lags. All these delays are important for the assessment of innovation support policies, which take about 15 years for their full impact to take place.

The model's dynamic can also be analyzed from the perspective of the different levels of granularity embedded in the model. For example, in the case of an increase in R&D expenditure, the impact mechanisms in the model can be traced as follows:

- At sectoral level, an increase competitiveness, output and employment.
- At inter-sectoral level, an increase in transaction flows and knowledge spillovers.
- At the aggregate level, the general equilibrium impact on variables such as wages, consumption and savings of the previous effects, are also captured.

Hence, there are three main layers of economic indicators: (i) macroeconomic, such as GDP and its components (final consumption, gross fixed capital formation, exports, imports, etc.), unemployment rates, etc.; (ii) sectoral, such as output, value added and employment per sector, and (iii) those related to national agent accounts: government, non financial corporations, financial corporations, households, and the external sector. Beyond economic indicators, the NEMESIS energy-environment module also captures results on energy supply and demand by fuel type and technology, and on CO_2 emissions.

7.2.2 *Supply Block and Innovation Mechanisms*

Next, to provide a clear description of the mechanisms at play in the model when simulating innovation policy shocks, we examine the specific sectoral production functions, followed by a detailed discussion of the innovation flows, which are one of the inputs into these production functions.

7.2.2.1 The Nested CES Production Function Framework

Figure 7.2 illustrates the nested nature of the production functions used. In each sector, output (in yellow) results from the combination of four variable inputs (in green) and two quasi-fixed inputs (in red). The variable inputs are materials (M), energy (E), lowly qualified labour (L_L)

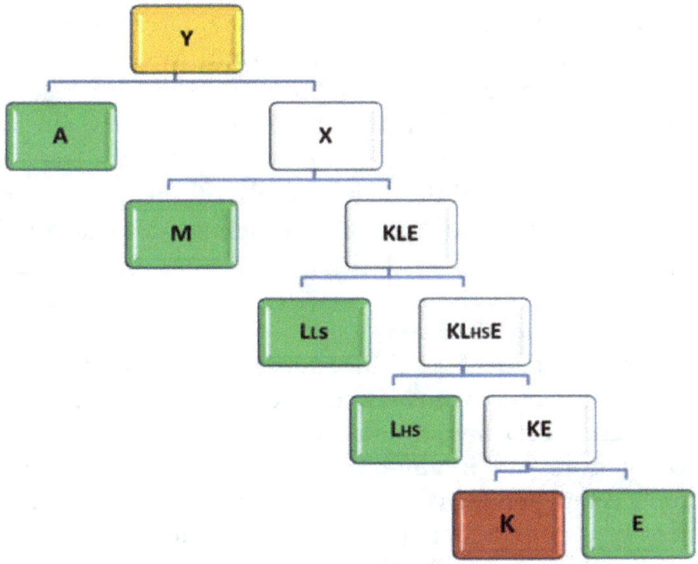

Fig. 7.2 The nested CES production function

and highly qualified Labour (L_H) (ISCED 5 and 6).[3] Quasi-fixed inputs are physical capital stock (K) and innovation services (A). The other inputs (in white) are the compound inputs - or 'intermediate outputs'- corresponding to the different levels of the nested CES function.

In the current version of the nested production function, innovation services enter at the first level, meaning that they proportionally increase marginal productivity of ordinary production factors, represented by the variable X that groups together the physical capital stock, the two categories of labour, and energy and materials. The impact of innovation on the production function is consequently Hick's neutral as it does not affect the balance between production factors.

This first level of the nested production function has the following analytical expression:

$$Y = C \cdot \left[\delta_A^{1+\rho_Y} A^{-\rho_Y} + \delta_X^{1+\rho_Y} X^{-\rho_Y}\right]^{-\frac{1}{\rho_Y}} \tag{7.1}$$

[3] Low and high labour qualifications correspond to ISCED levels 1-4 and 5-6, respectively.

where C is a scale parameter, δ_A is the share parameter for A, representing the share of innovation services in total output, δ_X is likewise the share parameter for X (by definition $\delta_X = 1 - \delta_A$), and ρ_y is the parameter that determines the partial elasticity of substitution between innovation services and X, equal to $\sigma_Y = \frac{1}{1+\rho_Y}$.

The functional forms of the other levels of the nested production functions are symmetric, and thus the the definition of factor shares are analogous.

7.2.2.2 Innovation Mechanisms

In the new version of the NEMESIS model, the flow of innovations in the different sectors and countries, do not result any more only from public and private R&D investments, but also from investments in ICT and in two categories of intangible other than R&D, namely training and software.[4] As in previous vintages (Brécard et al., 2006), the model distinguishes between product and process innovations.

The theoretical approach builds on the semi-endogenous and fully endogenous growth theory (Ha & Howitt, 2007). This approach has been adapted to be bridged with the concept of ICT as general purpose technology, as proposed by Bresnahan and Trajtenberg (1995). In this new framework, there are sources of externalities other than investments in R&D. In particular, externalities can also arise from the interactions between: (1) producers and users of ICT, (2) ICT users' co-inventions, and (3) ICT users' investments in complementary intangible assets.

In practice, these modifications affect the model in two main ways: (1) the modification of the innovation functions in the different sectors (now three dimensional), and (2) the modeling of knowledge externalities relative to different innovation assets. The calibration was based on existing empirical studies on the impacts of R&D, ICT and other intangibles (OI) investments on productivity and employment, at the macro, sectoral and micro levels (see Le Mouël et al., (2016). This new version of the model permits a more precise representation of innovation dynamics in the service sectors. It thus enlarges considerably the range of R&I policies whose macroeconomic impacts can be assessed with the model.

[4] This new version was first used in 2017 to support the ex-post assessment of FP7 and the interim evaluation of the Horizon 2020 Framework Programme (see (European Commission, 2017b; PPMI, 2017).

Three dimensional innovation functions

The flow of innovations in sector i in country c, A_{cit}, is a CES combination of three sub-innovations, denoted as innovation components, which are, in turn, investments in R&D, (AR_{cit}), investments in ICT, (AT_{cit}), and investments in OI, (AI_{cit}). The algebraic expression for the production function of innovation flows is:

$$A_{cit} = SC_{Aci} \cdot \Big[\delta_{ARci}^{1+\rho_{Aci}} AR_{cit}{}^{-\rho_{Aci}} + \delta_{ATci}^{1+\rho_{Aci}} AT_{cit}{}^{-\rho_{Aci}} + \delta_{AIci}^{1+\rho_{Aci}} AI_{cit}{}^{-\rho_{Aci}}\Big]^{-\frac{1}{\rho_{Aci}}} \tag{7.2}$$

where SC_{Aci} is a scale parameter, δ_{ARci}, δ_{ATci} and δ_{AIci} are distribution parameters and ρ_{Aci} determines the elasticity of substitution between AR_{cit}, AT_{cit} and AI_{cit}, $\sigma_{Aci} = \frac{1}{1+\rho_{Aci}}$.

In turn, production of the three innovation components is governed by the following expression:

$$Aj_{cit} = SC_{Ajci} \cdot KNOWj_{cit}^{\lambda_{jci} \cdot \frac{j_{cit}}{VA_{cit}}}, \tag{7.3}$$

where $j = R, T, I$, and SC_{Ajci} are scale parameters.

They are positive functions of a sector-country specific knowledge stock, $KNOWj_{cit}$, and of a specific knowledge absorption capability, $\lambda_j \cdot \frac{j_{cit}}{Y_{cit}}$.[5] This knowledge absorption capability is, with $\lambda_j > 0$, a linear positive function of the investment intensities in R&D, ICT or OI.

Knowledge stocks: The role of knowledge spillovers

Knowledge stocks, $KNOWj_{cit}$, are modeled as weighted sums of the stocks of assets (R&D, ICT, OI) across all sectors and countries.[6]

For all three innovation components, knowledge in sector i of country c, $KNOWR_{cit}$, is defined as the sum of the innovation component capital stocks $SR_{p,s,t-\Delta}$ from all country-sector pairs (p, s), weighted by a coefficient of diffusion $\Psi_{p,s\rightarrow c,i}$. This coefficient captures the relative

[5] This functional specification represents a departure from the related literature, where the elasticity of the flow of ideas with respect to the knowledge stock is commonly assumed to be a calibrated or estimated constant, rather than an object endogenously determined by investment intensity.

[6] The depreciation rates used come from Corrado et al. (2012). These are 0.15 for R&D, 0.315 for ICT, 0.315 for software and 0.4 for training.

propensity of knowledge from sector *s* in country *p* to be useful to innovate in sector *i* in country *c*.[7] It is also assumed that investments start producing knowledge after a delay Δ (two years). In algebraic terms,

$$KNOWj_{c,i,t} = \sum_{p,s} \Phi_{p,s-c,i} \times Sj_{p,s,t-2} \quad \forall \quad j \in R, T, I \qquad (7.4)$$

Public investments in R&D (*PIRD*) are allocated towards the different sectors in proportion to the share of each sector in overall business R&D expenditure.[8]

Process and product innovation

In NEMESIS, innovations cannot, by assumption, be exchanged on a market. They are not an asset that can be capitalized, but rather a flow of services that is produced according to equation 7.2 above.[9] Two effects of innovations can be distinguished in the model:

- From equation 7.1, the first level of the nested CES production function, 'process innovations' decrease the *ex-ante* use of X_{cit}, the compound input for ordinary production factors per unit of output, with an elasticity α_{ci};
- 'Product innovations', on the other hand, also increase, *ex-ante*, the quality of products, with an elasticity α'_{ci}, but without decreasing the use of X_{cit} per unit of output.

This distinction between product and process innovation is central for at list two reasons. On the one hand, in most empirical studies, private returns to process R&D have been shown to be higher than for product

[7] Diffusion parameters are calibrated on patent citations between sectors and countries, following the methodology developed by Verspagnen (1997). See also Belderbos and Mohnen (2013) for more details.

[8] In addition, public R&D investments are considered to be productive after a longer lag than private R&D (2 years later).

[9] Innovations are also supposed to begin producing their effects after a delay of one year.

R&D.[10]. As reported by Hall et al. (2010), there exist several explanations. For instance, product innovations often involve a "*start-up and debugging phase*" that reduce their returns in the short run. Additionally, the measurement of product R&D effects are difficult because of the currently poor translation of of quality improvements into changes in price indices, which is especially true for the goods and services produced by the public sector. On the other hand, output and employment impacts of product and process innovations are also dissimilar. Hall (2011) shows that the impact of product innovations on firms' revenue growth is always positive, while the impact of process innovations is small or even negative. They also found similar results on the impacts of these two types of innovations on employment. In particular, Peters et al. (2014) show that the employment impacts of process and organizational innovations are smaller than the ones of product innovations. Focusing on the distinct impacts of innovations on employment in service industries, Damijan et al. (2014) conclude that empirical studies generally find a positive impact of product innovations, and a negative impact of process innovations, while no major differences between manufacturing and services seem to emerge from the literature.[11]

Algebraically, these elasticities read:

$$\begin{aligned} \alpha_{c,i} &= \frac{\partial ln(X_t)}{\partial ln(A_t)} \\ \alpha'_{c,i} &= \frac{\partial ln(D_t)}{\partial ln(A_t)} \end{aligned} \tag{7.5}$$

where D_t is the demand faced by the representative firm.

In addition, it is assumed that in each sector the *quality* of output evolves in proportion with process innovation: $\alpha'_{cit} = m_{ci}\alpha_{cit}$.

7.2.3 Endogenous Growth Properties

This sub-section analyzes in more detail the endogenous growth properties resulting from the innovation mechanisms of the model. For that,

[10] Hall et al. (2010) quote several studies in this respect: Clark and Griliches (1984), Griliches and Lichtenberg (1984), Link (1982), Terleckyj (1980), Scherer (1982, 1983), and Hanel (1994)

[11] See also Harrison et al. (2014) and Bogliacino and Pianta (2010).

let us start by obtaining the expression for the long term growth rate of sectoral output. By differentiating the equation for sectoral output (Eq.7.1) expressed in natural logarithms with respect to time, we obtain:

$$\frac{dln(Y_{cit})}{dt} = \varepsilon^{Y_{cit}}_{A_{cit}} \cdot \frac{dln(A_{cit})}{dt} + \varepsilon^{Y_{cit}}_{X_{cit}} \cdot \frac{dln(X_{cit})}{dt} \tag{7.6}$$

where:

$$\varepsilon^{Y_{cit}}_{A_{cit}} = \frac{\partial ln(Y_{cit})}{\partial ln(A_{cit})} = SCY_{ci}^{-\rho Y_{ci}} \cdot \delta A_{ci}^{1+\rho Y_{ci}} \cdot \left(\frac{Y_{cit}}{A_{cit}}\right)^{\rho Y_{ci}} \tag{7.7}$$

$$\varepsilon^{Y_{cit}}_{X} = \frac{\partial ln(Y_{cit})}{\partial ln(X_{cit})} = SCY_{ci}^{-\rho Y_{ci}} \cdot \delta X_{ci}^{1+\rho Y_{ci}} \cdot \left(\frac{Y_{cit}}{X_{cit}}\right)^{\rho Y_{ci}} \tag{7.8}$$

are the elasticities of sectoral output with respect to innovations services, (A), and the bundle of traditional production inputs, (X), respectively.

The long term growth of sectoral output can therefore be decomposed in two components:

1. An endogenous one, driven by the growth of innovation services:

$$\frac{dln(Y^{A}_{cit})}{dt} = \varepsilon^{Y_{cit}}_{A_{cit}} \cdot \frac{dln(A_{cit})}{dt} \tag{7.9}$$

2. An exogenous one, driven by the growth of traditional production factors:

$$\frac{dln(Y^{E}_{cit})}{dt} = \varepsilon^{Y_{cit}}_{X_{cit}} \cdot \frac{dln(X_{cit})}{dt} \tag{7.10}$$

Hence,

$$\frac{dln(Y_{cit})}{dt} = \frac{dln(Y^{A}_{cit})}{dt} + \frac{dln(Y^{E}_{cit})}{dt} \tag{7.11}$$

It follows from equation (7.11) that the endogenous growth rate of sectoral output can be assimilated to a 'pure' TFP effect. We can thus write:

$$\frac{dln(Y^{A}_{cit})}{dt} = \frac{dln(TFP_{cit})}{dt} = \frac{dln(Y_{cit})}{dt} - \frac{dln(Y^{E}_{cit})}{dt} \tag{7.12}$$

or equivalently:

$$\frac{dln(TFP_{cit})}{dt} = \frac{dln(Y_{cit})}{dt} - \varepsilon_{X_{cit}}^{Y_{cit}} \cdot \frac{dln(X_{cit})}{dt} \tag{7.13}$$

According to the latter, growth in TFP, which captures the slack between the growth of output and the growth of traditional production factors, can be explained by endogenous investments in innovation inputs and the accompanying knowledge externalities. In practice, the TFP indexes that are computed from national account data lump together the joint influence of many mechanisms.

By keeping Y_{cit} constant in equation 7.1, we can define the 'TFP effect' as *minus* the elasticity of demand of production inputs with respect to innovations services, as follows:

$$\alpha_{cit} = -\frac{\partial ln(X_{cit})}{\partial ln(A_{cit})} = \frac{\varepsilon_A^{Y_{cit}}}{\varepsilon_X^{Y_{cit}}} \tag{7.14}$$

This 'TFP effect' is different from the definition given in equation 7.13 and must be interpreted as a measure of the transformation of the set of production possibilities resulting from the growth of innovation services over time, for a given level of output.

The second channel via which innovations services affect output growth is linked to the increase in the demand faced by firms arising from the gradual improvement of the characteristics of their products. This 'Quality effect' is defined as:

$$\frac{dln(Q_{cit})}{dt} = \alpha'_{cit} \cdot \frac{dln(A_{cit})}{dt} \tag{7.15}$$

In each sector, the *quality* of output is assumed to evolve in time proportionally to the 'TFP effect' (with a coefficient m_{ci}), so that:

$$\alpha'_{cit} = m_{ci} \cdot \alpha_{cit} \tag{7.16}$$

In NEMESIS, these two distinct *innovation effects* act on the sectoral output of firms through the price elasticity of demand, $\varepsilon_{cit}^D < 0$. In particular,

1. Process innovations reduce the unit costs with an elasticity α_{cit}, which leads to a proportional reduction in prices charged by firms, implying in turn an increase in demand with elasticity $-\varepsilon^{D}_{cit} \cdot \alpha_{cit}$.
2. Product innovations increase demand directly, according to an elasticity $-\varepsilon^{D}_{cit} \cdot \alpha^{'}_{cit}$

In equilibrium, the level of output must be equal to the level of demand, and thus the 'endogenous' part of output growth, which results from the growth of investment in the different types of innovation, $\frac{dln(Y^{A}_{cit})}{dt}$, is equal to:

$$\begin{aligned}\frac{dln\left(Y^{A}_{cit}\right)}{dt} &= \left(-\varepsilon^{D}_{cit} \cdot \alpha_{cit} - \varepsilon^{D}_{cit} \cdot \alpha^{'}_{cit}\right) \cdot \frac{dln(A_{cit})}{dt} \\ &= -\varepsilon^{D}_{cit} \cdot (1 + m_{cit}) \cdot \alpha_{cit} \cdot \frac{dln(A_{cit})}{dt} \end{aligned} \tag{7.17}$$

This 'endogenous' growth rate of sectoral output, encompasses three combined effects that go beyond the pure TFP effect in equation 7.14:

1. A TFP effect through the elasticity α_{cit} ;
2. A *quality* effect through the elasticity $\alpha^{'}_{cit} = m_{ci} \cdot \alpha_{cit}$;
3. A demand effect through the elasticity ε^{D}_{cit}.

A further decomposistion can be made in order to investigate the distinct contributions of the three innovation components on the long term endogenous growth rate. To do so, we start by differentiating equation 7.2 for innovation services, with respect to time:

$$\frac{dln(A_{cit})}{dt} = \sum_{j} \varepsilon^{A}_{Ajcit} \cdot \frac{dln(Aj_{cit})}{dt}, \ j = RD,\ ICT,\ OI \tag{7.18}$$

with:

$$\varepsilon^{A}_{Ajcit} = SCA_{ci}^{-\rho A_{ci}} \cdot \delta Aj_{ci}^{1+\rho A_{ci}} \cdot \left(\frac{A_{cit}}{Aj_{cit}}\right)^{\rho A_{ci}} \tag{7.19}$$

By assuming that the investment rates of innovation assets (in % of output) at sectoral level are constant in the long term, the growth rates of innovation components can be further decomposed from equation 7.3 as follows:

$$\frac{dln(Aj_{cit})}{dt} = \lambda_{jci} \cdot \frac{j_{cit}}{Y_{cit}} \cdot \frac{dln(KNOWj_{cit})}{dt} \tag{7.20}$$

By substitution of 7.20 into 7.18:

$$\frac{dln(A_{cit})}{dt} = \sum_j \varepsilon^A_{Aj_{cit}} \cdot \lambda_{jci} \cdot \frac{j_{cit}}{Y_{cit}} \cdot \frac{dln(KNOWj_{cit})}{dt}, \quad j = RD,\ ICT,\ OI \tag{7.21}$$

And by substitution of 7.21 into 7.17:

$$\frac{dln(Y^A_{cit})}{dt} = -\varepsilon^D_{cit} \cdot (1 + m_{ci}) \cdot \alpha_{cit} \cdot \sum_j \varepsilon^A_{Aj_{cit}} \cdot \lambda_{jci} \cdot \frac{j_{cit}}{Y_{cit}} \cdot \frac{dln(KNOWj_{cit})}{dt}, \quad j = RD,\ ICT,\ OI \tag{7.22}$$

The implications of equation 7.22 on the properties of the growth rate in output are:

- First, there is no endogenous growth in NEMESIS without growth in knowledge externalities. From a theoretical perspective, this property links the modeling of innovations in the model to the semi-endogenous growth literature where the ultimate source of growth is the size of the stock of R&D, which benefit from knowledge externalities. This property of the semi-endogenous growth models was simply extended in NEMESIS to sources of externalities other than R&D. The implication of this is that growth in the model is strongly dependent on the assumptions made on the growth of knowledge externalities. In the *business-as-usual scenarios*, it is assumed that the investment rates of the innovation assets stay constant in the medium to long term, and that growth in knowledge follows the growth of economic activity in the different world regions.
- Second, the long term endogenous growth rate is an increasing, but bounded, function of the investment rates in innovation assets, which can be influenced by policy instruments.
- Third, from the previous two points, policies aimed at increasing innovation, such as the EU's R&I programmes, affect the long term endogenous growth rate in the model through two channels:

1. An *intensity* effect, by raising the ability of firms to exploit existing knowledge
2. A *knowledge* effect, by which the creation of new knowledge increases the intrinsic productivity of innovation inputs.

7.3 An Example: Simulating the Ex-ante Impact of Horizon Europe

7.3.1 Context of the assessment

The NEMESIS model has been used for several socio-economic impact assessments of European R&I support policies and mainly for *ex-ante* studies, but also in *ex-post* analysis PPMI (2017) and European Commission (2017b). Recently, the model has also supported the socio-economic and environmental impact assessments of the future EU R&I Programme: Horizon Europe. We present here two of the four batches of policy options assessed with the NEMESIS model.[12]

For the simulation of the expected impacts of the Horizon Europe programme, the following scenarios were considered:

1. The "*Continuation*" scenario in which Horizon 2020, the previous programme, continues for the next multi-annual financial framework (2021–2027). This is compared with a scenario without EU R&I programme after 2020.
2. And a set of alternative scenarios on the design of the future Horizon Europe and regrouped in two scenarios called "*more impact*" and "*more openness*". These are compared with the "*Continuation*" scenario.

Starting with the description of the methodology used for the socio-economic impact assessment of Horizon Europe conducted with the NEMESIS model, we proceed with the presentation of the main macro-economic results for the "*Continuation*", followed by two other scenarios on the design options of Horizon Europe, namely "*more impact*" and "*more openness*".

[12] The contents of this section draw primarily from Annex 5 in European Commission (2018). For an in-depth analysis, see Boitier et al. (2018).

7.3.2 *Implementation of Horizon Europe in the Model*

Before running the model, we must define two different sets of variables or parameters. The first set of variables for the implementation of the Horizon Europe programme in NEMESIS is related to budget allocations, not only the overall amount and its temporal allocation, but also the decomposition between 'basic' and 'applied' research, as well as geographical and sectoral allocations. The second set of important factors for the analysis of EU R&I policy is related to the innovation mechanisms. The original parameters have been calibrated based on the empirical literature (Le Mouël et al., 2016). In order to assess any EU R&I programme, the key challenge is to evaluate how these parameters need to be modified when research activities are carried out at the European-wide level. The essential parameters are: (i) the leverage or direct *crowding-in* effect, giving the increase in private R&D expenditures following a one euro subsidy, (ii), the *knowledge spillovers* and, (iii), the *economic performance* of research. As a specific re-calibration of the knowledge spread parameters for EU R&I programmes is currently unfeasible, the ones currently present in the model are used, and for the case of different knowledge spillovers stemming from Horizon Europe, it is assumed that part of European-wide knowledge spillovers can be assimilated to a modification of the economic performance parameters.

7.3.2.1 Key Assumptions Behind the Impact Assessment Exercise

As touched upon before, the key assumptions in NEMESIS for assessing the impact of the Framework Programme are related to budget size, budget allocation and the value of key parameters such as leverage and economic performance. Table 7.1 shows the main assumptions behind the "*Continuation*" of H2020:

In this "*Continuation*" scenario, the budget size and its allocation are assumed to be the same as in Horizon 2020 in constant prices, minus the contribution from the UK (assumed to be 15% of the budget). The Horizon Europe programme is assumed to be financed through a reduction in national public investment. Regarding the direct leverage effect, the assumptions used are supported by a survey on research units involved in the 7th Framework Programme and by a body of empirical literature. A sensitivity analysis shows that the former parameter does not significantly drive the results produced by this impact assessment, for the values used in this study. Economic performance in NEMESIS is calibrated

Table 7.1 Key assumptions for the "*Continuation*" scenario (continuation of Horizon 2020)

Budget	*Continuation of Horizon 2020 budget in constant prices - 15 %*
Budget allocation across years, countries and sectors	Horizon 2020 allocation
Knowledge spillovers	inter-sectoral and international spillovers modelled using patent citation techniques with no additional specificity for the Framework Programme
Direct leverage effect	Direct leverage: – Basic research: 0 – National funding of applied R&I: 0.1 – EU funding of applied R&I: 0.15 Indirect leverage: firms keep their investment effort constant in the long term.
Economic performance	Higher performance of EU funding (+15%) compared to national funding
Financing	Reduction in public investment

by country and sector on the basis of the available empirical literature. Higher leverage and performance parameters for EU funding compared to national funding reflects the EU added value of the programme. The values for these parameters are supported by the existing quantified evidence on publications, patents and revenues from innovation.[13]

In order to assess the impact of the various changes in the design of Horizon Europe with respect to its predecessor programme, a set of scenarios have been assessed with the NEMESIS model either enhancing the impact of the programme, or reinforcing its openness. In each scenario, the changes envisaged in terms of the expected higher impact and wider openness were translated into variations of the values of certain parameters in NEMESIS. Therefore, different cases were considered, from low to high, by using ranges in the variation of the parameters. These ranges rely on plausible values found in the literature, with extreme values showing how impactful Horizon Europe can be under the most ambitious conditions. All these scenarios have been combined in the

[13] For details on the points made in this paragraph, see European Commission (2017a) and Boitier et al. (2018).

Table 7.2 Key departures from the assumptions in the "*Continuation*" scenario

Changes for more impact	*This assumes...*	*Range*
Higher economic performance	Focus on R&I with higher economic impacts andd on breakthrough innovations	Higher performance of EU funding compared to national funding: +0 (baseline) to +5 percentage points
Lower knowledge obsolescence	More focus on breakthrough knowledge	14% to 13% obsolescence rate compared to 15% in the baseline.
Stronger complementarities with other innovative assets	More cross-technological and cross-sectoral R&I	5% to 10% stronger than in the baseline
Higher direct leverage of private R&D	Betteraccess to finance of innovative firms, especially for SMEs	0.1 (baseline) to 0.15
Changes for more openness	*This assumes...*	*Range*
Higher complementarities with national support to R&D	Increased complementarities through partnerships	Increased leverage for Basic research: 0.05 to 0.1 compared to 0 in the baseline
Stronger knowledge diffusion	Facilitated knowledge diffusion nationally between the different categories of research organisations and/or internationally	5% to 10% stronger than in the baseline

two "*more impact*" and "*more openness*" different scenarios. Table 7.2 summarises the changes relative to the "*Continuation*" scenario:

7.3.2.2 Results

The macroeconomic effects in NEMESIS shown in Fig. 7.3 can be divided into three main phases:

1. The investment phase: this is a 'demand phase' in which the dynamics are induced by the change in R&D expenditures, with moderate impacts on innovation (as innovations only appear with a lag). This phase is hence dominated by the effect of the Keynesian multiplier embdedded in the model.

2. The innovation phase: the arrival of innovations (process and product) reduces the production costs of new products and/or raises the

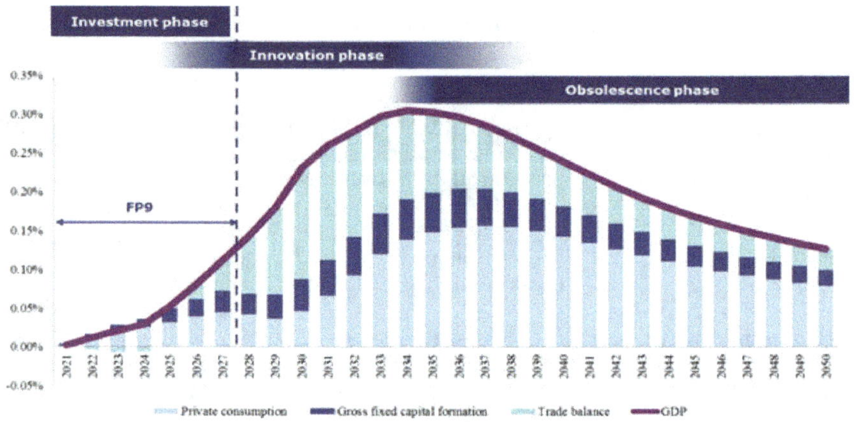

Fig. 7.3 GDP impacts under the "*Continuation*" of Horizon 2020 scenario (deviation in % from a counterfactual scenario without Framework Programme) *Source* Boitier et al. (2018)

quality of existing ones, inducing an increase in both external and internal demands.

3. The obsolescence phase: progressively, newly achieved knowledge declines over time due to knowledge obsolescence. In the long-term, the economy returns back to the reference scenario.

Thus, Horizon Europe as defined in the "*Continuation*" scenario could provide an increase of EU GDP up to +0.3% in 2035. This gain of EU GDP is mainly driven by the private consumption that contributes to half of the EU GDP deviation in 2035, while the external balance contributes to 35%. During the innovation phase, EU GDP gains are primarily driven by increasing market share of EU economy on global markets, rather than by the expansion of the internal market. Thereafter, productivity gains progressively spread throughout the European economy, inducing an increase in real wages that in turn reinforces the relative contribution of private consumption. In 2050, around two thirds of EU GDP deviation (i.e. +0.13%) can be ascribed to private consumption, with external balance explaining around 20% of EU GDP gains.

To summarise, the implementation of Horizon Europe, as defined in the "*Continuation*" scenario, delivers an increase of EU GDP by € 47 billion (constant euro 2014) i.e. maximum +0.3% in 2035. And the cumulative EU GDP gain from 2020 to 2050 in the "*Continuation*" reaches € 850 billion that is to say an average EU GDP raise of € 27 billion per year.

Over the period of the Horizon Europe programme, up to a hundred thousand jobs are expected to be directly created in R&D activities (see Figure 7.4). During this period, while the programme has a positive effect on jobs in the R&D sector, the decrease in national public investment that is assumed in the scenario is mechanically accompanied by a comparable decrease in non R&D-related jobs. The positive net indirect impact of the programme on jobs materialises starting at 2030, with the creation of more than two hundred thousand jobs after 2035, including more than eighty thousand highly-qualified jobs. From 2021 to 2050, Horizon Europe could create, on average, more than one hundred thousand employments per year, which correspond to jobs in the research sector at the beginning, and then transform into high- and low-qualified jobs with time.

Turning to the impact of the changes envisaged in the design of the Horizon Europe programme, in the "*more impact*" scenario, the deviation in EU GDP, in comparison with "*Continuation*", could reach up to +0.07% in 2040, with on average, from 2021 to 2050, a EU GDP deviation of €7.3 billion per year in 2014 constant euro (see Figure 7.5). In terms of employment, the gains are estimated at twenty eight thousand jobs yearly (average between 2021 and 2050). In the "*more openness*" scenario, the expected impact on EU GDP is lower and

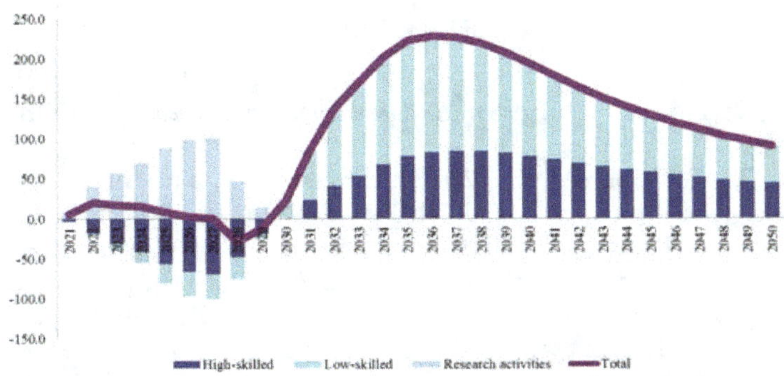

Fig. 7.4 Employment impact of the "*Continuation*" of Horizon 2020 (deviation in thousand jobs from a counterfactual scenario without Framework Programme) *Source* Boitier et al. (2018)

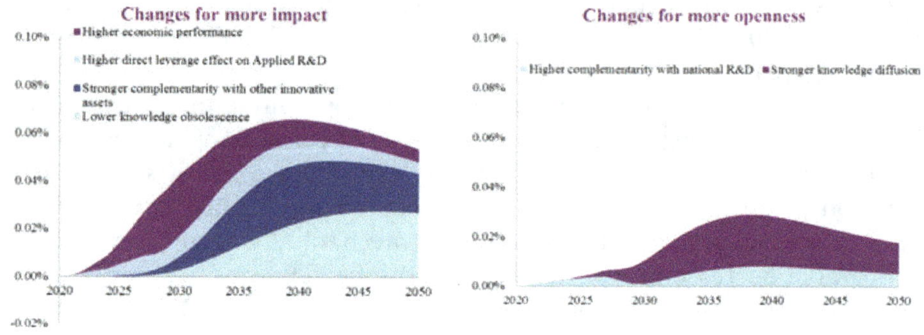

Fig. 7.5 Decomposition of total EU GDP impact into changes in the *more impact* and *more openness* scenarios (deviation in % from the "*Continuation*" scenario of Horizon 2020) Scenarios based on highest values of parameter ranges. *Source* Boitier et al. (2018)

reaches a maximum of +0.03% in 2040. On average, from 2021 to 2050, yearly EU GDP gains are about €2.7 billion whereas yearly employment gains are around nine thousand. Combining the "*more impact*" and "*more openness*" scenarios yields EU GDP gains of up to 0.1% in the most optimistic case, around +€12 billion per year, with an additional employment at EU level of a maximum of sixty seven thousand, in comparison with the "*Continuation*" scenario.

References

Aghion, P., & Howitt, P. (1998). *Endogenous growth theory*. Cambridge, MA: MIT Press.

Belderbos, R., & Mohnen, P. (2013). Intersectoral and international R&D spillovers. Working paper 2, EU 7th FP—SIMPATIC Project.

Bogliacino, F., & Pianta, M. (2010). Innovation and employment: A reinvestigation using revised Pavitt classes. *Research Policy*, *39*(6), 799–809.

Boitier, B., Le Mouël, P., Zagamé, P., Winjes, R., Mohnen, P., Ricci, A., Brozaitis, H., Espasa, J., & Stanciauskas, V. (2018). *Support for the assessment of socio-economic and environmental impacts (SEEI) of European R&I programmes: The case of Horizon Europe. Technical report, European Commission*. Luxembourg: Publications Office of the European Union. ISBN 978-92-79-92736-2.

Brécard, D., Chevallier, C., Fougeyrollas, A., Le Mouël, P., Lemiale, L., & Zagamé, P. (2004). *A 3% R&D: An analysis of the consequences using the Nemesis model*. DG RTD: Technical report.

Brécard, D., Fougeyrollas, F., Le Mouël, P., Lemiale, L., & Zagamé, P. (2006). Macro-economic consequences of European research policy: Prospects of the Nemesis model in the year 2030. *Research Policy*, *35*(7), 910–924.

Bresnahan, T., & Trajtenberg, M. (1995). General purpose technologies: Engines of growth. *Journal of Econometrics*, *65*(1), 83–108.

Chevallier, C., Fougeyrollas, A., Le Mouël, P., & Zagamé, P. (2006). A time to sow, a time to reap for the European countries: A macro-econometric glance at the RTD national action plans. *Revue de l'OFCE*, *97*(5), 235–257.

Clark, K. B., & Griliches, Z. (1984). *Productivity growth and R&D at the business level: Results from the PIMS data base*, Chapter 19, pp. 393–416.

Corrado, C., Haskel, J., Jona-Lasinio, C., & Iommi, M. (2012).*Intangible capital and growth in advanced economies: Measurement methods and comparative results* (Working paper, EU 7th FP–INTAN-INVEST Project).

Corrado, C., Haskel, J., Jona-Lasinio, C., & Iommi, M. (2014). *Intagibles and industry productivity growth: Evidence from the EU*. INTAN-Invest Paper: Technical report.

Damijan, J. P., Kostevc, C., & Stare, M. (2014). *Impact of innovation on employment and skill upgrading* (SIMPATIC Working paper 7, SIMPATIC EU Project).

Delanghe, H., & Muldur, U. (2007). Ex-ante impact assessment of research programmes: The experience of the European Union's 7th Framework Programme. *Science and Public Policy*, *34*(3), 169–183.

European Commission. (2005). *Annex to proposal for the Council and European Parliament decisions on the 7th Framework Programme (EC and Euratom)—Impact assessment and ex-ante evaluation*. Technical Report SEC(2005) 430, Commission Staff Working Paper.

European Commission. (2012). *The Grand Challenge—The design and societal impact of Horizon 2020*. Directorate-General for Research and Innovation: Technical report.

European Commission. (2017a). Taxes in Europe database v3.*Database*.

European Commission. (2017b). Assessment of the union added value and the economic impact of the EU framework programmes (FP7, Horizon 2020). Directorate-General for Research and Innovation, B-1049 Brussels.

European Commission. (2017c, May). *In-depth interim evaluation of horizon 2020*. Commission Staff Working Document. Directorate-General for Research and Innovation.

European Commission. (2018). Commission staff working document: Impact assessment. SWD(2018) 307 final, Part 2/3 . Brussels, 7.6.2018.

Eurostat. (2018a). *Annual national accounts (ESA 2010)*. Database.

Eurostat. (2018b). *Annual sectors accounts*. Database.

Eurostat. (2018c). *Labor force survey*. Database.

Eurostat. (2018d). *Research and development statistics*. Database.

Fougeyrollas, A., Le Mouël, P., & Zagamé, P. (2010). *Consequences of the 2010 fp7 budget on European economy* (Technical report, SEURECO—Demeter Working Paper).

Fougeyrollas, A., Le Mouël, P., & Zagamé, P. (2011). *Consequences of the fp7 2012 call on European economy and employment* (Technical report, SEURECO—Demeter Working Paper).

Griliches, Z., & Lichtenberg, F. (1984). *R&D and productivity growth at the industry level: Is there still a relationship?*, Chapter 21, pp. 465–502.

Ha, J., & Howitt, P. (2007). Accounting for trends in productivity and R&D: A schumpeterian critique of semi-endogenous growth theory. *Journal of Money, Credit and Banking*, *39*(4), 733–774.

Hall, B. H. (2011). *Innovation and productivity* (Working Paper 17178, National Bureau of Economic Research).

Hall, B. H., Mairesse, J., and Mohnen, P. (2010). *Measuring the returns to R&D*, Volume 2 of *Page ii*, Chapter 24, pp. 1033–1082.

Hanel, P. (1994). R&D, inter-industry and international spillovers of technology and the total factor productivity growth of manufacturing industries in Canada, 1974–1989. *Cahiers de recherche*, 94–04.

Harrison, R., Jaumandreu, J., Mairesse, J., & Peters, B. (2014). Does innovation stimulate employment? A firm-level analysis using comparable micro-data from four European countries. *International Journal of Industrial Organization 35*(C), 29–43.

Le Mouël, P., Le Hir, B., Fougeyrollas, A., Zagamé, P., & Boitier, B. (2016). *Toward a macro-modelling of European innovation union: The contribution of NEMESIS model*. In 9th Conference on Model-based Evidence on Innovation and Development (MEIDE) the 16–17 June 2016 in Moscow, Russia.

Link, A. N. (1982). *A disaggregated analysis of industrial R&D: Product versus process R&D*.

OECD. (2017). *Business enterprise R&D expenditure by industry*.

Peters, B., Dachs, B., Dünser, M., Hud, M., Köhler, C., & Rammer, C. (2014). *Firm growth, innovation and the business cycle: Background report for the 2014 competitiveness report*. Number 110577 in ZEW Expertises. ZEW—Zentrum für Europäische Wirtschaftsforschung.

PPMI. (2017). *Assessment of the union added value and the economic impact of the EU framework programmes—Final report*. Technical report.

Scherer, F. M. (1982). Interindustry technology flows and productivity growth. *Review of Economics and Statistics*, *64*, 627–634.

Scherer, F. M. (1983). Concentration, R&D and productivity change. *Southern Economic Journal*, *50*, 221–225.

Terleckyj, N. (1980). *Direct and indirect effects of industrial research and development on the productivity growth of industries.*

Timmer, M. P., Dietzenbacher, E., Los, B., & Stehrer, R. (2015). An illustrated user guide to the world input-output database: The case of global automotive production. *Review of International Economics*, *23*(3), 575–605.

Verspagnen, B. (1997). Estimating international technology spillovers using technology flow matrices. *Review of World Economics*, *133*(2), 226–248.

Zagamé, P. (2010). *The costs of a non-innovative Europe: What can we learn and what can we expect from the simulations works*. SEURECO: Technical report.

Zagamé, P., Fougeyrollas, A., & Le Mouël, P. (2012). *Consequences of the 2013 fp7 call for proposals for the economy and employment in the European union* (Technical report, SEURECO—DEMETER working paper).

8

Reviewing the Major Conclusions

Cristiana Benedetti Fasil, Miguel Sanchez-Martinez and Julien Ravet

8.1 Policy Context

EU-level investment in Research and Innovation (R&I) focuses on excellence through EU-wide competition and cooperation. Successive EU Framework Programmes have aimed at supporting training and mobility for scientists, creating transnational, cross-sectoral and multidisciplinary collaborations, leveraging additional public and private investment, building the scientific evidence necessary for EU policies, and strengthening national research and innovation systems. Over the years, the political narrative has put more and more emphasis on ' shaping the future' through R&I policy and funding, thereby lending even more

C. Benedetti Fasil (Deceased) (✉) · M. Sanchez-Martinez
European Commission, DG JRC, Brussels, Belgium
e-mail: cristiana.benedetti-fasil@ec.europa.eu

M. Sanchez-Martinez
e-mail: miguel.sanchez-martinez@ec.europa.eu

J. Ravet
European Commission, DG RTD, Brussels, Belgium
e-mail: julien.ravet@ec.europe.eu

importance to the assessment of the funding programmes' economic impact.

Horizon Europe is the European Commission' s proposal for the 2021–2027 Framework Programme for EU R&I policy, succeeding the Horizon 2020 Programme (active between 2014–2020).[1] With a proposed budget of about 100 billion euros for the period 2021–2027, Horizon Europe is the most ambitious R&I funding programme ever. This Programme builds on lessons learnt from previous evaluations, as well as on feedback from experts and from other stakeholders.[2] It will be an evolution, not a revolution, focusing on a few design improvements to further increase openness and impact. These changes in design aim at making this Programme achieve even more impact than its predecessor (through, i.e., the European Innovation Council and mission-orientation) and more openness (through strengthened international cooperation, a reinforced Open Science policy, and a new policy approach to European Partnerships).

8.2 Macroeconomic Modelling, EU R&I Framework Programmes and the EU Policy Cycle

Assessing the impact of the Framework Programmes is crucial for policymakers in order to inform their strategic decisions. There is a general consensus (Hall et al., 2009; Di Comite & D'Artis, 2015; European Commission, 2017c) that R&I policies are decisive in fostering productivity growth. However, putting a precise figure on the expected benefits of large R&I programmes such as the EU Framework Programmes is a challenging task with a lot of uncertainties, especially in an ex-ante approach. This is rendered even more difficult by the long-term horizon that a proper analysis of these impacts requires.

In this context, macroeconomic modelling is an essential tool to support policymaking, since it attempts at quantifying the impact of the Programmes and assessing policy options. Depending on when the assessment takes place in the policy cycle (Figure 8.1), this can be done in

[1] See European Commission (2018).

[2] These notably include: (i) the interim evaluation of Horizon 2020 (European Commission, 2017a) and, (ii) a high-level group chaired by Pascal Lamy set up by the European Commission in order to provide advice on how to maximise the impact of the EU's investment in research and innovation (European Commission, 2017b).

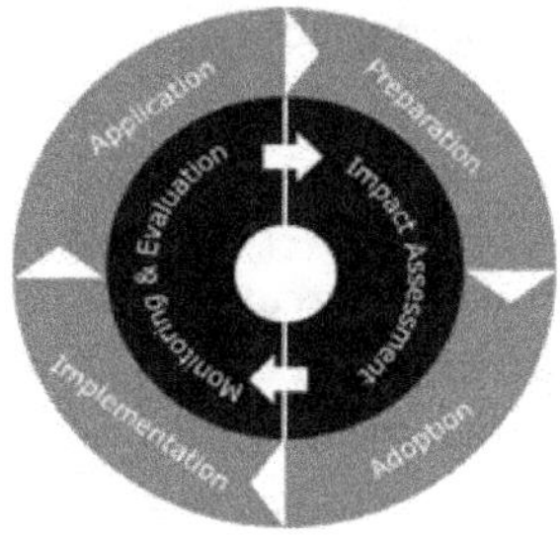

Fig. 8.1 The EU policy cycle (*Source* adapted from the EU better regulation guidelines (European Commission (2015)))

an ex-post/interim (monitoring and evaluation of a programme) or ex-ante/design (impact assessment) fashion, with policy options examined during impact assessments only in order to feed the preparation phase of the Programmes.

The first ever ex-ante impact assessment of any EU policy initiative in the field of research was the impact assessment of the 7th Framework Programme (FP7) (Muldur et al., 2006; Delanghe & Muldur, 2007). This exercise relied on historical data (e.g. publications and patents) and on simulations based on a macroeconomic model. The NEMESIS model was used for this impact assessment, and subsequently for the impact assessment and interim evaluation of Horizon 2020 (European Commission, 2012; European Commission, 2017a). Since FP7, macroeconomic models have evolved and lessons from previous impact assessments can help policymakers in using these models for current and future assessments.

The latest assessment of a EU R&I Framework Programme is the impact assessment of Horizon Europe (European Commission, 2018). A key novelty in the approach for this assessment is the use of three different macroeconomic models for assessing the continuation of the Programme ('baseline' scenario), which are the models presented in the previous chapters: QUEST III, RHOMOLO and NEMESIS.

8.3 How much is the Continuation of Horizon 2020 Worth?

Quantifying the impact of R&I policies at a macroeconomic level requires modelling tools that appropriately capture how R&I translates into economic gains. By relying on three models, namely QUEST III, RHOMOLO and NEMESIS, the impact assessment of Horizon

Europe (European Commission, 2018) was aimed at leveraging on their respective strengths while partly counterveiling some of their limitations.

The strengths of these models rely on their specificities, and differences between the models can help address specific needs of policymakers. Di Comite and D'Artis (2015) consider that NEMESIS is the richest model in terms of the types of innovation types captured and the number of policy-sensitive elasticities when compared to other standard macroeconomic models for R&D and the number of innovation policies. This means that policymakers can easily design and evaluate a wide range of policy options related to specific innovation types or innovation channels when using this model. On the other hand, the forward-looking, dynamic approach of QUEST makes the model most appropriate for assessing the impact of R&D and innovation policies over time. This is particularly important as the effects of initial investments are expected to bear fruit only after the period covered by the Programme, which calls for a model that can measure long-term impacts with precision. Finally, by modelling regional economies and their spatial interactions, RHOMOLO is the most suitable model to address questions related to the geographic concentration of innovative activities and spatial knowledge spillovers, which is also a crucial aspect for policymakers.

When using and interpreting the results produced by these models, it is also essential to acknowledge their main limitations. Any model allows only for a partial representation of reality, subject to the assumptions made. RHOMOLO balances its detailed spatial and regional dimensions by keeping optimisation problems static and, hence, not capturing the inter-temporal consequences of innovation decisions. These are binding constraints for ensuring the tractability of the model. In addition, it does not distinguish between private and public innovation or between different types of endogenous innovation. On the other hand, QUEST III, not being a multisector macroeconomic model, groups all R&D activities in a unique R&D sector without capturing the complexity and diversity of the type of R&D investments, such as private and public R&D activities, product and process innovation, non-R&D and disruptive innovations. These elements are also not present in RHOMOLO, albeit the latter features more extensive sectoral and geographical details. Lastly, NEMESIS is based on empirically observed relationships among variables as well as on adaptive expectations instead of forward-looking ones, allowing for more degrees of freedom in behaviour than in other models. This may generate inconsistencies with recent developments in macroeconomic theory. As opposed to the other two models, however, NEMESIS incorporates private and public R&D activities, product and process innovation, and non-R&D investments.

With these caveats in mind, Figure 8.2 shows the comparisons of the simulated impact of Horizon Europe on the GDP trajectory discussed in the previous chapters.

Overall, Figure 8.2 shows that NEMESIS, QUEST and RHOMOLO present consistent results in terms of the sign and temporal pattern of the GDP gain from the Framework Programme (compared to the discontinuation of the Programme) over 2021–2050. The three models show a strong increase in GDP especially after the period covered by the Programme, with highest impacts predicted between 2029 and 2034. The size of the GDP gain is highest for the simulations based on the NEMESIS model. This can be explained by the fact that the three models use different sets of innovation channels and elasticities.

Furthermore, the parameters and mechanisms in QUEST and RHOMOLO do not directly take into account the higher leverage and

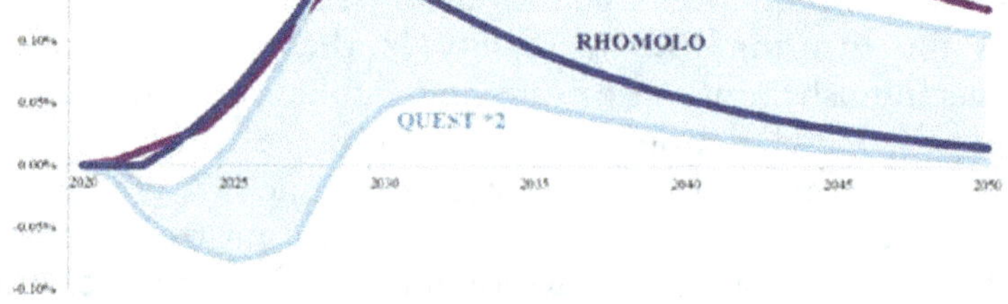

Fig. 8.2 GDP impact of horizon 2020 continuation (% deviation from a baseline, no framework programme scenario) (*Source* European Commission (2018); *Note* EU+ indicates that NEMESIS uses higher performance and leverage for EU funding compared to national funding as a reflection of the EU added value of the Programme. QUEST *1 assumes that financing of the Programme relies on VAT increases. QUEST *2 assumes that financing relies on lowering public investment)

performance expected from EU funding of R&I compared to national funding, which are acknowledged in NEMESIS as an illustration of the EU added value of the Framework Programme. This can potentially explain a significant part of the difference between the results from NEMESIS and the other models. Several studies (Delanghe et al., 2011; Vullings et al., 2014; Rosemberg et al., 2016; ECDG & Elsevier, 2017; PPMI, 2017) provide empirical evidence that shows that EU funding could be expected to perform ' intrinsically' better at EU level compared to national level due to factors that are not directly captured by these models, such as multidisciplinary transnational collaborations or critical mass. However, the way this EU added value is translated in a model, i.e. the size of the effect, is not trivial and requires caution in its interpretation.

Another essential aspect for all models is the mode of financing of the Framework Programme. Money spent for the Framework Programme can come from different sources, and it is tempting but rather unrealistic and undesirable to not model how the funds are financed. In this regard, both RHOMOLO and NEMESIS assume that the financing of the Programme can be reflected by lower national expenditure. The results from QUEST highlight the difference between two funding scenarios: (i) raising additional VAT revenues across Member States and (ii) lowering national public investment. It is shown that VAT funding should be unambiguously more beneficial compared to the second scenario as it allows Member States to continue public investment in productive uses.

In short, the three models used for the impact assessment of Horizon Europe are based on different modelling strategies, assumptions and parameters specifications and values, which results in different quantitative estimates of the economic impact of Horizon Europe. Nevertheless, the comparison of results across different models is essential to ascertain the consistency of a policy intervention, in this case Horizon Europe. This comparison is also required to understand the different aspects and mechanisms at play within the models, which partially mirror those determining the actual impact of Framework Programmes.

8.4 Modelling for Policymaking

Overall, past experience demonstrates the growing importance of macroeconomic modelling in the evaluation and impact assessment of EU R&I policy. The need for state-of-the-art modelling approaches all along the policy cycle has never been as pressing today. However, the complexity of the modelling exercise can make it challenging for policy-makers and modelers to collaborate effectively. In this regard, modelers also have a role to play to help policymakers understand the key aspects and assumptions that they need to reflect upon when using and interpreting models and their results. For instance, while *discontinuation* versus *continuation* scenarios can be straightforward to interpret and can inform policymakers on the 'cost of non-Europe', it can be challenging to translate policy options regarding the design or implementation of a Programme into assumptions in the models if there is lack of collaboration or understanding from the different parties involved.

References

Delanghe, H., & Muldur, U. (2007). Impact assessment of research programmes: The experience of the European Union's 7th framework programme. *Science and Public Policy, 34*(3), 169–183.

Delanghe, H., Sloan, B., & Muldur, U. (2011). European research policy and bibliometrics indicators, 1990–2005. *Scientometrics, 87*(2), 389–398.

Di Comite, F., & D'Artis, K. (2015). *Macroeconomic models for R&D and innovation policies*. IPTS Working Papers on Corporate R&D and Innovation.

ECDG & Elsevier. (2017). *Overall output of select geographical group comparators and related FP7- and H2020 -funded publication output*. Final Report https://frama.link/C7wPJhGp.

European Commission. (2012). *The grand challenge: The design and societal impact of Horizon 2020. Directorate-General for Research and Innovation.* https://doi.org/10.2777/85874.

European Commission. (2015). *Better regulation guidelines*. Staff Working Document. SWD(2015)110 final.

European Commission. (2017a). *In-depth interim evaluation of horizon 2020.* SWD(2017) 220.

European Commission. (2017b). *LAB—FAB—APP investing in the European future we want: Report of the independent high level group on maximising the impact of EU research & innovation programmes*. Directorate-General for Research and Innovation. https://publications.europa.eu/en/publication-detail/-/publication/ffbe0115-6cfc-11e7-b2f2-01aa75ed71a1.

European Commission. (2017c). *The economic rationale for public R&I funding and its impact*. Directorate-General for Research and Innovation, Policy Brief Series. https://doi.org/10.2777/047015.

European Commission. (2018).*Commission staff working document: Impact assessment*. SWD(2018) 307 final, Part 2/3. Brussels, 7.6.2018.

Hall, B., Mairesse, H. J., & Mohnen, P. (2009). *Measuring the returns to R&D*. NBER Working Paper No. 15622.

Muldur, U., Corvers, F., Delanghe, H., Dratwa, J., Heimberger, D., Sloan, B., & Vanslembrouck, S. (2006). *A new deal for an effective European research policy: The design and impacts of the 7th framework programme*, 1–289. https://doi.org/10.1007/978-1-4020-5551-5.

PPMI. (2017). *Assessment of the Union added value and the economic impact of the EU framework programmes* (FP7, Horizon 2020). https://frama.link/o6oBPRZU.

Rosemberg, C., Wain, M., Simmonds, P., Mahieu, B., & Farla, K. (2016). *Ex-post evaluation of Ireland's participation in the 7th EU framework programme*. Technopolis Group, June: Final Report.

Vullings, W., Arnold, E., Boekholt, P., Horvat, M., Mostert, B., & Rijnders-Nagle, M. (2014). *European added value of EU science, technology and innovation actions and EU-member state partnership in international cooperation*. Main Report. Technolopis Group. https://doi.org/10.2777/1193.

9

Alternate Innovation Policies and Modeling Approaches

Cristiana Benedetti Fasil, Giammario Impullitti and Miguel Sanchez-Martinez

9.1 Introduction

This chapter contains a thorough discussion of the results of two simulation exercises on the macroeconomic implications of changes in entry barriers and R&D tax credits, assessed using the QUEST III model.[1] Next we provide a brief introduction to the policy context and relevance

[1] The discussion on this chapter draws from Benedetti Fasil et al. (2017) and Sanchez-Martinez et al. (2017).

C. Benedetti Fasil (Deceased) · M. Sanchez-Martinez (✉)
European Commission, DG JRC, Brussels, Belgium
e-mail: miguel.sanchez-martinez@ec.europa.eu

C. Benedetti Fasil (Deceased)
e-mail: cristiana.benedettifasil@ec.europa.eu

G. Impullitti
University of Nottingham, Nottingham, UK
e-mail: Giammario.Impullitti@nottingham.ac.uk

of these two types of innovation-related issues, before proceeding to the technical discussion of the results in the next section.

Entry barriers play a key role in business dynamism by conditioning the flow of entry of new firms into markets and the transformation of new ideas into marketable products. These processes lie at the core of economic and productivity growth through the reallocation of resources from shrinking and exiting firms to new entrants and growing firms.[2,3] A study from the European Commission covering France, Italy, Germany, Ireland, Portugal and Spain over the 1997–2003 period, estimated that a 1% increase in the entry rate of firms would increase GDP growth by 0.6% and employment growth by 2.67% based on data from the same period.[4]

Following the launch of the Lisbon Strategy, most Member States began to reduce the costs of starting a business.[5] Nevertheless, the levels of entry barriers are still very heterogeneous across Member States and some countries, such as Italy, Cyprus, Malta and Poland, face costs to start a business that are, relative to income per capita, up to 70 times higher than the best EU performers, namely Denmark, United Kingdom and Ireland (Ciriaci, 2014, Table III.1). The OECD's indicator on product market regulation also provides evidence of country heterogeneity in terms of barriers to entrepreneurship (OECD, 2015). Over time, most countries have made considerable progress in removing entry barriers, although this pace has slowed down since 2008. Hence, in several Member States policymakers still have room for significant interventions directed towards creating more dynamic and competitive industries. As a result, policies in favour of Small- and Medium-sized Enterprises (SMEs),

[2] Nicoletti and Scarpetta (2003) using a panel of 18 OECD countries between 1984 and 1998, were the first to estimate that lower entry barriers would result in a faster catch up with the technology frontier. This is now widely established in the empirical literature.

[3] Several papers assess the growth contribution of the reallocation of resources from exiting to entering firms. For instance, Luttmer (2007) and Gabler and Licandro (2009) estimate that this selection effect can explain between 20% and 50% of US GDP growth. These estimates are consistent with Scarpetta et al. (2002), who find that entry and exit contributed to between 20% and 40% of aggregate productivity growth in a panel of OECD countries.

[4] See Cincera and Galgau (2005).

[5] See Ciriaci (2014, Table III.2). The World Bank definition of the costs of starting a business comprises three main elements; the number of procedures, the number of days and the cost as percentage of income per capita necessary to start a business. These are the so-called *red tape* entry barriers

in particular those policies that may create the right conditions for the flourishing of the so-called High Growth Innovative Enterprises (HGIE) are receiving greater attention. An important, related policy issue is to understand and measure the impact of policies aimed at reducing entry barriers.[6] Both large companies and SMEs are bound to benefit from a reduction in entry barriers. However, large companies are often better able to cope with entry barriers than SMEs due to having access to a larger pool of resources, including easier access to finance. Consequently, policies aimed at a reduction of entry barriers notably support SMEs and, in particular, young enterprises, as these are the types of firms most negatively affected by entry barriers. This is a particularly important policy issue in order to increase productivity and employment growth, as most of the job creation by young firms is carried out by new firms entering the market (Haltiwanger, 2013). Criscuolo et al. (2014) in a study with 18 OECD countries estimate that the share of total employment creation due to SMEs that are less than three years old is disproportionately larger relative to their size.

Firm size is also closely related to business dynamism. The European Commission's Product Market Review (European Commission, 2013) highlights a non-linear relationship between firm size at both entry and exit and an efficient allocation of resources between and within firms. In particular, they find that, on average, an increase in the size of a firm by just one employee, when entering the market, is associated with an increase in efficiency by 1.6%. In addition, such a relation exhibits an inverted U-shape, peaking at 10 employees at entry. This indicates that policies geared toward increasing the average size of small start-ups give rise to efficiency gains.

Concerning fiscal incentives to promote R&D investment, 25 Member States currently employ some form of tax break instruments, as a means to ultimately support economic growth and employment. Strong commitment for public intervention to spur investment in R&D can be traced back to the 2003 action plan 'Investing in Research', whereby the European Commission recommended supporting private investments in research. In particular, concerning tax measures, it recommended to 'improve fiscal measures for research on the basis of formal evaluations,

[6] At the European level, Sapir (2004) stressed that too much policy attention is paid to incumbent firms to ensure fair competition, whereas entrants and young firms tend to be neglected.

mutual learning and the application of principles of good design such as simplicity, low administrative cost and stability' (European Commission, 2003).

Some Member States such as France were already making use of R&D tax credits at the time of the action plan, but this recommendation was subsequently adopted by many others, making tax credits a widely used instrument in the EU as a way to subsidise the conduct of R&D. The total amount of foregone tax revenue due to R&D tax breaks is estimated at more than EUR 12 billion (OECD, 2014). In some countries, such as Belgium and France, the total value of foregone tax revenue via tax credits is higher than the value of government direct expenditures on R&D subsidies.

Despite the increasing relevance of tax credits as a stimulus tool for R&D investment in the EU, ex-ante evaluations of their potential macroeconomic effects are scarce. In particular, studies in the same vein as the one presented below do not provide an investigation of the structural factors behind the observed cross-country differences in the impact of R&D tax credits on macroeconomic outcomes. As noted in Veugelers (2016), 'where the macro models are as yet underexploited and where they would be a very useful R&D policy instrument is in assessing which framework conditions need to be in place to improve the impact of public R&D funding instruments, such as grants and tax credits'.

The next sections provide a summary of two exercises that focus precisely on tackling this last point by providing insights on the structural factors of EU Member States that condition the macroeconomic effects of policies addressed at lowering entry barriers and increasing fiscal incentives for R&D investment, respectively. In the final section, possible complementary refinements and extensions to these two analyses are discussed at a technical level.

9.2 The Macroeconomic Impact of Entry Barriers and R&D Tax Credits

This section, building on the content of Chapter 5, presents and discusses two examples of policy shock simulations undertaken using the QUEST III model: (i) a reduction equal to 0.1% of GDP in entry barriers for intermediate firms (see Benedetti Fasil et al., 2017) and (ii) a 0.1% increase of GDP in tax-credited R&D investment (see Sanchez-Martinez et al., 2017).

In this literature, and in the specific case of QUEST III, entry barriers are treated as sunk costs paid by intermediate firms upon entry, while tax credits impact directly on the user cost of intangible capital. Intuitively, the general mechanism through which these policies propagates in the model's economy is the following: a reduction in entry barriers or an increase in tax credits stimulate entry in the intermediate good sector and the demand for new patents. This leads to a gradual increase in R&D activities, resulting in the production of more patents, which can be used to develop new product lines. On the labour market, this is accompanied by a reallocation of high-skilled workers from the production to the research sector due to increased demand for this type of workers in the latter. If the drain of high-skilled workers from the final good sector to the R&D sector is sufficiently large, final good-producing firms might reduce output even if they increase hiring of low- and medium-skilled workers. Indeed, because of the reallocation of high-skilled workers, the initial effects on GDP can be positive or negative depending, among other things, on the elasticity of substitution among the different types of labour. Nevertheless, the size of these effects is small in the short term. Substantial, positive output effects materialise in the longer term, once R&D activities yield their fruits in the form of marketable products. Despite the increase in the efficiency of all factors of production in all countries, brought about by the higher stock of ideas, employment (at all skill levels) is higher in the new equilibrium. This is due to the surge in aggregate demand ensuing from higher incomes for households, which more than compensates for the labour-saving effect of the increase in TFP.

The key equation behind the aforementioned mechanism is the free entry condition of intermediate firms.[7] That is,

$$PR_{x,t} = \frac{i_{A,t} P_{A,t}}{DEF_t} + FC_A(i_{A,t} + C_{A,t}) \tag{9.1}$$

where FC_A represents the level of entry costs, $PR_{x,t}$ is the profit earned by design/firm x, $P_{A,t}$ is the price for licencing a patent, DEF_t is the GDP deflator, and $i_{A,t}$ represents the user cost of intangible capital.[8]

[7] Free entry means that intermediate firms will enter the market and thus buy new patents until the value of profits in a given period equals the entry costs plus the net value of patents.

[8] C_t^A is an auxiliary term related to the change of the price of patents over time.

While fixed entry costs enter this equation directly, tax credits do so indirectly via $i_{A,t}$.

This equilibrium equation shows that high entry barriers or low R&D tax credits (i.e., high cost of intangible capital) must be compensated for by high expected profits or by a lower licencing price for the patent, or by a combination of both, for the decision to enter the market to be economically sensible. The profits of intermediate firms are positively related to the inverse of the mark-up charged by final good producers, $\eta_{y,t}$, and negatively related to the number of patents issued, A_t:

$$PR_{x,t} = \left(\frac{1-\theta}{\theta}\right)\frac{i_{k,t}P_{C,t}x_t}{DEF_t} = (1-\theta)\frac{p_{x,t}x_t}{DEF_t} = (1-\theta)\frac{\eta_{y,t}(1-\alpha)(Y_t+FC_Y)}{A_tDEF_t} \quad (9.2)$$

where θ is the elasticity of substitution between intermediate good inputs in the final good production function, α is the fixed-cost-adjusted elasticity of labour in final good technology, Y_t is aggregate output from the final good sector, FC_Y are fixed costs in final good production, $i_{k,t}$ is the user cost of tangible capital, $P_{C,t}$ is the price index of final goods. As each intermediate firm buys only one patent to produce one intermediate product, the number of patents equates the number of intermediate firms and represents, together with the mark-up, a measure of market competition. Hence, the more concentrated markets are, the higher the profits for each intermediate producer.

The price of patents, determined optimally in the R&D sector, is positively related to the unit labour cost of researchers and inversely related to the elasticity of R&D output with respect to research labour, λ:

$$P_t^A = \frac{DEF_t}{\lambda}\frac{W_{H,t}L_{A,t}}{\Delta A_t} + MADJ_t \quad (9.3)$$

Substituting 9.2, 9.3 and 6.18 into 9.1, we can rewrite the latter as follows

$$(1-\theta)\frac{\eta_{y,t}(1-\alpha)(Y_t+FC_Y)}{A_tDEF_t} = i_t^A\left(\frac{W_{H,t}L_{A,t}}{\lambda\nu A_{t-1}^{\varphi}L_{A,t}^{\lambda}} + \frac{MADJ_t}{DEF_t}\right) + FC_A\left(i_{A,t}+C_{A,t}\right) \quad (9.4)$$

A decrease in the user cost of intangible capital drives an initial positive wedge between period profits and entry costs, attracting new firms into the sector until profits are driven down to exactly match costs, so that no more profits from arbitrage can be realised. This implies that, in countries with relatively high capital income taxes, a reduction in the user cost of capital alleviates the costs faced by intermediate good firms to a greater extent than in countries with lower tax rates, fostering the creation of new intermediate businesses and thus more purchases of patents from households.

In fact, it can be shown that the impact of an increase in the R&D tax credit rate on the user cost of intangible capital increases with the level of the (*tangible*) capital income tax rate. This can be seen algebraically from the equilibrium condition of the user cost of R&D capital:

$$i_{A,t} = \frac{(1-\tau_A)\Big(1+i_t-\big(1+g_{P_A}\big)(1+\pi_{A,t+1})(1-\delta_A)\Big)-t_K\delta_A}{1-t_K} + rp_{A,t} + \epsilon_t^{rp_A} \tag{9.5}$$

where τ_A represents the R&D tax credit rate and t_K is the capital income tax rate. This equation has an intuitive interpretation, as it shows that the user cost of capital depends, among other things, negatively on the tax credit rate and positively on the risk premium demanded by capital owners, $rp_{A,t}$, the risk-free interest rate and the rate at which the stock of ideas depreciates, δ^A. Moreover, it can be shown that a higher capital income tax rate in a given country means that hiring either type of capital in the economy is more expensive than in other countries. Thus, a decline in the user cost of capital leads to a proportionally higher demand for patent licences arising from intermediate good firms (see Sanchez-Martinez et al., 2017).

9.2.1 Simulation Results

Before presenting delving into the simulation exercises, the reader should be aware of a number of caveats. First, the current version of QUEST III models innovation exclusively via the patents generated by R&D efforts. Thus, it does not account for investments and innovations which do not result in patents. This is a somewhat limited view of both R&D and innovation. Second, for relatively long time horizons, the simulations are likely to underestimate the impact of R&D, because the model does not capture disruptive innovations. Third, some countries have already made considerable progress on entry barrier reductions and have very large starting levels of R&D tax credit rates. For these Member States, further reductions of entry barriers or further increases in tax credits are likely to yield small impacts, due to low marginal returns of continuous improvements. Fourth, there may be a discrepancy between the estimated entry barriers in the model and the actual entry costs faced by individual firms which depend on size, geographical location and other country-specific characteristics that the model does not account for. Finally, the version of QUEST III model used for the simulations is a three-country model characterising an individual Member State versus the EU27 and the rest of the world. Thus, the effects of potential simultaneous cross-country policies or spillovers generated by, for instance, common deregulation policies or the effect of tax competition cannot be studied. With these caveats in mind, as we are mainly interested in highlighting the macroeconomic factors impacting the effectiveness of the two R&D policies discussed in the chapter, the cross-country comparison made below is yields interesting insights, not least because, as pointed out in Bravo-Biosca et al. (2013), it highlights the potential for further improvements across countries.

Moreover, to explain the cross-country differences in the results of the simulations it is key to understand the differences in the values of the structural parameters that capture the *deep* characteristics of the economy of each Member States. The most important structural parameters and variables, that affect the impact and transmission of shocks to entry barriers and tax credits, are summarised for each Member State in Table 9.1.

9.2.1.1 Reduction in Entry Barriers

The first policy scenario discussed is a reduction in the value of fixed entry costs for intermediate firms equal to 0.1% of GDP (see Benedetti Fasil et al., 2017).[9] In each simulation, the shock is applied to the fixed costs of a given country only; the other Member States and the rest of the world

[9] Even though the original entry barrier costs are calculated in GDP per capita terms in Djankov et al. (2008), all quantities in the model are expressed in terms of GDP (which is the numeraire). Hence the reason for the choice of the size of the shock in GDP terms instead of GDP per capita.

Table 9.1 Cross-country values of selected parameters and initial steady-state values of key variables *(QUEST calibration January 2017)*

	FC_A	τ^A	λ	ν	$R\&D_{int}$	$L_{A,0}$	φ	t^K
AT	0.063	0.119	0.398	0.213	0.034	0.012	0.619	0.250
BE	0.060	0.108	0.465	0.309	0.027	0.010	0.555	0.355
BG	0.054	0.126	0.645	1.282	0.009	0.004	0.386	0.235
CY	0.144	0.134	0.551	1.077	0.006	0.002	0.476	0.260
CZ	0.100	0.185	0.496	0.484	0.022	0.010	0.478	0.180
DE	0.048	0.010	0.496	0.298	0.032	0.012	0.548	0.222
DK	0.011	0.019	0.473	0.255	0.036	0.016	0.548	0.235
EE	0.022	0.139	0.482	0.416	0.016	0.007	0.542	0.081
EL	0.058	0.088	0.652	1.301	0.010	0.004	0.377	0.239
ES	0.090	0.276	0.777	1.745	0.014	0.007	0.257	0.253
FI	0.049	0.031	0.441	0.231	0.036	0.015	0.578	0.299
FR	0.019	0.232	0.526	0.404	0.026	0.010	0.497	0.469
HR	0.064	0.133	0.672	1.598	0.009	0.004	0.361	0.235
HU	0.084	0.156	0.595	0.776	0.016	0.006	0.435	0.214
IE	0.016	0.241	0.595	0.580	0.017	0.008	0.456	0.130
IT	0.153	0.049	0.777	1.752	0.015	0.007	0.257	0.370
LT	0.015	0.139	0.582	0.751	0.011	0.006	0.447	0.098
LU	0.046	0.020	0.594	0.659	0.008	0.008	0.432	0.239
LV	0.030	0.139	0.738	2.027	0.008	0.005	0.299	0.099
MT	0.179	0.135	0.773	2.091	0.009	0.006	0.265	0.235
NL	0.057	0.171	0.547	0.431	0.022	0.011	0.477	0.137
PL	0.196	0.022	0.542	0.738	0.011	0.004	0.684	0.190
PT	0.028	0.263	0.773	1.700	0.015	0.007	0.261	0.295
RO	0.041	0.126	0.879	7.658	0.004	0.002	0.164	0.235
SE	0.025	0.070	0.335	0.152	0.040	0.014	0.679	0.306
SI	0.016	0.159	0.477	0.331	0.028	0.011	0.546	0.196
SK	0.045	0.102	0.685	1.439	0.010	0.005	0.349	0.167
UK	0.013	0.166	0.495	0.363	0.019	0.010	0.527	0.357

are only indirectly affected via trade and financial links. The following graphs show the impulse response functions (IRF) of GDP, employment and TFP for the 28 Member States (Figs. 9.1, 9.2, 9.3).

High entry barriers preclude some intermediate good-producing firms from entering the market. This results in a low demand for patents and a low level of intangible capital. Hence, the marginal productivity of intangible capital is higher than in an equilibrium with more patents, due to decreasing returns. Other things equal, a shock that reduces entry barriers

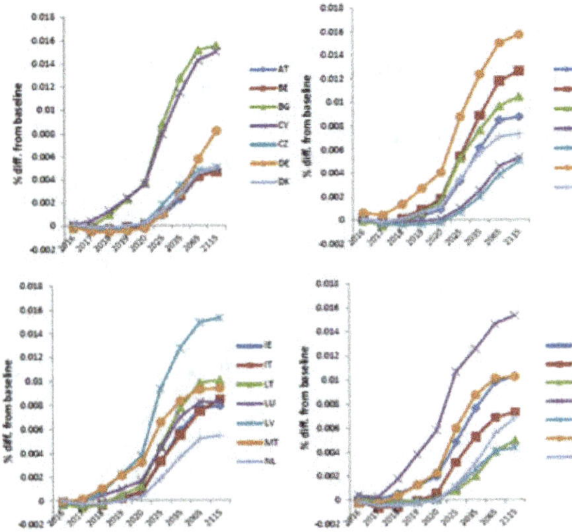

Fig. 9.1 Response of GDP to a reduction in fixed costs equal to 0.1% of GDP

yields higher output effects the higher the marginal productivity of intangible capital, i.e., the higher the initial level of entry barriers. A symmetric argument, again owing to diminishing returns, holds for the share of research labour; a lower share of labour devoted to research means that the effect on output will be larger when entry barriers are reduced. In both cases the output effect is amplified by higher R&D efficiency levels, and higher elasticities of R&D with respect to researchers. Moreover, differences in the magnitude of impacts are better understood by investigating the role played by the different variables and parameters involved, particularly the ones reported in Table 9.1.

Poland, Malta and Italy exhibit the highest entry barriers among all countries, while also characterised by very low R&D intensity and initial low quantity of researchers. The high marginal return on intangible capital and researchers' productivity results in a lower short-term reduction in GDP and in a long-term trajectory for output characterised by a higher slope compared to, for example, Slovenia and Portugal. As another example, the efficiency level of the Italian R&D production function, coupled with a relatively high value of the share of researchers in total labour, constitutes an advantage, as comparatively fewer researchers are needed to increase the production of knowledge, thereby relaxing the pressure on wages and sustaining a higher level of employment also in the long run. Nevertheless, due to comparatively higher wages in Italy,

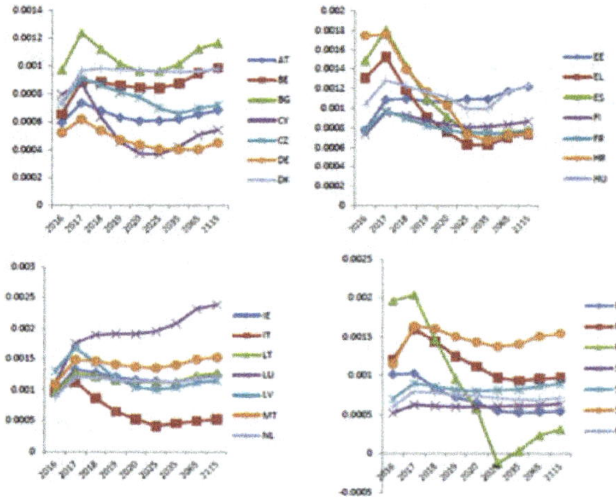

Fig. 9.2 Response of aggregate employment to a reduction in fixed costs equal to 0.1% of GDP

Italian TFP reacts to a lesser extent than Maltese and Polish TFP, leading to a slightly higher GDP response for Poland and Malta in the very long run.

Denmark is characterised by the lowest level of fixed costs and the highest share of initial research labour and R&D intensity. Given this leadership position, a shock to fixed costs has only a marginal impact on GDP. Total employment reacts positively upon impact, mainly due to an increase in the share of low-and medium-skilled workers. The long-term effect on employment is however negligible. Also, the initial high share of R&D employment mitigates the negative impact on GDP resulting from the reallocation of high-skilled labour from the final good sector to the R&D sector. This also implies a comparatively moderate impact on TFP (see Fig. 9.3).

GDP and employment in Slovenia, Finland, Belgium, France and the Netherlands react only marginally to a shock on entry costs. Similar trajectories are also displayed by the Czech Republic, despite its higher entry costs. In this case, the reaction to the shock is hampered by a comparatively higher risk premium on investment in intangibles.

Portugal and Ireland, characterised by both fairly low entry costs and fairly low shares of research labour, display a steep long-run GDP trajectory, while TFP and employment react similarly to other countries. The effect of the positive long-run productivity effect of a reallocation of high-skilled labour towards the research sector, which also causes the initial

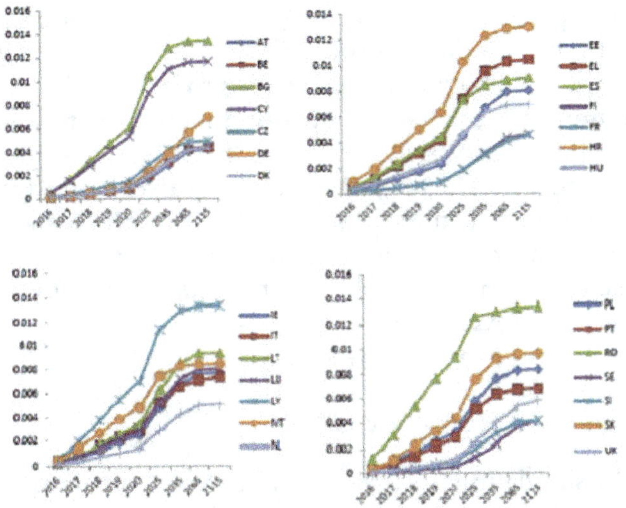

Fig. 9.3 Response of TFP to a reduction in fixed costs equal to 0.1% of GDP

drop in GDP, is hindered by a relatively high-risk premium. This slows down TFP growth, but sustains GDP as the final sector still benefits from a relatively higher number of skilled workers whose recruitment in the R&D sector is partially blocked by high-risk premia.

Slovakia and Lithuania have relatively low entry barriers and very low R&D intensity and labour dedicated to research. On the other hand, they have a relatively high elasticity of R&D with respect to research labour and also display a relatively strong efficiency of the R&D production function. Consequently, the transmission of the shock is amplified and exhibits trajectories similar to Malta and Poland, which start with much higher entry costs. The same reasoning holds for Spain, whose economy is characterised by fairly high entry costs, a fairly low share of researchers and R&D intensity, but an overall efficient R&D technology.

Germany has a robust R&D sector with a high initial R&D intensity and share of research labour. A reduction in fixed costs, which are higher than the ones prevailing in Denmark, results in a positive long-term impact on GDP, TFP and employment. This is particularly strong after 20 years from the initial shock when the trajectories of TFP and GDP become the steepest among all countries, owing to the more important role played by structural factors such as the production technology.

Romania is a particular case, with the lowest R&D intensity and share of research labour employed in the R&D sector together with fairly low initial entry costs. The high marginal returns to research labour, combined with a calibration of the R&D production function that indicates an efficient use of inputs, draw skilled workers from the final good sector to the research sector. However, GDP reacts positively already in the short run as the strong short-run increase in TFP offsets the reallocation effect. As TFP increases, more low and medium-skilled workers are hired in the final good sector, and total employment reacts comparatively more than in other countries. Over time, upward pressure on wages substantially erodes the initial gains in employment.

9.2.1.2 Increase in R&D Tax Credits

We proceed by simulating, for each Member State, the impact of a 0.1% of GDP permanent increase in tax credits for R&D (see Sanchez-Martinez et al., 2017).[10] By analysing the differences in outcomes for individual Member States we gain important insights into how different macroeconomic contexts influence the effectiveness of R&D tax credits. Because of structural differences, the impact of such policy differs substantially across Member States. The following graphs show the deviations from baseline in the path followed by GDP, employment and TFP, over both the short-to-medium and long terms in all 28 Member States.

Inspection of Table 9.1 and the impulse response functions in Figs. 9.4, 9.5, and 9.6 reveals a number of important points. The effects of a more generous R&D tax credit policy vary significantly across countries. A country that deserves special attention is Germany, as it is the only one without an initial tax credit policy in place. Germany's path for GDP exhibits a steep slope after 2025. This can be explained by the trajectory for TFP, which is the ultimate precursor of income growth over the long term. In fact, it can be seen from Figures 9.4 and 9.6 that the evolution of GDP is a mirror image of that for TFP, and that the path for the latter variable is steepest also for Germany. The reason why Germany is able to reap larger benefits in the very long run compared to the rest of the EU

[10] To be precise, the simulated shock consists of an increase in tax credit rates such that, for each country, the additional R&D investment generated equals 0.1% of GDP (i.e. in the new scenario, *tax-credited* R&D investment is 0.1% of GDP higher compared to baseline).

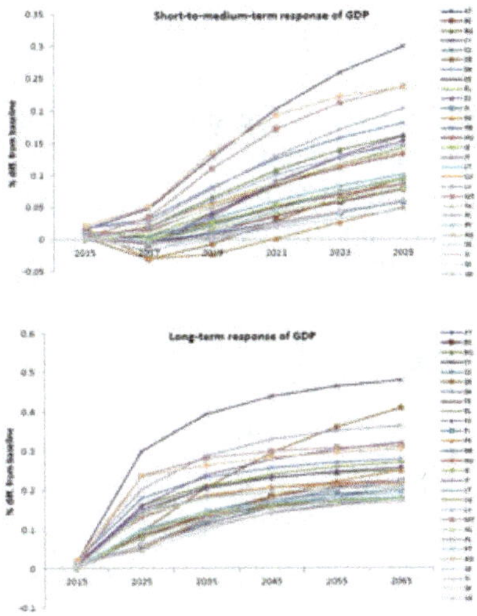

Fig. 9.4 Response of GDP to an increase in the tax credit rate such that tax-credited additional R&D investment equals 0.1% of GDP

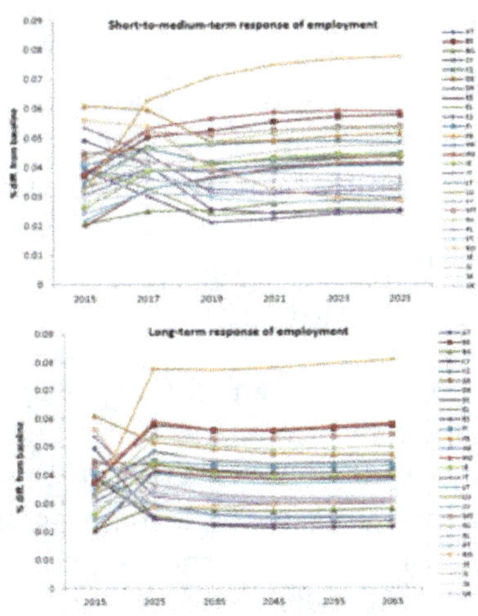

Fig. 9.5 Response of aggregate employment to an increase in the tax credit rate such that tax-credited additional R&D investment equals 0.1% of GDP

is that it departs from the highest levels in terms of the stock of knowledge and TFP among all Member States, thus being able to converge to a higher level of overall productivity in the new equilibrium. Because of the higher productivity and the bounded supply of all types of workers, real wages in Germany also reach the highest level among all countries in the long run. This deters the hiring of new workers to a greater extent than

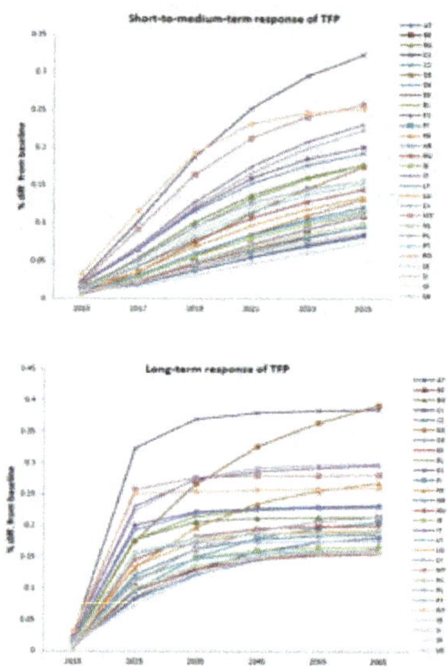

Fig. 9.6 Response of TFP to an increase in the tax credit rate such that tax-credited additional R&D investment equals 0.1% of GDP

in other countries, and thus the rise observed in German employment in the long run is somewhat in the middle of the distribution of the size of employment effects in the sample of countries considered. Employment levels are boosted most strongly in Luxembourg, both in the short and medium-to-long terms, owing to a combination of factors, including relatively low increases in real wages.

France is another special country in the sample, as it exhibits the highest value of the R&D tax credit rate. As apparent from Figure 9.4, the initial response of GDP in France is among the most negative ones (along with Germany's), remaining subdued over the medium term and picking up only towards the longer term. This response in output mainly owes to the relatively more intense outflow of labour input from the final good production sector to the R&D sector. The reason for this high sensitivity of employment to the policy shock is in turn partly related to the very high initial value for the capital income tax rate in France.

In short, the results of the simulations show that, by 2035, the countries which exhibit the largest GDP gains are Cyprus, Poland, Malta and Romania. These countries' R&D intensities in the initial period are among the lowest relative to the other countries in the sample, which makes them experience larger changes, all else equal.[11] However, this does not invalidate the fact that countries such as Italy and Cyprus, which depart from relatively sizeable levels of both R&D intensity and the physical capital income tax rate, rank rather high in terms of the size of GDP impacts. This is especially true in the very long run, as the influence of the initial value for R&D intensity fades away over time and deep parameters gain more importance. Also, these structural factors can partly offset the effect of the dissimilar magnitude of the tax credit shock across countries, even after only 20 years from now. This can be seen in the particular case of Italy. Despite departing from a middle-range value for R&D intensity, relatively higher values of (i) the elasticity of R&D output to the number of researchers, λ; (ii) the efficiency level of R&D, ν ; and (iii) the capital income tax rate, yield a GDP impact in 2035 which is the fifth highest.

Therefore, we can conclude that deep parameters in the R&D production function as well as policy parameters play a more important role for macroeconomic outcomes in the long run. By contrast, the starting level of variables such as R&D intensity are more important determinants over the short to medium run. Our results and the explanations behind cross-country differences in outcomes are thus consistent with the findings in D'Auria et al. (2009).

9.3 Alternative Approaches to Modelling the Impact of R&D Tax Credits and Entry Barriers

In this section, other modelling approaches aimed at addressing the problem of providing sound structural evaluations of the macroeconomic implications of policies, inducing changes in R&D tax incentives and entry barriers in EU countries, is presented. This is an important challenge in view of, among other issues, the sluggish productivity performance of many European countries in the recent decades. First, a discussion is provided on some of the specific issues arising from the analyses presented in the last section. Based on this, a broader view on

[11] Indeed, as discussed in DAuria et al. (2009), '...countries with low R&D intensity (R&D investment as a percentage of GDP and research labour, L_A) gain the most from R&D promoting policies. This is partly due to the fact that the 0.1% of GDP policymeasure implemented to boost the knowledge sector represents a proportionally stronger shock for countries investing less in R&D and is proportionally smaller for the R&D intensive countries...'.

possible alternative and complementary lines of future research on this topic is suggested.

Growing availability of firm-level data in the last two decades has triggered a revolution in the field of international trade and is slowly changing the macroeconomic-modelling landscape. Long-run growth models have already started incorporating several dimensions of firm heterogeneity, but short-run models are still lagging behind. Most existing DSGE macroeconomic models do not embed firm heterogeneity, as the purpose they were originally designed for does not necessitate such structure. However, recent research shows that firm heterogeneity is particularly relevant for analysing the macroeconomic impact of innovation policies, such as the ones exemplified in the last sections on increasing R&D tax credits and implementing measures to reducing market entry barriers (Acemoglu et al., 2017). For the purpose of policy evaluation exercises, it would be quite challenging to estimate/calibrate large-scale DSGE models with micro-data, since many EU countries still do not have high-quality data at a fine-grain level. With the growing availability of high-quality microdata, however, this could be a fruitful long-run avenue for future research. As a first step, it is interesting to explore the new potential channels brought about by new, smaller scale quantitative models featuring firm heterogeneity.

9.3.1 The Treatment of R&D Tax Credits and Subsidies

Regarding the modelling of R&D tax credits performed in Sanchez-Martinez et al. (2017), it is important to note that the growth engine embedded into the representative-firm DSGE model used is that of horizontal innovation (Romer, 1990), where growth is driven by the introduction of new products by new firms. Innovation is conducted by firms that were not producing before having discovered/invented and patented the new product. Hence, by construction, in this model incumbent firms do not innovate. Policy to stimulate innovation then must act on the entry margin, whereas tax credit is the appropriate policy only for incumbent firms. The authors circumvent this problem by interpreting the tax credit as acting on the cost to households of purchasing the patent resulting from innovation. The credit can then be seen as a subsidy to the acquisition of intangible capital (patents). This is an indirect way to introduce a tax subsidy in the model, which does not directly affect the firms' innovation decisions, but rather acts through the financial market affecting the user cost of (intangible) capital. It is not a priori clear whether this modelling choice leads to an under or overestimation of the effects of the R&D tax credits, but it makes it virtually undistinguishable from a (physical) capital tax credit. A more direct way to model R&D tax credits would be to use a Schumpeterian type of growth model, where innovation is performed by incumbent firms.

Furthermore, in the Romer class of models firms underinvest in innovation due to two types of dynamic inefficiencies. First, there exist knowledge spillovers and, second, there is a form of endogenously incomplete markets; there is no way to purchase a *machine* that is not yet produced, hence the set of Arrow-Debreu commodities is not complete, because it is endogenous. It follows that it is always optimal to subsidise innovation, and the model cannot accommodate cases of over-investment that can arise from strategic competition across firms. In policy debates, there is often no consensus on whether any type of investment should be subsidised. A quantitative economic framework where firms can potentially under or over-invest in R&D depending on their own characteristics and on those of the sectors where they operate can address these issues, subject to the discipline imposed by the data. Schumpeterian models formalise the idea that firms compete vertically, so that successful innovation by one firm allows it to replace another firm. This process of *creative destruction* generates a negative externality in the form of over-investment, as in its innovation decision the successful firm does not take into account the damage inflicted to other firms. In these models then, innovation subsidies can have a positive or negative economic impact depending on the characteristics of the sector and the economy. This class of models thus permits the analysis of those cases where the market produces *too much* innovation.

As an example of this family of macro models featuring firm dynamics, Akcigit et al. (2018) offer a model which belongs to the strand of research considering smaller size models compared to large DSGEs, focusing on a more detailed analysis of the macro and micro channels through which innovation policies affect aggregate outcomes. These models often depart from the representative firm framework to incorporate rich firm-level heterogeneity which is carefully calibrated to the data, thereby exploiting the wealth of microdata that has become available in recent decades. Some key papers in this literature are Akcigit and Kerr (2017), Acemoglu et al. (2017), and Akcigit et al. (2016), among others.

In Akcigit et al. (2018), new evidence is provided using data from the US Patent Office of stronger competition experienced by American firms as a result of higher patenting by Japanese and European firms in most sectors of the economy during the 1970–1981 period. These developments, together with Reagan's introduction of R&D subsidies at the time motivate the construction of a dynamic model of international technology competition, which is employed to perform a quantitative comparative analysis of the economic effects of that innovation policy *vis-a-vis* a counterfactual, protectionist policy.[12]

The model builds on *step-by-step* Schumpeterian innovation, which allows for strategic interaction among competitors.[13] International markets are separated by transportation costs and tariff barriers. Slow international diffusion of ideas in the form of knowledge spillovers represents a potential engine of convergence across countries.

The model is calibrated to reproduce the convergence in patenting experienced by the United States in the 1970s and used to evaluate both the R&D subsidy policy introduced in 1981 and an alternative, counterfactual, protectionist policy. The authors find that a 50% increase in US import tariffs produces welfare gains for Americans lasting for about 20 years and losses afterwards. In the short run, trade barriers help firms in import-competing sectors recoup profitability sheltering them from foreign competition. This artificial protection reduces firms incentives to innovate which, in turn, impacts negatively the country's long-run growth prospects. This results hold under the assumption that US trade partners do not retaliate. Under retaliation, that is in the case where foreign countries exactly match the US policy change, even the short-run gains disappear. Figure 9.7 illustrates the results.

In Fig. 9.7 the welfare effects of the unilateral tariff and, in the second panel, the effect of the tariff on US incumbent firms' innovation, are shown. The Figure plots the incumbent firms' distribution of innovation in the steady state across technology gaps. Positive (negative) gaps illustrate technology classes (sectors) where US (foreign) firms hold a leading position in patenting. US firms accelerate their innovation efforts close to the import cut-off, the left peak before which their products' quality

[12] This type of evaluation serves to illustrate how similar EU innovation policy evaluations could potentially be conducted based on this family of models.

[13] The global economy is dominated by large and innovative firms (Bernard et al., 2017; Hottman et al., 2016) so that the strategic interaction between large firms is crucial.

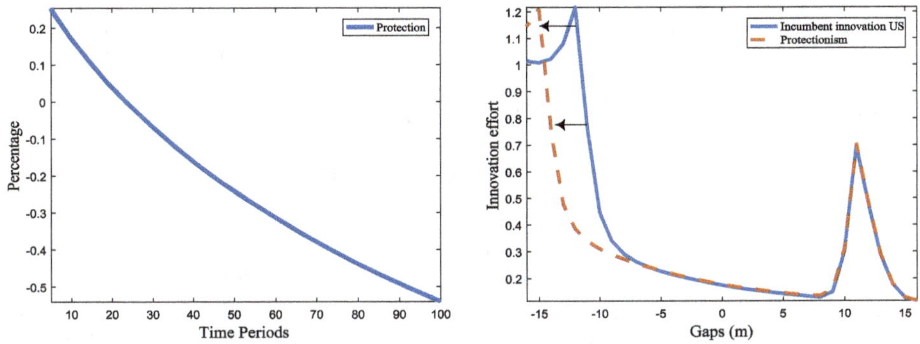

(a) Protectionist vs. benchmark welfare (b) Steady state incumbent innovation

Fig. 9.7 Unilateral 50% increase in US trade tariffs (Akcigit et al., 2018)

is not high enough to beat foreign competitors on their own turf. The incentive to obtain more quality improvements and conquer the domestic market stimulates innovation. This effect is dubbed *defensive innovation*. American incumbent firms accelerate innovation also before entering the export market, the right peak. Here the incentive to go one step further is the conquest of the foreign market and it is dubbed the *expansionary innovation* effect. The increase in US tariff reduces the domestic cut-off, thereby allowing easier survival of US firms in their own market. This is the source of the short-run gains reported on the left panel of the Figures for the 20 years after the policy. In an imperfectly competitive world, tariff protection shifts profits (and in an extended version of the model also wages) away from foreign firms (and workers) towards US firms (and workers). The side-effect of protectionism is that US firms in the import competing industries reduce their innovation effort, thereby reducing the growth prospects of the US economy and leading to welfare losses in the long run.

Figure 9.8 reports the effect of a trade war, where a 50% US tariff hike is met by a similar hike from their commercial partners. As it can be seen in the left panel, even the short-run gains now disappear, and protectionism becomes a bad policy even for very short-sighted policymakers. Moreover, comparing the magnitude of the effects in the scenarios with and without retaliation, the latter are one order of magnitude larger, ranging from about 1 to over 2% of consumption per year. The right panel shows the economic mechanism behind this results. Retaliation affects US

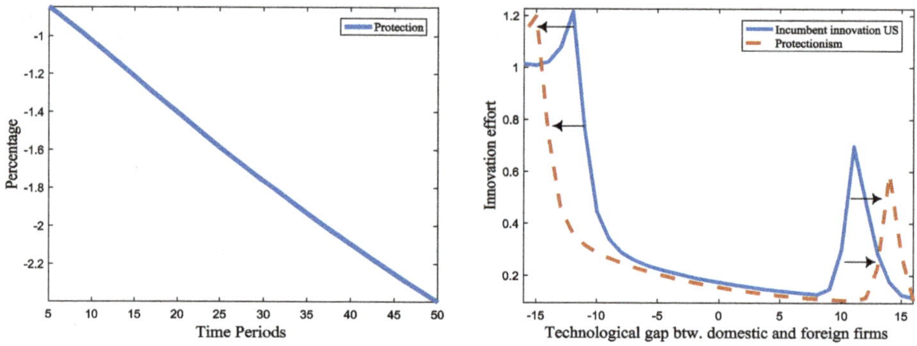

(a) Protectionist vs. benchmark welfare

(b) Steady state incumbent innovation

Fig. 9.8 50 per cent increase in US trade tariffs under retaliation (Akcigit et al., 2018)

exporters, which find it harder to penetrate foreign markets. In the figure the export cut-off moves to the right, and some US firms exit the export market. Since American firms find it harder to compete in foreign markets, they are discouraged in their innovation efforts, which drops substantially for a large set of firms.

The R&D subsidy change introduced in 1981 generates welfare gains both in the short and in the long run, as shown in Figure 9.9. Differently from the protectionist response, R&D subsidies increase US incumbent

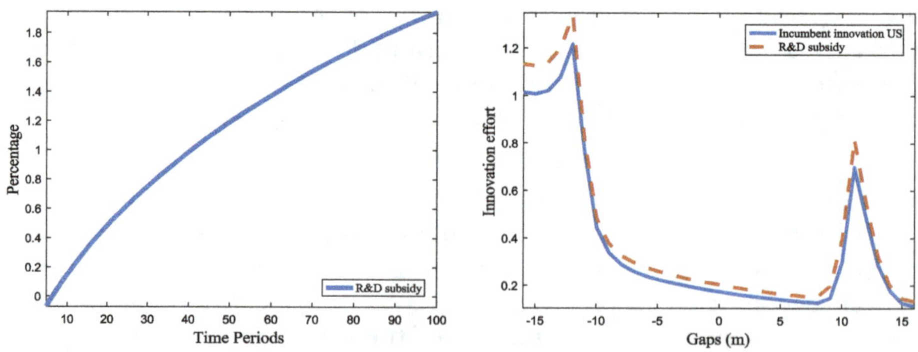

(a) Policy change vs. bench. welfare

(b) Steady state incumbent innovation

Fig. 9.9 US R&D subsidy increase in 1981 (Akcigit et al., 2018) firms' innovation in all sectors, thereby allowing policymakers to support national competitiveness without giving up the gains from trade. Welfare gains increase in time after the policy change as the growth effect of innovation has a stronger impact in the long run when the full potential of the innovation stimulus is realised.

Finally, Figure 9.10 shows the optimal US R&D subsidy over different time horizons and in a 35 years horizon at different levels of multilateral openness. It follows from inspection of the Figure that longer policy horizons imply higher optimal R&D subsidies, as a longer horizon allows larger gains from policy-induced growth to materialise. Moreover, more openness leads to lower optimal levels of innovation subsidies. Intuitively, a more open economy provides stronger incentives for US firms to innovate and there is less need for the government to subsidise innovation.

Although this model is more stylised along some dimensions than business-cycle DSGE models, it permits a clear illustration of some key mechanisms through which the R&D subsidy policy operates. Moreover, it highlights the importance of the interaction between innovation policy and trade policy. The last result of the paper seems to suggest that the more integrated EU countries are (both in terms of tariff and non-tariff barriers) the weaker the need for a strong innovation subsidy policy. Moreover, for trade between EU countries and their non-EU trade partners, the results imply that any increase in trade barriers, due for

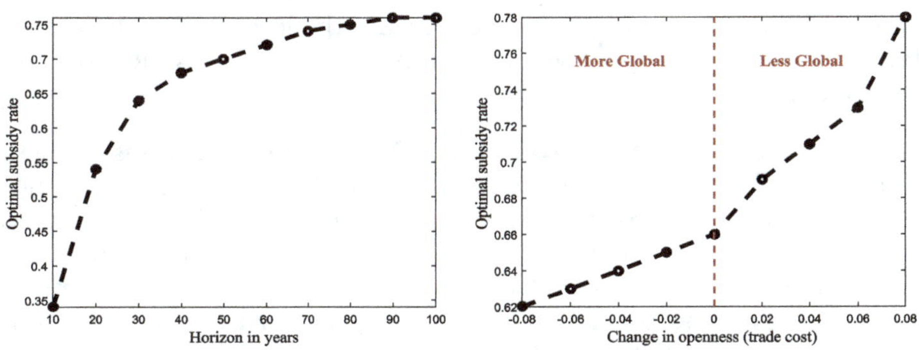

(a) Optimal subsidy over horizons (b) Optimal subsidy over openness (35y h.)

Fig. 9.10 Optimal US R&D subsidy, over different horizons and levels of openness (Akcigit et al., 2018) example to tariff wars, would increase the need for stronger EU support to innovation.

Another relevant example of the analysis of the impact of R&D tax credits is presented in Borota et al. (2016). These authors analyse R&D tax credit policies in the European Union via a multi-country Schumpeterian growth model,featuring cross-country technological heterogeneity. In technologically more advanced countries, firms have access to frontier production and innovation technologies, while less developed countries lag behind the frontier but can potentially catch up through technology diffusion and innovation. Countries may also differ in other dimensions such as size, human capital and other policies.

The authors first analyse the growth channels in the model, where different countries are integrated through trade and foreign direct investment, and explore the benefits and costs of R&D tax incentives. Second, they identify and describe the optimal R&D tax subsidy from each country's perspective, and from the perspective of the overall European economy. The latter identifies optimal policies under various scenarios of policy cooperation between countries. Policymakers may use R&D tax incentives to promote the competitiveness of national firms in the global economy, at the expense of foreign firms. The strategic nature of this policy leads naturally to consider possible national and supra-national *gains from cooperation.* Since countries are different in this economy, costs and benefits from competition and cooperation in innovation policy differ across countries. A key point of the analysis is to show how countries' differences in size, technology and the level of economic integration within the EU, shape their incentives to set innovation policies cooperatively.

Evidence is presented showing that Western European firms' foreign direct investment to the East is strongly correlated with R&D and innovation by Eastern European firms. In the model this is formalised as knowledge diffusion: when Western firms move their production to the east some of their technology spills over locally allowing local firms to start innovating and potentially *leapfrogging* Western firms. The incentives for FDI are driven by lower labour costs in the East, and the disincentives are related to technology diffusion that might allow local firms to imitate their technology and even leapfrog them. The paper looks at the R&D subsidy game between Western European countries, bunched in a single region for simplicity, and a region of Eastern European countries. Moreover, the gains from innovation policy cooperation, defined as a unified subsidy at the European level, are also explored.

In this economy, as in the standard Schumpetarian model Aghion and Howitt (1992), the optimal subsidy is governed by two externalities, one leading to underinvestment and one to overinvestment in R&D. First, once an innovation is introduced it benefits present and future consumers because future innovators build on it, this is the *standing on the shoulder of gians* type of externality, also known as the *intertemporal spillover* effect. Since innovating firms do not take these effects on consumers into account, they tend to underinvest in innovation and the intertemporal spillover generates a motive to subsidise R&D. Second, when quality laggard firms successfully innovate, they drive incumbent leaders in their product lines out of business. The innovating firm does not take this into account and is therefore bound to overinvest in R&D. The open economy dimensions of this model add a new key external effect. Successful Western innovation, for example, drives Eastern firms out of business and shifts profits towards the West, thereby increasing domestic income and welfare. Similarly, when an Eastern firm successfully innovates, it drives a Western firm out of business, and the related shift of profits across countries increase national welfare. Since home R&D firms do not take this effect into account when innovating, a bias towards underinvestment obtains. This is the *international business-stealing* effect, and pins down the strategic motive for subsidising R&D in an open economy. Table 9.2 summarises the results focusing on the long-run equilibrium of this economy.

The non-cooperation scenario is the one where each region sets its subsidy to maximise its own welfare given the other region's subsidy, and the result is the Nash equilibrium of this game. The cooperation equilibrium is obtained assuming that a European level planner sets a common

Table 9.2 The effect of cooperation

	s^W	s^E	W^W	W^E	W^{EU}	growth
Non-coop (s_n^W, s_n^E)	0.44	0.46	9.15	6.24	15.39	1.16
Unified (s_{uni})	0.78	0.78	8.84	7.45	16.29	3.23
Welfare gain			−0.017	0.080	0.028	

subsidy to maximise European welfare. The paper assumes that there is no ex-post scheme available to winners to compensate the losers. Therefore, cooperation will be implemented only when it benefits both regions.

Cooperation allows the internalisation of the international business stealing effect, neutralising the strategic role of subsidies. Cooperation leads to a higher level of subsidies compared to the non-cooperation scenario in both countries. Global growth rates are higher, as well as total European welfare. However, the West loses from cooperation and, in the absence of a compensation scheme, it does not have incentives to cooperate. Further simulations in the paper show that the incentives to cooperate for the West increase when the cost of offshoring production to the East declines. Intuitively, in a more integrated European market, Eastern firms represent more of a threat for Western firms, as cheaper offshoring increases technology transfer to the East thereby exposing Western firms to more intense technological competition.

This model adds hence a new perspective to the evaluation of R&D subsidies. Accounting for strategic innovation policy competition across European countries provides a framework for evaluating a common EU R&D tax policy.

9.3.2 *The Treatment of Entry Barriers*

As an example of an alternative approach to modelling the impact of a reduction in entry barriers, within the same family of models with heterogeneous firms, Impullitti and Licandro (2018) use a version of this type of model to assess the effects of both a reduction in entry costs and credit frictions. The model represents a two-country world with symmetric technologies, preferences and endowments, where both countries produce exactly the same set of differentiated goods which can be traded at an iceberg trade cost. Within a given variety, firms from both countries compete *à la* Cournot for market shares. At entry, firms draw a productivity level from a given distribution. After entry, they invest in innovation to increase their productivity. The innovation technology features within variety knowledge spillovers at the country level generating sustained growth under a stationary productivity distribution. In steady state, the productivity distribution permanently moves to the right as a travelling wave at the long-run growth rate. In what follows the analysis is restricted to the steady-state equilibrium. Notice that, as opposed to Romer-style endogenous growth models, the growth engine in this model comes from innovation by incumbent firms rather than entrants. Hence, policies affecting the cost of entry would impact growth only indirectly, through their effect on product market competition. Hence, all the mechanisms shown here are complementary to those present in representative-firm DSGE models.

The model is calibrated to match some key aggregate and firm-level facts of the US economy. These targets lay in rather standard ranges, and so their numerical values can be deemed as relevant for large EU countries too. The following exercises are performed: first, the effects of changing the entry cost parameter for a sufficiently wide range of values around the benchmark value is simulated. The effects on firm selection, markups, innovation, growth and welfare, are shown. In order to show the role of firm heterogeneity, the exercise is repeated, shutting down the selection channel. The second exercise is to reduce financial constraints on the fixed operating costs. Finally, notice that only policy changes implemented symmetrically in both countries are considered. This would be equivalent to a coordinated EU-level policy on entry barriers and credit constraints reductions in a EU-wide model such as QUEST III.

9.3.2.1 *Reducing Entry Barriers*

Figure 9.11 shows the effect of wide changes in the entry cost around the benchmark value which is 0.1, corresponding to about 7% of GDP. Changes in key endogenous variables in the baseline model and in a version of the model where the selection effect is shut down are reported. That is, changes in policy parameters that affect the survival cut-off, which is set constant at the benchmark level, are assumed away. Hence, the economies with and without selection have by construction the same equilibrium at the benchmark entry cost.

The simulations show that a reduction in entry costs generates larger pro-competitive effects in the benchmark economy than in the economy without selection. When entry cost is reduced, the number of firms in each product line increases more and the average markups drops more in the baseline economy than in the economy without selection. Intuitively, lower entry costs induce more firms to enter the market, thereby reducing markups. Stronger product market competition forces the less productive, less profitable firms, out of the market, thereby generating tougher firm selection which leads to a lower firm survival probability. By contrast, in the model without selection firm survival is unchanged. The pro-competitive effect leads to higher market efficiency which in

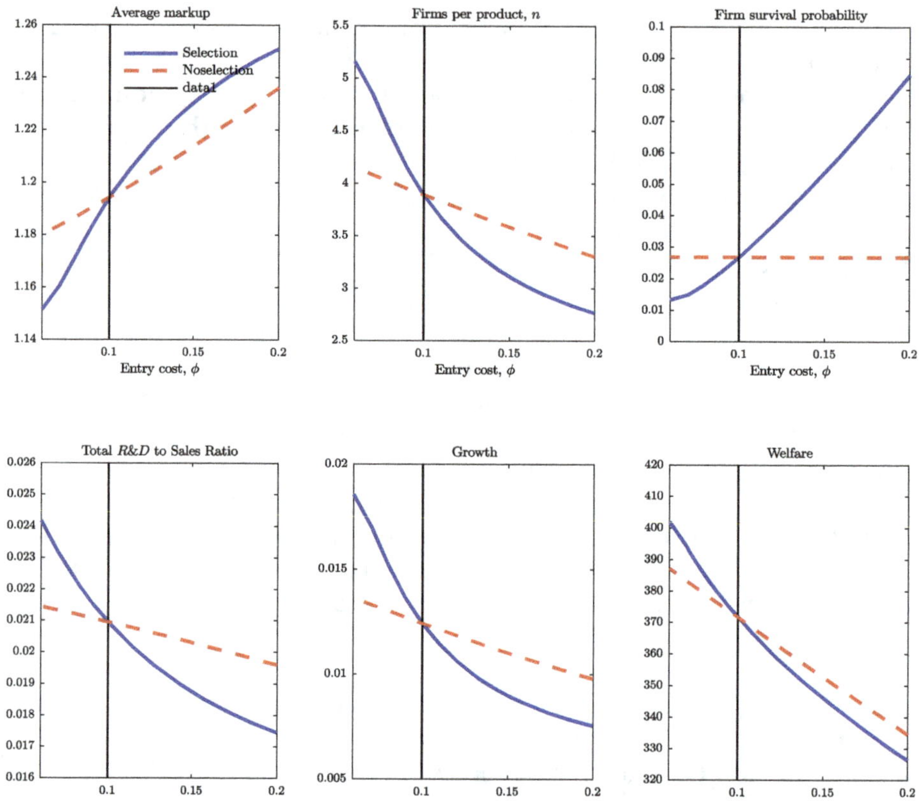

Fig. 9.11 Entry costs, selection and growth

turn yields a higher equilibrium size of the firms. In this economy, firms perform cost-reducing (or productivity-enhancing innovation), and the return to innovation scales with the quantity produced by the firm. Hence, a large firm size leads to greater innovation and faster productivity growth. The increase in firm size is feasible because of the presence of a homogenous good sector from which the more efficient differentiated good sector attracts resources. In the heterogeneous firm model there is an additional reallocation from exiting, less productive firms to surviving, more productive firms. This reallocation leads to higher incentives to innovate and faster productivity growth than in the model without selection. Finally, there are several channels of welfare gains in this economy. The economy without selection features welfare improvements from a reduction in entry costs coming from the reduction in markups, and the induced increase in productivity growth. The economy with selection adds additional static and dynamic gains due to the adjustments on the extensive margin. First, selection further increases the static efficiency of the economy; second, by stimulating innovation, it fuels an additional surge in long-run productivity growth.

9.3.2.2 Reducing Financial Constraints

The original model does not feature credit constraints but they can be easily introduced. In order to introduce credit constraints, it is assumed that while variable costs can be funded internally, firms must borrow a fraction $d \in (0, 1)$ of their fixed operating costs λ upfront. In order to cover this upfront cost, firms borrow from financial institutions pledging a fraction $\gamma \in (0, 1)$ as collateral.[14] Higher d and lower γ indicate stronger financial vulnerability of the firm or sector. Neither cross-sector nor cross-firm heterogeneity along this dimension is assumed for simplicity. Because of the imperfect ability to insure risk away, credit institutions can expect to be repaid by firms with probability $\chi \in (0, 1)$, which embodies the strength of financial institutions or their willingness to enforce credit contracts. For simplicity, it is assumed that firms are credit constrained only in financing the fixed cost for producing domestically.[15] To embed this credit friction, the firm's problem of the original model must be augmented with the following constraints:

$$
\begin{aligned}
LC &: \; r(\tilde{z}_t) - h(\tilde{z}_t) - (1-d)\lambda \geq F(\tilde{z}_t), \\
PC &: \; -d\lambda + \chi F(\tilde{z}_t) + (1-\chi)\gamma\lambda \geq 0,
\end{aligned}
$$

where $r(\tilde{z}_t)$ are the revenues net of variable production costs of a firm with productivity $\tilde{z}_t$, $h(\tilde{z}_t)$ is the R&D expenditure, and $F(\tilde{z})$ is the payment due to the financial institution in case the contract is enforced. The liquidity constraint (LC) states that in case of repayment firms can pay up to their net revenues. The participation constraint (PC) implies that the financial institution is willing to enter the contract only if the expected

[14] In purchasing intermediate inputs, paying salaries to workers, and paying rents for land use and equipment, firms often have to incur in expenses previous to production and sales.

[15] The model can be easily extended to include frictions on fixed export costs.

returns exceed the outside option, which for simplicity is normalised to zero.

The optimal decision of firms is to adjust their payment F to take the investors to their participation constraint, which in equilibrium holds with equality. Substituting this into the liquidity constraint (LC), the domestic survival cut-off of this economy can be determined. Focusing on the steady-state equilibrium, where z is the stationary productivity level of firm z, the survival cut-off z^* can be expressed as:

$$r(z^*) - h(z^*) = \hat{\lambda},$$

where $\hat{\lambda} = \left[1 + \frac{1-\chi}{\chi}(d - \gamma)\right]\lambda$ is the effective fixed cost which includes the cost of borrowing in imperfect financial markets. A more financially constrained economy is one in which credit institutions are less likely to be repaid, γ is low, and therefore offer firms contracts with high cost of credit which imply a high effective fixed cost. Hence, the effects of financial constraints in this economy can be analysed by focusing on the induced changes in the fixed operating cost they produce.

In Figure 9.12, the effects of wide changes in the fixed operating cost are simulated around the benchmark value which is 0.01 (corresponding to about 3.9% of GDP). A reduction in the fixed operating cost is shown to generate an anti-selection effect, that is it makes firm survival easier. In every model with firm heterogeneity, high fixed cost serves as a discipline devise since they make survival harder for less productive firms. Hence, the probability of firm survival increases as fixed costs decrease. In our model, more productive firms innovate more, and since higher survival rates leave firms with low productivity on the market, this leads to lower aggregate innovation and growth.

9.3.2.3 Policy Comparison

Table 9.3 reports some quantifications of the effects of the policy changes considered above, allowing for a direct comparison of their impact on key outcomes. First the effects of a 10% reduction in the entry cost are computed, from its benchmark value of 0.1 to 0.09, a reduction equivalent to 0.7% of GDP. Although the markup declines only by one per cent, the selection effect is strong and reduces the probability of firm survival at entry by 18%. The total R&D to sales ratio increases by 3% and growth and welfare rise by about 9%. Repeating the same exercise in the model without selection it can be seen that the effects are substantially smaller:

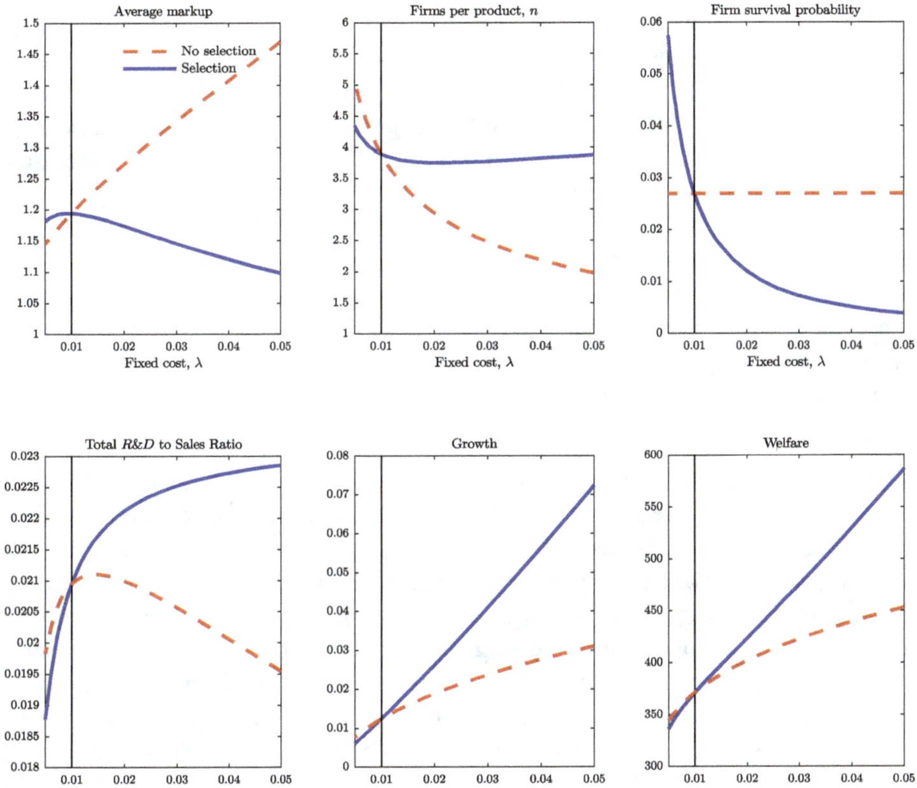

Fig. 9.12 Credit constraints, selection and growth: Domestic fixed cost

Table 9.3 Effect of a 10% reduction in entry and fixed cost (percentage change)

	Benchmark		*No selection*	
	Δ entry cost	Δ fixed cost	Δ entry cost	Δ fixed cost
Markup	−1	0.01	−0.3	−0.7
Survival probability	−18.6	11.8	0	0
R&D/sales	3	−1.2	0.6	-0.5
Growth	9.6	−11.2	2.4	−6.8
Welfare gains	9.1	−7.5	5.2	−5.6

the growth effect is three times smaller than in the baseline model and the welfare effect is about half of that in the baseline model.

The effect of a 10% reduction in the fixed operating cost is also reported. In this case both models suggest non-negligible losses, but in line with the previous policy exercise, the losses when the selection channel is operative are substantially larger.

9.3.2.4 *Extensions*

Relaxing financial constraints to the fixed operating costs of producing domestically has a negative effect on growth as it makes the economy less selective. Different results can be obtained if the credit constraint is on the fixed operating cost. Proceeding as above, the credit friction leads to an effective fixed export cost of $\hat{\lambda_x} = \left[1 + \frac{1-\chi}{\chi}(d - \gamma)\right]\lambda_x$. Figure 9.13 explores the effects of financial constraints on exports. A reduction in the fixed cost of exporting, triggered by a reduction in credit constraints, reduces the survival probability, therefore generating more selection, more innovation and faster growth. The economic mechanism is straightforward. Easier access to foreign markets allow marginal, non-exporting firms to start selling abroad, thereby boosting their sales and increasing their incentives to innovate. The productivity improvements made by these new exporters increase their competitiveness also on their domestic market where they see their market shares increase at the expense of the local non-exporting firms. As a consequence, the latter find it harder to survive and the least productive of them exit.

Finally notice that firms could also be credit constrained in financing their entry costs. The model can be easily extended to include this possibility. It could be assumed that firms borrow to finance the entire entry cost and that they face credit constraints on this activity. Financial institutions can expect to be paid the full firm profit with probability $\chi < 1$, or only a fraction $t_e \in (0, 1)$ of it with probability $1 - \chi$. Free entry in the financial market leads to

$$E_z(\phi(z)) = \frac{\phi}{\chi + (1-\chi)t_e} = \hat{\phi}$$

where $\hat{\phi}$ is the entry cost inclusive of the cost of borrowing, and $E_z(\phi(z))$ the expected profit at entry. Higher credit constraints imply higher cost of borrowing to finance entry and therefore higher entry costs. Policies aimed at improving firms' access to credit facilitate entry of new firms and,

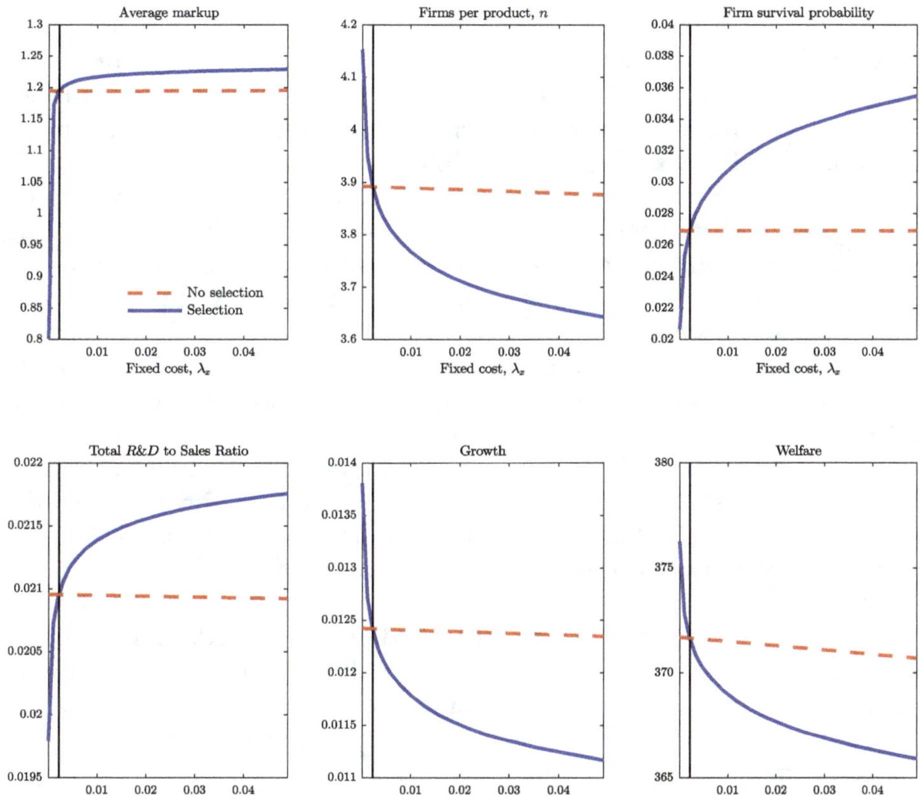

Fig. 9.13 Credit constraints, selection and growth: Export fixed cost

consequently, have the same impact on selection, innovation and growth as the reductions in entry costs are explored in Figure 9.11. Easier access to credit to finance entry leads to an economy that is more competitive, more selective and more innovative, resulting in a faster pace of aggregate growth and higher welfare.

9.3.2.5 Conclusion

A substantial share of the EU budget is directed at funding and bailing out incumbent (often large) firms (Acemoglu et al., 2017; Criscuolo et al., 2014). Recent frontier quantitative macroeconomic analysis of industrial policy has highlighted the importance of policies promoting selection and reallocation across firms with heterogeneous productivity and innovation capacity. Acemoglu et al. (2017) show that any horizontal policy aimed a stimulating production and/or innovation by all firms ultimately hinders selection and reallocation, as it facilitates survival of inefficient and non-innovative firms. The open economy dimension of the model that was used in the simple policy analysis above adds an important qualification to those results. Reducing credit constraints on non-exporting firms makes the economy less selective thereby hindering efficiency-improving reallocations of market shares towards more productive and more innovative firms. This is in line with Acemoglu et al.'s (2017) results. Lowering financial constraints on exporting firms, though, has the opposite effect, generating more selection, more reallocation and faster growth. This is a relevant guidance to avoid firm-specific or sector-specific policies which are often open to 'pork-barrel' distortions. By facilitating access to credit to exporting firms, policymakers let the market pick the winners. The second conclusion that can be drawn from the experiments above is that slashing financial and non-financial barriers to entry has unambiguously positive effects on competition, selection and growth.

Relating the results here with the findings in Benedetti Fasil et al. (2017), a number of conclusions can be drawn: first, a reduction in entry barriers can affect innovation and growth even in a model where new firms are not a direct engine of growth; hence, this is a new channel complementing the one in Romer-type models. Second, endogenous markups allow entry policies to have substantial efficiency effects on the economy. Third, models that disregard firm heterogeneity and extensive margins of adjustment, both on the domestic and the export market, may underestimate the effects of entry and regulation policies on growth and welfare. Finally, financial incentives to incumbent firms have different implications for growth depending on whether they are directed to domestic or to exporting firms.

References

Acemoglu, D., Akcigit, U., Alp, H., Bloom, N., & Kerr, W. R. (2017). *Innovation, reallocation and growth* (National Bureau of Economic Research Working Paper 18993).

Aghion, P., & Howitt, P. (1992). A model of growth through creative destruction. *Econometrica, 60,* 323–351.

Akcigit, U., Hanley, D., & Stantcheva, S. (2016). *Optimal taxation and R&D policies* (National Bureau of Economic Research Working Paper 22908).

Akcigit, U., & Kerr, W. R. (2017). Growth through heterogeneous innovations. *Journal of Political Economy, 126*(4), 1374–1443.

Akcigit, U., Sina, A., & Impullitti, G. (2018). *Innovation and trade policy in a globalizing world* (NBER Working Paper No. 24543).

Benedetti Fasil, C., Sanchez-Martinez, M., Christensen, P., & Robledo-Bottcher, N. (2017). *Entry barriers and their macroeconomic impact in the EU: An assessment using QUEST III* (JRC Technical Report EUR 28857 EN).

Bernard, A. B., Jensen, J. B., Redding, S. J., & Schott, P. K. (2017). Global Firms. *Journal of Economic Literature, 56*(2), 565–619.

Borota, T., Defever, F., & Impullitti, G. (2016). *Innovation policy in an interdependent world: A European perspective.* Mimeo.

Bravo-Biosca, A., Criscuolo, C., & Menon, C. (2013). *What drives the dynamics of business growth?* (OECD Science, Technology and Industry Policy Papers, 1).

Cincera, M., & Galgau, O. (2005). *Impact of market entry and exit on EU productivity and growth performance* (DG ECFIN, European Economy—Economic Papers 2008–2015).

Ciriaci, D. (2014). *Business dynamics and red tape barriers* (DG ECFIN, European Economy. Economic Papers 432).

Criscuolo, C., Gal, P. N., & Menon, C. (2014). *The dynamics of employment growth: New evidence from 18 countries* (NBER Working Papers 17842).

Criscuolo, C., Martin, R., Overman, H., & Van Reene, J. (2014). *The causal effects of an industrial policy* (OECD Science, Technology and Industry Policy Papers No. 14).

D'Auria, F., Pagano, A., Ratto, M., & Varga, J. (2009). *A comparison of structural reform scenarios across the EU member states: Simulation-based analysis using the QUEST model with endogenous growth* (DG ECFIN, European Economy. Economic Papers 392).

Djankov, S., La Porta, R., Lopez De Silanes, F., & Shleifer, A. (2008). *The regulation of entry: A survey* (CEPR Discussion Papers 7080).

European Commission. (2003). *Investing in research: An action plan for Europe* (Communication from the Commission SEC/489/2003).

European Commission. (2013, December). *Product market review 2013—Financing the real economy: Annex 5* (DG ECFIN, European Economy 8).

Gabler, A., & Licandro, O. (2009). *Firm dynamics support the importance of the embodied question* (CEPR Discussion Paper 7486).

Haltiwanger, J. R., Jarmin, S., & Miranda, J. (2013). Who creates jobs? Small versus young. *Review of Economics and Statistics, 95*(2), 347–361.

Hottman, C. J., Redding, S. J., & Weinstein, D. E. (2016). Quantifying the sources of firm heterogeneity. *Quarterly Journal of Economics, 131*(3), 1291–1364.

Impullitti, G., & Licandro, O. (2018). Trade, firm selection, and innovation: The competition channel. *Economic Journal, 128,* 189–229.

Luttmer, E. G. J. (2007). Selection and growth, and the size distribution of firms. *Quarterly Journal of Economics, 122*(3), 1103–1144.

Nicoletti, G., & Scarpetta, S. (2003). *Regulation, productivity and growth: OECD evidence* (Policy Research Working Paper Series 2944).

OECD. (2014). OECD R&D Tax Incentives Indicators. OECD—Directorate for Science, Technology and Innovation. Science, Technology and Industry Scoreboard.

OECD. (2015). *OECD science, technology and industry scoreboard 2015: Innovation for growth and society* (Technical Report, OECD). Directorate for Science, Technology and Innovation. Science, Technology and Industry Scoreboard.

Romer, P. M. (1990). Endogenous technological change. *Journal of Political Economy, 98,* 71–102.

Sanchez-Martinez, M., Benedetti Fasil, C., Christensen, P., & Robledo-Bottcher, N. (2017). *R&D tax credits and their macroeconomic impact in the EU: An assessment using QUEST III* (JRC Technical Report, EUR 28858 EN).

Sapir, A. (2004). Structural reforms and economic growth in the EU: Is Lisbon the right agenda? (ULB Institutional Repository, 8126).

Scarpetta, S., Hemmings, P., Tressels, T., & Woo, J. (2002). *The role of policy and institutions for productivity and firm dynamics: Evidence from micro and industry data* (OECD Economics Department Working Paper Series 329).

Veugelers, R. (2016). *Getting the most from public R&D spending in times of austerity: Some insights from Simpatic analysis* (Bruegel Working Paper, No. 1).

Conclusions

This book provides an extensive overview of the latest theoretical and empirical insights surrounding the macroeconomic modelling of R&D and innovation policies. It also contains several examples of model-based impact simulations of actual policies implemented by the EU, with a particular focus on the European Commission's future Framework Programme, *Horizon Europe*. This last chapter provides a comprehensive synthesis of the main conclusions concerning the latest empirical observations and macroeconomic modelling strategies discussed, and their inter-linkages with innovation policy. The insights emerging from the discussions on macroeconomic modelling are given higher prominence, reflecting their correspondingly greater weight throughout the volume.

Regarding the empirical literature and its policy implications, some of the most salient recent observations include the positive linkages between innovation and wider societal dimensions, such as happiness and social mobility. However, greater innovation is also associated with increasing inequality, especially in top-income segments. Optimal policy measures must thus take these facts into consideration. More specifically, the main policy lessons stemming from the most recent empirical studies are:

- International competition spurs innovation by providing direct and indirect incentives for it. Barriers to international competition are hence prone to reduce the growth rate of technological progress.

- Innovation policies, such as R&D subsidies, require patience on the side of policymakers, as these only have a significant impact on the economy in the medium-to-long run.
- Industrial policy needs to consider the effects on firm composition and factor reallocations in the economy when opting for different policy options. Bailing out unproductive firms could slow down factor reallocation from unproductive incumbents to more productive entrants.
- The rate of successful inventions has been observed to be highly correlated with the pool of inventors, which is in turn dependent on as wide as possible access to education. Education policy should thus focus on providing as much equal opportunities for education as possible, thereby improving the quality of the inventor pool and therefore overall innovation capacity.
- Innovation policy generally emphasises tax credits on the income of firms more than on the income of inventors and researchers. One promising policy direction is to couple corporate income tax with tax breaks or research grants to inventors in order to offset the potential disincentive effects of overall taxation.
- The widespread use of new technologies is at least as important as their invention for increasing the economic impact. Hence, it is important to develop well-functioning secondary markets for technologies, in particular on the sale and licensing of technology.

Capturing these stylised facts in a robust modelling framework, which also needs to capture the intricacies embedded in the plethora of innovation policies that can be evaluated, has been the primary subject of this book. In the remainder, a summary of the very rich and thorough insights offered in this manuscript on the sound macroeconomic modelling of innovation policies is offered.[1]

The overarching principle that should govern any attempt at modelling the macroeconomic effects of innovation policy is that the latter should act as the ultimate guide for the former. This means that in order to evaluate different programs and policies, it is critical to start

[1] The points underlined are presented in an order congruent with their ranking in terms of their relevance for optimal model design. They are also ordered from more general to more specific.

from a clear description of these measures, so as to understand the channels through which they are expected to operate to achieve their goals. In this sense, crucial for the description of these channels are the views and *priors* of the policymakers involved in the design and implementation of the programs, as well as other experts working closely with policy institutions in the design of programs and policies. The importance of this resides in ensuring the pertinence and usefulness of the simulated effects as an accurate representation of the actual effects on innovation, growth and productivity, among others, that can be expected from the policies under evaluation. In this sense, a transparent dialogue between practitioners in these institutions and the academics and others responsible for modelling is of utmost importance.

In addition, an important principle in model design is that it needs to be question and data-dependent. Large Dynamic Stochastic General Equilibrium models used, for example, by central banks and other institutions have often been designed for the purpose of analysing fiscal and monetary policies. However, the necessary elements contained in these models might differ from the ones needed for the goal of studying the impact of innovation policies. As an example, it is common practice among DSGE models to treat the whole economy as consisting of a single sector. Even though this simplification may be adequate for other types of policies, it may not be suitable to fully capture the effects of R&D and innovation policies, where there may be a need for a more detailed approach to modelling the sectors of production in the economy.

With these key tenets in mind, together with the basic principle that models should be tailored to the exact outcome variables policymakers wish to explore, the following exhaustive list provides a set of the main elements that a macroeconomic model designed for innovation policy evaluation should have:

- **Core model ingredients.** A fundamental principle in the construction of macroeconomic models is that they should be kept as tractable as possible, while maximising their explanatory capacity on the specific economic issues for which they are devised. In this regard, the basic elements any first attempt at building a macroeconomic model should depart from are:

- *The nature of economic growth.* In particular, should economic growth be modelled as exogenous, endogenous or semi-endogenous? Since policymakers are mainly concerned with the impact on main economy-wide variables, such as GDP growth, models of endogenous growth should be at the top of the agenda, since they permit to trace the impact of a certain policy shock on final macroeconomic outcomes. However, the debate should not be so much about the nature of growth, as opposed to the empirical pertinence of existing endogenous growth models (i.e. observed stylised facts need to be replicated by the models).
- *The time dimension of the outcomes to be analysed.* One of the most common questions any macroeconomic model needs to answer from its onset is whether it should cover the short, medium or long run. While economic growth models are mostly concerned with long-term effects, innovation policies also require regular (short and medium-term) evaluation. In this sense, intermediary effects, such as those taking place during the transition from a balanced growth path to another, are critical for the evaluation of innovation policies.
- *Firm size as unit of analysis.* Given the existence of so-called *zombie* firms and leading firms, characterised by widely different employment shares and productivity levels, it is central to capture the changes in the size distribution of firms over time, because policies can have an important bearing on macroeconomic outcome variables by re-shaping this distribution. As highlighted in the examples in Part II, the family of models featuring firm dynamics provides a suitable modelling framework to capture the effect of changes to firm size.
- *The treatment of welfare and distributional effects.* This aspect has been traditionally absent in the innovation policy modelling debate. Yet, the creative destruction process inherent to innovation leads to new jobs often requiring new skills, as well as to job losses with subsequent distributional and welfare consequences. These may be unevenly distributed across sectors, regions and generations. For instance, R&D subsidies aimed at promoting investment in innovation may affect the variance of the productivity distribution across firms and regions. A better understanding of these types of effects is important to gauge

the distributional consequences of innovation policies. A model thus needs to capture these impacts.

- **Capturing the heterogeneity of agents based on microdata.** In order to identify the key channels through which innovation policy may affect growth performance, the use of models featuring heterogeneous agents, which feed from the latest microeconomic data available, is critical. As a general principle, a macroeconomic model is a good laboratory for the evaluation of economic policy if it is as close as possible to the data on those dimensions on which the policy is supposed to operate. Indeed, since innovation policies affect the incentives and performance of innovative firms, a macroeconomic model needs to capture firm dynamics and be disciplined by microdata at the firm level. This requires the description at the firm level of their innovation behaviour, the entry of new innovative firms and the exit of the less innovative ones. The risk of not including this is to miss the relevant ways through which innovation policies influence growth and welfare. By the same token, in order to evaluate the redistributive effects of innovation policies, a model with heterogeneous individuals is needed, where differences in education and skills are captured. Innovation, by creating and destroying jobs and the value of associated skills, impacts earnings unequally. Phenomena like the rise in the skill-premium, job polarisation and skill obsolescence are intimately related to technical progress. Adequately accounting for these effects calls for modelling skill and education heterogeneity.
- **The role of product and process innovation.** Productivity levels vary across firms and evolve according to a complex process which involves different dimensions and stages: the *quality* of the products offered by the firm (as perceived by consumers or by firms using them in their production processes), the technical efficiency of the firm's production process (in the transformation of inputs into output) and the quality and price of inputs used in production. Innovation affects all these aspects of productivity. *Product* innovation mainly permits the development of new, higher quality products, whereas *process* innovation allows a reduction of production costs by improving technical efficiency, adopting better quality inputs or reducing the cost of these inputs. Different techniques have been developed in recent years to estimate the product value of firms and the production efficiency of the firm. An appropriate model to

evaluate innovation policy should be able to distinguish between these two major types of innovation in order to properly capture the nuanced linkages between innovation and productivity growth.

- **The role of basic and applied research.** It is safe to state that the current state of technological development and welfare would have been much more limited if applied research would have been undertaken in isolation from basic research. The close relationship between these two types of research is essential, not least because of their impact on the innovation process, including positive externalities stemming from collaboration between universities and the private sector. In the particular case of the EU, its leadership critically depends on the excellence of European universities and basic research centres. The modelling strategy has to embed these two types of fundamental activities, the channels via which they interact and the time delays involved. First, the different stages of the innovation cycles need to be captured. Importantly, the model should be able to accommodate the different impacts of radical innovations and general purpose technologies. Second, the time elapsed between basic and applied research, between first prototypes and economically profitable innovations, between first adoption and full diffusion, needs to be captured in accordance with the empirical evidence. It is critical to precisely identify the time delays present in any innovation process until they have an actual bearing on economic growth and the welfare of individuals. In this sense, a requirement is for the model to deliver some intermediary indicators, such as academic publications and citation indexes for basic research and patents, new products or new models or versions of existing products, for applied research. Third, diffusion and adoption of technologies across space and time and the different forms of technological spillovers and externalities need to be properly modelled too.
- **Multiple Modules.** In order to satisfy the objective of the model's tractability, a general model needs to be complemented by a series of *satellite*, specific micro models, which reflect sectorial, occupational and regional nuances. These micromodules should be interpreted as *blocks* of the *core* macromodel, via which general equilibrium effects will be able to operate. It is in these decisions concerning the model's structure that the principle of policymakers and experts as guides of the shape of the model plays a crucial role; they should identify the channels through which they expect incentives to affect innovation,

productivity and growth, as well as other outcomes such as labour market and income distribution effects.

- **Multiple countries and regions and the role of spillovers.** The model needs to mimic the multi-country, multi-region nature of the EU, including its trading links with the rest of the world. The degree of disaggregation should be determined by the level required by the specific policy under evaluation. Particularly important for innovation policy evaluation is to adequately embed channels through which innovations diffuse across Europe and other parts of the world. This strategy is critical to evaluate the growth and welfare gains from a number of important EU policies, including the Innovation Union, The European Research Area, the Single Market, the European Structural and Investment Funds. The former three require chiefly that institutional differences across Member States are properly captured, while the latter require a focus on regional spillovers. A special case of policies is that of the Framework Programme and European Structural and Investment Funds, whose aims are apparently opposed, as the former focuses on funding research excellence and the latter on economic convergence across regions. Nevertheless, the redistribution of productivity gains stemming from technological diffusion across European countries and regions is bound to play a major role in smoothing the apparent trade-off. The economic gains permitted by this diffusion process hence need to be accounted for in the model. With regard to the implications of the EU's position in a globalised world, competition and cross-country externalities play a crucial role and thus also need to be captured. Lastly, not only does technological diffusion need to be across regions and time, but also across the different economic sectors, in view of the ongoing secular structural shift, mainly from manufacturing to services.
- **Ancillary elements** Lastly, besides the principal ingredients outlined above, several extensions of the model and other issues that should be considered, from a holistic point of view, are:
  - **Human capital formation, skills and education.** Since a high proportion of technology is embedded in human capital, ideally the latter should be modelled consistently. In particular, human capital, education and the process of skill creation and destruction should be present. It has been observed that the

distribution of skills across the labour force is more persistent than the distribution of required skills by firms. Understanding these dynamics is important for policies relating to skill needs and the future of work.

- **Sources of misallocation.** A good policy should identify and be addressed to solve misallocations problems inducing an inefficient allocation of resources across firms and sectors. Financial frictions are among the main market failures inducing misallocation. Lack of competition in goods and labour markets, sometimes related to regulation, can also be very important. The introduction of different types of market failures into the modelling framework is thus also important to capture these inefficiencies.
- **Innovation and the environment.** Since R&D is partially addressed to reduce environmental challenges, an environmental module could be added to the model, in particular, if policymakers and other models' users are concerned about the extent to which policies contributes to resource efficiency and sustainability.
- **Measurement Issues.** A macroeconomic model is as good as the quality of the underlying data supporting it. Multiple measurement issues still exist in relation to innovation and its process. These issues call for an effort to coordinate official statistical offices to improve the measurement of, for instance, quality gains. Due to methodological difficulties, to improve on this area, a strong commitment from policymakers with a longer term view is necessary.

The aforementioned points are an attempt to provide a comprehensive reflection on the main guidelines for appropriate macroeconomic modelling of R&D and innovation policies, both from the academic and policy viewpoints. Both parties agree on the fact that R&D and innovation drive economic growth and prosperity. Academic research aids in shedding light on the *why* and the *how* by using sophisticated models. These models explain us the mechanisms through which R&D and innovation policies impact GDP, employment and welfare. Policymakers, on the other hand, define the *what*, by delineating policy targets (e.g., GDP, employment and welfare growth), by deciding on budgets, and by designing and implementing large R&D and innovation policies. These policies are often cumbersome and impact simultaneously different actors, sectors and regions. Hence, the main link between academic research and policymaking lies in the fact that macroeconomic models, even the most elaborate and abstract, are in need of data validation and a policy question to answer. Policymakers need robust and reliable modelling platforms able to guide them by quantifying the trade-offs and assessing the ex-ante and ex-post impact of different policies interventions.

No macroeconomic model on its own is able to capture all the complexity of these policies and their exact impact. For its very nature, every model is a simplification of reality and hence can only partially guide policymakers. Nevertheless, both parties, academics and policymakers, are ultimately held accountable for the impact of such policies on economic growth and prosperity. This book is an effort to bring the two worlds of academic research and policy making one step closer, and to present the reader with the conclusion that academic research and assessment of innovation policies are two faces of the same coin.

Permissions

All chapters in this book were first published by Springer; hereby published with permission under the Creative Commons Attribution License or equivalent. Every chapter published in this book has been scrutinized by our experts. Their significance has been extensively debated. The topics covered herein carry significant information for a comprehensive understanding. They may even be implemented as practical applications or may be referred to as a beginning point for further studies.

The contributors of this book come from diverse backgrounds, making this book a truly international effort. We would like to thank all the contributing authors for lending their expertise to make the book truly unique. They have played a crucial role in the development of this book. Without their invaluable contributions this book wouldn't have been possible. They have made vital efforts to compile up to date information on the varied aspects of this subject to make this book a valuable addition to the collection of many professionals and students.

This book was conceptualized with the vision of imparting up-to-date and integrated information in this field. To ensure the same, a matchless editorial board was set up. Every individual on the board went through rigorous rounds of assessment to prove their worth. After which they invested a large part of their time researching and compiling the most relevant data for our readers.

The editorial board has been involved in producing this book since its inception. They have spent rigorous hours researching and exploring the diverse topics which have resulted in the successful publishing of this book. They have passed on their knowledge of decades through this book. To expedite this challenging task, the publisher supported the team at every step. A small team of assistant editors was also appointed to further simplify the editing procedure and attain best results for the readers.

Apart from the editorial board, the designing team has also invested a significant amount of their time in understanding the subject and creating the most relevant covers. They scrutinized every image to scout for the most suitable representation of the subject and create an appropriate cover for the book.

The publishing team has been an ardent support to the editorial, designing and production team. Their endless efforts to recruit the best for this project, has resulted in the accomplishment of this book. They are a veteran in the field of academics and their pool of knowledge is as vast as their experience in printing. Their expertise and guidance has proved useful at every step. Their uncompromising quality standards have made this book an exceptional effort. Their encouragement from time to time has been an inspiration for everyone.

The publisher and the editorial board hope that this book will prove to be a valuable piece of knowledge for students, practitioners and scholars across the globe.

Index

www.ingramcontent.com/pod-product-compliance
Lightning Source LLC
LaVergne TN
LVHW051044220926
848485LV00001BA/6
* 9 7 8 1 6 4 7 2 5 4 5 0 6 *